# GET FREE CASH FOR COLLEGE

## Twelfth Edition

- A comprehensive scholarship strategy guide
- Step-by-step instructions on how to find, apply for and win scholarships
- Learn from the successes and failures of real students
- 175 scholarships anyone can win

## Gen and Kelly Tanabe

Winners of over $100,000 in scholarships and authors of
*The Ultimate Scholarship Book* and
*How to Write a Winning Scholarship Essay*

**Get Free Cash for College**
By Gen and Kelly Tanabe

Published by SuperCollege, LLC
2713 Newlands Avenue
Belmont, CA 94002
650-618-2221
www.supercollege.com

ISBN-13: 978-1-61760-159-0

Manufactured in the United States of America
10  9  8  7  6  5  4  3  2  1

**Library of Congress Cataloging-in-Publication Data**
Names: Tanabe, Gen S., author. | Tanabe, Kelly Y., author.
Title: Get free cash for college : secrets to winning scholarships / Gen
   and Kelly Tanabe.
Description: Twelfth edition. | Belmont, CA : SuperCollege, LLC, [2020] |
   Summary: "Guide for parents and high school and college students on how
   to win scholarships. Contains advice on finding the right scholarships,
   crafting applications, writing essays and asking the college for a
   financial aid reassessment. Also has a scholarship directory of 175
   awards; examples of winning scholarship applications, essays, and
   interview questions and answers are included"-- Provided by publisher.
Identifiers: LCCN 2019058570 | ISBN 9781617601590 (paperback)
Subjects: LCSH: Scholarships--United States.
Classification: LCC LB2338 .T36 2020 | DDC 378.3/4--dc23
LC record available at https://lccn.loc.gov/2019058570

# Contents at a Glance

# Table of Contents

## Chapter 10. Secrets to Writing Winning Essays / 137

## Chapter 11. Ace the Interviews / 155

## Chapter 12. Strategies for Specific Scholarships / 177

# Special Features

## Stories from Real Life

These stories about the successes and failures of real students are entertaining and enlightening. They serve as valuable lessons about how the scholarship process really works!

## Special Highlights

As a step-by-step strategy guide, we have created easy-to-follow practical methods for key areas of the scholarship process.

To our families for shaping who we are.

To Harvard for four of the best years of our lives.

To the many students and friends who made this book possible by sharing their scholarship experiences, secrets, successes and failures.

To all the students and parents who understand that paying for college is a challenging but worthwhile endeavor.

# How to Get Free Cash for College

In this chapter, you'll learn:

- How this book guides you through the entire scholarship process

- How this book is different from traditional scholarship books

- The seven myths of scholarships

- Why all financial aid is not created equal

- How scholarships are judged and what you can do to maximize your chances of winning

# How to Get Free Cash for College

When I received my acceptance letter from Harvard, I proudly showed it to my parents. After calming down from the excitement, they asked that question you don't really want to ask, "How are we going to pay for this education?" This is when my father—always the pragmatist—made me an offer that was difficult to refuse.

> **About the Authors**
>
> *Gen and Kelly Tanabe won more than $100,000 in scholarships and graduated from Harvard debt-free.*

"Son," he began, "why don't you go to our state university and I'll buy you a brand new car?" Given the price of a private college, it would have been much cheaper for my family to pay state tuition and buy a new car. In fact, for what Harvard charged, we could have purchased a whole fleet of cars.

So there I was: Harvard in one hand but a brand new ride in the other. It was a difficult decision.

When my coauthor, Kelly, received her acceptance letter from Harvard, she and her family were similarly torn. She had also been accepted to the University of Southern California and offered a full-tuition scholarship. Harvard, on the other hand, didn't offer any assistance.

So why, you might wonder as our parents certainly did, would we both choose to attend one of the most expensive colleges in the country and turn down (both literally and figuratively) free rides? We made the decision because we were fanatical in our belief that we could find scholarships to pay our mind-boggling tuition bills. There was only one, tiny problem with this decision: We had no idea where to start.

We began our journey the only way we knew. We bought a scholarship book. (Sound familiar?) After flipping through hundreds of pages of scholarships, we were disappointed to find that few awards fit us. Even more discouraging was that when we found a scholarship, we didn't have a clue on how to actually win the award. Through a long process of trial and error we slowly developed a workable system for finding and winning scholarships.

In the end we won more than $100,000 in scholarships, ranging from local awards from the Lions Club, high school PTA and local newspaper to national awards from Tylenol, Shell Oil Company and Knight Ridder newspapers. These scholarships allowed us not only to fulfill our dream of attending Harvard but (to our parents' delight) to graduate debt-free.

This book is based on the hard lessons we learned during our struggle to fund our own educations. In addition, we have done years of research collecting the strategies used by hundreds of students who have successfully won scholarships. (We've included samples of their scholarship applications, resumes and essays in this book.) We've interviewed scholarship judges to learn how they pick scholarship winners and what you can do to improve your chances in a competition. We then distilled these experiences, strategies and advice into a system that we believe will help you find and win scholarships. In short, this is the knowledge that we wish had been available when we were applying for scholarships.

## Scholarships Are Not Just for Superstars

Whether you are just starting out or are an experienced veteran of the battle for scholarships, this book has a great deal to offer. Each chapter is filled with valuable advice, strategies, shortcuts and real life examples. Through the lessons in this book you can emulate our successes while avoiding our most tragic blunders in your own scholarship quest.

Don't think you need to be the class valedictorian or star athlete to win a scholarship. If you have the desire, you have everything you need to win free cash for college. We will help you make this happen. The goal of this book is to teach you the skills and provide you with the resources to be able to pay for the college of your dreams and graduate, as we did, debt-free.

## Why Most Scholarship Books and Websites Can Be Soooooooooooooo Frustrating

Chances are that you found this book nestled among dozens of others on scholarships. If you look at the other books, you will notice something interesting: They all look like unabridged dictionaries. Flip through one, and you will find that it doesn't contain much more than award listings. This is the traditional format of the scholarship book, and it has been around for decades. The Internet has not done much to improve on things. You can go to various websites that list scholarships but again you are just viewing raw scholarships—and often many may not even fit you that well.

> ### Not a Superstar, Not a Problem
>
> *You don't have to be a straight-A student or star athlete to win a scholarship. The strategies in this book and the students you will meet clearly prove that any student can win a scholarship. What is required is the desire and willingness to put in the time and effort to find awards that fit your background and write applications that show scholarship judges why you deserve to win. Don't worry, you'll learn how in the following chapters.*

Unfortunately, it is this directory format that has caused so much dissatisfaction among students. While any single book or website may contain thousands of listings, few of those awards actually apply to you. To make matters worse, even when you do find an award, these books and websites leave you on your own to figure out how to create an application that will win the scholarship. What's the point of spending all this time and effort to find a scholarship when you don't know how to win it?

As we wrote this book, we vowed not to perpetuate the mistakes of other scholarship book authors. Go ahead and flip through a few chapters. What do you see? Holy cow! You see actual paragraphs and real examples of applications, scholarship resumes and essays. This whole book is a detailed scholarship strategy guide. You will learn all the ins and outs of scholarships, grants and financial aid. You will also learn what works when applying for scholarships and how to get the best financial aid offer. We have loaded this book with examples so you can see what a scholarship essay looks like and read a preview of questions you may be asked in a scholarship interview. We equip you with the knowledge and tools to actually win the scholarships that you spend valuable time finding.

*Get Free Cash for College* is our attempt to fix the outdated format of traditional scholarship books and websites that have been found lacking by so many students. In doing so, we believe that this book will provide you with the maximum advantage possible when it comes to finding and winning free cash for college.

## The Big Picture

Don't you hate it when you are given instructions on how to do something without knowing what the final result is supposed to be? We do too, which is why at the start of each chapter you will find what we call *The Big Picture*. This is an overview of our approach or strategy. Seeing the big picture first will help you understand how all the smaller pieces fit together.

So in the spirit of giving you the big picture, we would like to share our general view of scholarships. Through our own experience and that of helping thousands of students and interviewing dozens of scholarship judges, we have come to firmly believe that the biggest misconception about scholarships is that you have to be an academic, athletic or extracurricular superstar to win one.

**This is just plain untrue.**

There are scholarships that reward every background, talent and achievement that you can imagine. Plus, most don't even consider grades, or if they do, it is the least important factor. It is true that winning a scholarship is not easy. There will be competition because scholarships are essentially free cash with no strings attached. But like most everything in life, you can greatly improve your chances of winning by learning as much as you can about these competitions and applying what you learn to your applications. Matched with the right scholarships and armed with this knowledge, you can set yourself up to win.

The bottom line is that scholarship winners are not superstars but are students who have prepared and invested the time to create an application that highlights their strengths while minimizing their weaknesses.

It's really sad to see students who don't apply for scholarships because they mistakenly assume that they don't have a chance to win. The truth is that regardless of what kind of student you are, winning comes down to whether or not you have a solid strategy. We believe you can learn this strategy. In fact, we're sure of it!

## The Mind-Boggling Cost of a Good Education

We don't need to tell you that college is expensive. But have you actually seen the numbers? Are you ready for some major sticker shock? The price tag is staggering—an average of $21,370* per year for tuition and room and board at four-year public schools and $48,510* at private schools. These costs have grown approximately 30 percent over the past 10 years and have consistently risen faster than inflation. Ouch!

That is the bad news. The good news is that more than $241.3 billion was awarded in scholarships and financial aid last year. That's a lot of cash! You only need to get a small slice of this pie to be able to afford college. At this amount, even getting a small piece of crust is appealing!

So if you're ready to get your piece of the scholarship pie, let's begin by debunking some of the most common myths about scholarships that often prevent even the most motivated students from applying.

*The College Board

# Seven Scholarship Myths Busted

### Never Too Early or Too Late to Apply

There are scholarships for students as young as seventh grade and that go all the way through graduate school. As long as you are in school you should be applying for scholarships.

Did you know that Walt Disney is cryogenically frozen and awaiting the day medical science can revive him? Or, you do know to be careful when walking the city at night since there are gangs of organ thieves who will knock you unconscious and steal your kidneys, right? We have all heard urban legends like these, and on the subject of scholarships there are no shortages of such stories.

You may have heard myths like these: You need to have near zero dinero in order to qualify for a scholarship, or you have to be the record holder for three-point shots to win a full-ride award. To help you sort the truth from the tall tale, here are some common scholarship myths and the truth behind them:

## Myth #1: You need to be financially destitute to be eligible to apply for scholarships.

**The Truth:** While it is true that financial need is a consideration for some scholarships, the definition of "need" varies considerably. Given the cost of a college education, many families who consider themselves to be "middle class" actually qualify for need-based scholarships. Plus, there are many scholarships where financial need is not even a factor. These "merit-based" scholarships are based on achievements, skills, career goals, family background and a host of other considerations that have nothing to do with a family's financial situation. You really could be the son or daughter of Donald Trump and still win a scholarship.

## Myth #2: You can only win scholarships as a high school senior.

**The Truth:** It is never too early or too late to apply for scholarships. There are awards for students as young as seventh grade. (If you win these awards, the money may be paid to you directly or put into a trust account until you head off to college.) Also, many students stop applying for scholarships after they graduate from high school. Big mistake. There are many awards for college students. Once you are in college you should continue to apply for scholarships, especially those geared toward specific majors and careers.

**More Truth:** Most scholarships are aimed at students who are getting their first degree, regardless of age. If you're 92 and working toward your bachelor's degree, you are just as eligible for scholarships as the 17-year-old high school student. In fact, today more than 20 percent of all students on campus are over the age of 35, so it's easy to understand why the rules for many scholarships have been modified to no longer limit an applicant based on age.

## Myth #3: Only star athletes get scholarships, especially full-tuition scholarships.

**The Truth:** While full-tuition scholarships for star running backs often make the news, the majority of scholarships awarded by colleges are not for athletics. As you will start to see from the Scholarships (Almost) Anyone Can Win in the Directory, there are literally thousands of scholarships for those of us who don't know the difference between a touchdown and a touchback.

If you are an athlete, you might also be surprised to know that many colleges give scholarships to student athletes even if they are not the next Kevin Durant. Depending on the level of the school's athletic team, you may find that while at one college your soccer skill wouldn't earn you a place on the team as a bench warmer, at another school you would not only be a starter but also could earn a half-tuition scholarship.

## Myth #4: You need straight A's to win money for college.

**The Truth:** While straight A's certainly don't hurt your chances of winning, most students assume that grades are the primary means for picking scholarship winners. This is just not true. Most scholarships are based on criteria other than grades and reward specific skills or talents such as linguistic, athletic or artistic ability. Even for scholarships in which grades are considered, they are often not the most important factor. What's more important is that you best match the qualities the scholarship committee seeks. Most students who win scholarships do not have the highest GPA. Don't let the lack of a perfect transcript prevent you from applying for scholarships.

*Scholarships: The Ultimate in Financial Aid*

*Scholarships are the only form of aid that comes with virtually no strings attached and that you can receive regardless of your family's finances.*

## Myth #5: You should get involved in as many extracurricular activities as possible to win a scholarship.

**The Truth:** Scholarship competitions are not pie eating contests where you win through volume. They are more like baking contests in which you create an exquisite dessert with an appearance and flavor that matches the tastes of the judges. Scholarships are won by quality, not quantity.

Scholarship judges are looking for students who have made quality contributions. For example, for a public service scholarship, the judges would be more impressed if you organized a school-wide volunteer day than if you were a member of 20 volunteer organizations but did little to distinguish yourself in them. Scholarship judges are looking for meaningful involvement, not a laundry list of clubs that you've joined.

## Myth #6: You should apply to every scholarship you find.

**The Truth:** When you turn 35, you technically are eligible to run for President of the United States. This hardly means you should start packing your bags for the White House. Just because you are technically eligible for a scholarship does not mean you should apply for it. Why? You have a limited amount of time to spend on scholarship applications. It is necessary to allocate your time to those in which you have the best chance of winning. You may find that you are eligible for 500 scholarships. Unless you're willing to make applying to scholarships your full-time avocation, it's unlikely that you can apply to more than several dozen awards. Thus, you need to be selective about which scholarships fit you best. One caveat: This does not mean that you should only apply to two or three scholarships. You should still apply to as many scholarships as you can—just make sure you have them prioritized.

## Myth #7: There's nothing you can do to increase your chances of winning a scholarship.

**The Truth:** We would not be here today if it weren't for the fact that there are many techniques you can use to improve your chances of winning scholarships. In the following chapters you will learn how to select scholarships that best fit you and your background, create a powerful application, write winning essays and successfully present yourself in interviews. We will teach you what successful students have done that worked for them. While there is no magic formula that guarantees you'll win a scholarship, our strategies have worked for others and can work for you too.

## "How We Choose Our Scholarship Winners"
### Mary Hawkins, Scholarship Judge

The first thing you should understand about national scholarships like ours is the magnitude. We don't just get a box of applications for our scholarship. We get truckloads of applications. I am on the small team of people who sift through this mountain of paperwork.

Our first step is to make a quick first pass. We spend about 10 to 20 seconds taking a brief look at the applications. Even though we don't spend much time on each application, we quickly eliminate applications that don't meet the basic requirements. We purge applications that are not complete, missing information or materials, illegible or sloppily completed. We're pretty rigid in our decisions because we've found that if students don't even follow our award's simple directions, they probably aren't that attentive to their studies either.

After this first pass, we separate the applications into two piles. One is the pile of students we send thank you notes for entering. The other is the pile with potential. We spend on average between one and three minutes per application, hitting the highlights of the application form and reading the first few paragraphs of the essay. If we are impressed, we place the application in a separate pile.

Our last step is to separate the truly outstanding applications from the merely great ones. This is always the most difficult part. There are always so many more students with superb qualifications than we have scholar-

ships to give. It's not easy to point out exactly what makes an application rise above the rest, but here are some qualities I've found common to our winners:

**Academics.** There are some scholarships in which academics is not the most important factor. For us, academic excellence is a prerequisite. Students don't have to have perfect grade point averages, but they do have to be committed to their schoolwork and take challenging courses. This should be reflected in the application.

**Leadership.** We look for students who have made a difference by being leaders in their activities. You don't have to be student body president to be a leader. You can show leadership by serving your community, speaking out for what you believe in or being an example for other students. We want students who will make a difference both in college and beyond.

**Originality.** Students with an original approach to their essays rise to the top. Creativity shows intelligence and a readiness to think differently.

**Results.** In the students' activities, we seek students who have demonstrated that they can deliver results. We don't care what area these results are in (i.e., music, service, science, sports) but we do want to see that there are actions that support the applicants' words.

**Personality.** One of the most important things we want are students who we feel like we know after reading their applications. It's important that students convey a piece of who they really are and that we feel like we've gotten to know them a little better through their applications.

Some scholarship judges have the luxury of being able to interview their finalists. Personally, I think it would help to meet the person behind the application. However, I think we do a great job relying on the applications, essays and recommendations. It's amazing how well you can get to know someone just through their written words.

## What about Federal Financial Aid?

You may think that the terms *scholarship* and *financial aid* are interchangeable. They are not. Financial aid refers to money from the government (both federal and state) and the college. It comes in several forms. Each type of aid has its own requirements, advantages and disadvantages. When we talk about financial aid, we mean one of the following:

**Grants**: Money with no strings attached—meaning you don't have to pay it back. This is really the equivalent of hitting the financial aid jackpot. Grants are almost always based on financial need.

> *Advantages:* Grants do not need to be repaid.
> *Disadvantages:* They are limited to those with financial need.

**Student Loans**: Money you borrow and are required to pay back with interest. In most cases the terms are more generous than other types of consumer loans. Some student loans are also based on financial need.

> *Advantages:* Loans are usually the easiest form of financial aid to obtain. Often you do not need to repay them until after you graduate or leave school.
>
> *Disadvantages:* Unlike the other forms of financial aid, loans need to be repaid.

**Work-Study**: Money you earn the old-fashioned way—by working. This federal program subsidizes on-campus employment while you are enrolled in school. The program is based on financial need.

> *Advantages:* Work-study allows you to gain valuable work experience (like how to shelve books, scrub dishes or serve a mean cup of coffee) while in school and opens up employment opportunities that are not available to other students.
>
> *Disadvantages:* You will need to balance schoolwork with a part-time job. The program is limited to those with financial need.

In this book we will explain how financial aid works and what you need to get your share. We will also cover some important techniques on how to make sure you are receiving the most financial aid that you deserve from the college. To successfully pay for college, keep all your options open by applying for both financial aid and scholarships.

## The Big Disadvantage of Federal Financial Aid

With so much financial aid available, why would anyone want to apply for a scholarship? The downside to financial aid is that most of the programs are based on need. This means that a family's income and assets are examined. Unfortunately, many middle class families find that they don't qualify for grants. Or, even if they do qualify, the amount they receive falls far short of what they need. This is where scholarships can be a lifesaver. Most scholarships don't consider a family's finances and therefore can bridge the gap between what a family has saved (including what they get from financial aid) and what the college actually costs them.

## Scholarships: The Real Financial Aid Jackpots

While financial aid is important, we consider scholarships to be the true jackpots. With few, if any, strings attached to the money, scholarships represent free cash that does not have to be paid back. Best of all, students can win scholarships regardless of their parents' income!

In general, scholarships range in size from $500 to more than $100,000. Scholarships come from diverse organizations including schools, colleges, churches, state and local governments, companies and civic, political, service and athletic organizations. Often, these groups provide awards to promote their cause. For businesses, the cause may be to contribute to the communities in which they operate or to build relationships with future potential employees. For colleges, the motive may be to recruit certain types of students, to create a diverse student population by attracting those with different backgrounds or to encourage students to enter nontraditional fields. Local and civic organizations often promote the missions of their organizations. For example, an equestrian club might sponsor a scholarship to reward students who love horseback riding.

The possibilities are truly limitless. And here's a secret: For practically every cause, occupation, hobby and passion that exists there is at least one scholarship. Often there are more. With some detective work, you can find many awards that match your particular skills, talents, achievements, goals and background. As you are searching, you will discover that most scholarships can be divided into two major categories: Need-based and Merit-based.

> **Need-based** scholarships are those in which financial need is a criterion. The importance of financial need and the definition of financial need in the selection process vary by scholarship. For some scholarships, financial need may be the most important factor or may be required for eligibility. For others, it may be one of many factors that are used to pick a winner. Also, the definition of a student with financial need varies widely. One scholarship may consider a family that makes less than $75,000 a year "needy" while another may set the limit at $150,000.

> Most scholarships are **merit-based**, which means financial need is not a requirement to apply. These scholarships are based on qualities such as skills, talents or accomplishments. "Merit" does not automatically equal academic merit, either. In the context of scholarships, "merit" can really mean anything from being a part of a specific ethnic group to being able to ride a skateboard. The only thing a merit-based scholarship really signifies is that your family's financial status is not a consideration.

It's no secret that we believe scholarships are the best way to pay for college. This does not mean that you should ignore other forms of financial aid, however, there are some real advantages that scholarships offer over other forms of financial aid.

> **Scholarships Are Everywhere**
> ───────
> *There are scholarships for practically every cause, talent and interest. While some are based on your financial background (need-based) others are based on almost any criteria that you can imagine (merit-based).*

**First, you don't have to hold down a job to win a scholarship.** For work-study, you need to work part-time. For loans, you need to toil after graduating to pay them off. Scholarships are free cash that does not need to be paid back. We love it (and so will you)!

**Scholarships are open to students from all financial backgrounds.** Most financial aid programs are based on your parents' and your financial background, something that you have little control over. While some scholarships are based on financial need, the vast majority are not.

**Scholarships may be renewable.** You need to apply for financial aid each year that you are in college. What you receive for your first year may not be the same for your second, third or fourth years. However, if a scholarship is "renewable" as long as you meet the requirements (often maintaining a 3.0 GPA) you will get the money each and every year that you are in school. A $1,000 "renewable" scholarship may actually be worth $4,000 over the course of your college career.

**Most important, unlike other types of financial aid, scholarships allow you the greatest opportunity to control your chances of winning.** You create the application, write the essay and control how you present yourself to the scholarship judges during the interview. The bottom line is that you determine through your own efforts the chances of receiving free cash for college.

## Scholarship Competitions Are Not Lotteries

Unlike a lottery jackpot, scholarships are not based on luck. To win scholarships, you need to show the scholarship judges how you fit the award. Often this is through the scholarship application, essay and interview. In fact, almost all scholarship competitions come down to one key factor—how well you can show that you fit the mission of the scholarship. In this respect you have tremendous influence over the outcome. Through what you choose to highlight (and ignore) in the scholarship application, you are able to show your fit with the scholarship's mission. We hope that you feel empowered by the fact that you have so much control over the scholarship process!

In the following chapters you will learn how to use this opportunity to tailor your application to fit a scholarship's mission and thereby maximize your chances of winning it. Now turn the page and let's get started!

## Chapter 1 Summary: How to Get Free Cash for College

**Not a superstar? Not a problem.** Remember that you don't have to be an academic, athletic or extracurricular superstar to win scholarships. Different scholarships reward different strengths. However, you do need a solid strategy for applying for scholarships. Discover the ins and outs of creating a winning strategy in the next chapters, including selecting scholarships that fit, creating outstanding applications and keeping the money you win.

**Benefit from the experiences of others.** The best way to learn anything is to study and draw from the knowledge of those who have already been through a similar experience. We will share the successes (and a few disasters) of students who have been through the scholarship process. You can choose to emulate their feats and avoid their failures.

**Not all money is the same.** Financial aid comes in a number of different forms, each with its own advantages and disadvantages. Loans are repaid while grants and scholarships are not. Work-study allows you to hold a part-time job while attending college.

**Debunk scholarship urban legends.** Separate the truth from the tall tales about scholarships. Among the truths in this chapter are

the following: You don't have to be financially destitute, participate in every extracurricular activity or apply for every scholarship for which you remotely qualify.

**Scholarships for everyone.** There are scholarships for almost every skill, experience, career aspiration and field of study you can imagine.

**Take advantage of your influence.** Scholarships are based on factors such as your fit with the mission, essays, interviews, recommendations and financial need. Understand that you can positively affect nearly all these requirements.

**Know what the judges want.** In the first round, superficial factors such as neatness and completeness are important. Next, judges divide applications between good and excellent based on factors such as academics, leadership, originality, strength, results, maturity and personality.

**Judging criteria.** One of the most important things to remember when applying for scholarships is that you must show how you fulfill the mission of the award. In the following chapters, you will learn more about defining the mission and using it to your advantage throughout your applications, essays and interviews.

# Find the Best Scholarships You Can Win

CHAPTER 2

• • • • • • • • • • • • • • • • • • • • • • • • • • • • •

**In this chapter, you'll learn:**

- **The best places to find scholarships**

- **Truly outrageous scholarships**

- **How to determine which scholarships you have the best chance of winning**

- **How to read the minds of the judges**

- **The magic number of scholarships**

• • • • • • • • • • • • • • • • • • • • • • • • • • • • •

## Where to Find the Best Scholarships

There's a saying: "If you give a man a fish, you feed him for a day. If you teach a man to fish, you feed him for life." In the second part of this book you will find our list of Scholarships (Almost) Anyone Can Win. That's our way of starting you out with a barrel full of fish! We do, however, want to make sure that we also teach you how to catch your own scholarships. So before you skip to the directory, master the techniques in this chapter to guarantee yourself a lifetime supply of scholarships.

Learning how to find scholarships is a skill. Unfortunately, we learned this through painful trial and error. For example, when we first started to search for scholarships, we applied for nearly every one that we found as long as we remotely met the eligibility requirements. Big mistake. We wasted a lot of time filling out applications that we should have passed on. Even worse, we spent a lot of time tracking down scholarships that we later discovered were listed in resources that were free for the asking. But we did learn from each mistake and eventually developed an efficient strategy for finding scholarships.

In this chapter we will teach you everything we learned about unearthing scholarships, including how to avoid common time-wasting mistakes. Let's begin with an overview of our scholarship-finding technique.

## The Big Picture

Our approach to finding scholarships consists of two important steps. First, you must create a list of as many scholarships as possible that fit you. The list of Scholarships (Almost) Anyone Can Win in the second part of this book is a great place to start. However, don't stop here. Use the techniques in this chapter to seek out other scholarships—especially local awards given in your community. The goal is to compile as large a list as possible from as many sources as possible.

Second, once you have a big list of scholarships, prioritize the awards. Here is where you will do some detective work. Decide which scholarships from the list are most worth your time in filling out applications. To help process your choices and maximize your time, you need to learn as much as you can about each scholarship and the goal of the awarding organization. You also need to determine if your own background, skills and experience match what the scholarship wants to reward. Don't worry, this is much easier than it sounds and we'll show you how to do it quickly.

By following this two-step technique you will end up with a prioritized list of scholarships that are closely matched to your background and achievements. So, even before you fill out a single scholarship application form, you have greatly improved your chances of winning. Plus, you saved time by not wasting energy on awards that you won't win.

## The Best Places to Find Scholarships

When we began to look for scholarships, we made what is perhaps the biggest mistake of every novice scholarship hunter—we started by looking as far away as possible. We were mesmerized by the big prizes of the large (and often well-publicized) national awards. We even thought, "If I won just one of these national scholarship competitions, I'd be set and could end my search." This turned out to be a big mistake and an even bigger time-waster. It seemed that everyone and his brother, sister and second cousin were also applying to these competitions. The Coca-Cola scholarship competition, for example, receives more than 100,000 applications each year.

It turned out that the last place we looked for scholarships was our most lucrative source. Best of all, this place turned out to be in our own backyard!

## Fantastic Backyard Scholarships

What are backyard scholarships and where do you find them? Think about all the groups, clubs, businesses, churches and organizations in your community. Each of these is a potential source for scholarships. (If you are already in college, you have two communities: your hometown and the city in which you go to school.) Since these awards are usually only available to students in your community, the competition is a lot less fierce.

You may be thinking, "Yeah, but what good is a $500 Lions Club scholarship when my college costs 20 grand a year?" It's true that local scholarships don't award the huge prizes that some of the national competitions do. You already know that we won over $100,000 in scholarships. What we haven't told you is that the majority of this money came from local scholarships! We literally won $500 here and $1,500 there. By the time we graduated from Harvard and added up all the awards, it turned out to be a huge amount. Plus, some of the local scholarships that we won were "renewable," which meant that we received

> **Be a Detective**
>
> Take off your "thinking cap" as your elementary school teacher used to call it and put on your "detective hat." When researching scholarships, be willing to look high and low to find out whatever you can about the mission of the award and goal of the organization that is giving away the money.

that money each year we were in college. So a $500 renewable scholarship was really worth $2,000 over four years.

If you still can't get over the fact that some of the local awards seem small compared to the cost of tuition, try this exercise: Take the amount of the award and divide it by the time you invested in the application. For the $500 Lions Club award, let's say that you spent one hour each night for three days to complete the application and write the essay. $500 divided by three hours works out to a little over $166 per hour. (Now imagine that the award was for $1,000 instead. That would make it $333 per hour!) Surprised? If you can find a job that pays you more than $166 an hour, then take it and forget applying to scholarships. If not, then get back to applying for scholarships–even the little ones!

As you begin the search for scholarships, make your community the first place you look. Begin with the following places to find your own backyard scholarships:

**High school counselor or college financial aid office.** If you are a high school student, start with your counselor. Ask if he or she has a list of scholarship opportunities. Most counselors have a binder filled with local scholarships, or they post them on your school's website. It's helpful if before your meeting you prepare information about your family's financial background as well as special interests or talents you have that would make you eligible for scholarships. Don't forget that your own high school will have a variety of scholarships from such places as the parent-teacher organization, alumni group and athletic booster clubs.

If you are a college student, make an appointment with your school's financial aid advisor. Before the appointment, think about what interests and talents you have and what field you may want to enter after graduation. If you have one, take a copy of your Free Application for Federal Student Aid (FAFSA) as background. Mention any special circumstances about your family's financial situation. Ask your advisor for recommendations of scholarships offered by the college or by community organizations.

It's important whenever you speak to a counselor (either in high school or college) that you inquire about any scholarships that require nomination. Often these scholarships are easier to win since the applicant pool is smaller. You have nothing to lose by asking, and if anything, it shows how serious you are about financing your education.

**High school websites.** You may not visit your school's website daily, but when you are looking for scholarships, it pays to search the site for lists of scholarships. Most high schools post scholarship opportunities for students on their websites. (You may have to dig down a few levels to find this list.) If your school does not do this, surf over to the websites of other high schools in the area. You'll find that many are a wealth of scholarship resources.

**Department of your major.** Especially if you are already in college and have declared a major, check with the department's administrator for any awards that you might be eligible to win.

**Nearby colleges.** While your college has great scholarship resources, wouldn't it be great if you had double or triple these resources? You can. Simply seek the resources of other local colleges. Ask permission first, but you'll find that most neighboring schools are more than willing to help you. If you are in high school, nothing prevents you from visiting all the local colleges and asking for scholarship information. Because you are a prospective student, these colleges will be happy to provide whatever assistance they can.

**Student clubs and organizations.** Here's a reason to enjoy your extracurricular activities even more. One benefit of participating may be a scholarship sponsored by the organization. Inquire with the officers or advisors of the organization about scholarship funds. Bands, newspapers, academic clubs, athletic organizations and service organizations often have scholarships that are awarded to outstanding members. If the organization has a national parent organization (e.g. National Honor Society), visit the national organization website. There are often awards that are given by the parent organization for members of local chapters.

**Community organizations.** If you've ever wondered why community organizations have so many breakfast fundraisers, one reason is that some provide money for scholarships. You usually don't have to be a member of these organizations to apply. In fact, many community groups sponsor scholarships that are open to all students who live in the area. As we have mentioned, college students really have two communities: your hometown and where you go to college. Don't neglect either of these places.

How do you find these organizations? Many local government websites list them. Visit the websites for your town, city and state. Also visit

> ### Find the Binder
>
> *Your counselor probably has a binder full of local scholarships. Many high school counselors we spoke with lament the fact that not very many students take advantage of the legwork they have done compiling local scholarships. Make your counselor's day and ask to see their list of scholarships.*

**Ask to Be Nominated**

*Sometimes the biggest hurdle to winning a scholarship from your school or college is that you need to be nominated. Don't be afraid to ask teachers or professors if they will nominate you.*

or call your community association or center. Local or state affiliates should be able to provide the names and contact information for groups that disburse college funds to deserving students. If contact information is lacking for some of the groups, follow up by going online to look up the organizations. Some local websites even have a calendar of annual events that are sponsored by various civic groups. Finally, don't forget to pay a visit to the public library and ask the reference librarian for help. Here is a brief list of some of the more well-known civic groups to track down:

- Altrusa
- American Legion and American Legion Auxiliary
- American Red Cross
- Association of Junior Leagues International
- Boys and Girls Clubs
- Boy Scouts and Girl Scouts
- Circle K
- Civitan
- Elks Club
- Lions Club
- 4-H Clubs
- Fraternal Order of Eagles
- Friends of the Library
- Kiwanis International
- Knights of Columbus
- National Exchange Club
- National Grange
- Optimist International
- Rotary Club
- Rotaract and Interact
- Ruritan
- Sertoma International
- Soroptimist International of the Americas
- U.S. Jaycees
- USA Freedom Corps
- Veterans of Foreign Wars
- YMCA and YWCA
- Zonta International

**Local businesses.** Businesses like to return some of their profits to employees and students in the community. Many offer scholarships as a way to reward students who both study and work. Ask your manager if your employer has a scholarship fund and how you can apply. Some companies–particularly large companies that have offices, distributor-ships or factories in your community–offer scholarships that all students in the community are eligible to win. Check with the chamber of commerce for a list of the largest employers in the area. You can contact the public relations or community outreach department in these companies to inquire about any scholarship opportunities. Visit the large department and chain stores in the area and ask the store manager or customer service manager about scholarships.

**Parents' employer.** Your parents may hate their bosses, but they'll love the fact that many companies award scholarships to the children of their employees as a benefit. They should speak with someone in the human resources department or their direct managers about scholarships and other educational programs offered by their company.

**Parents' or grandparents' military service.** If your parents or grandparents served in the U.S. Armed Forces, you may qualify for a scholarship from a military association. Each branch of the service and even specific divisions within each branch have associations. Speak with your parents and grandparents about their military service and see if they belong to or know of these military associations.

**Your employer.** Flipping burgers may have an up side. Even if you work only part-time, you may qualify for an educational scholarship given by your employer. For example, McDonald's offers the McDonald's Scholarship to reward the accomplishments of its student-employees with awards of up to $2,500. If you have a full- or part-time job, ask your employer about scholarships.

**Parents' union.** Some unions sponsor scholarships for the children of their members. Ask your parents to speak with the union officers about scholarships and other educational programs sponsored by their union.

**Interest clubs.** Performing arts centers, city orchestras, equestrian associations and amateur sports leagues are just a few of the many special interest clubs that may offer scholarships. While some limit their awards to members, many simply look for students who are interested in what they support. A city performing arts center, for example, may offer an award for a talented performing artist in the community.

**Professional sports teams.** They may not have won a World Series since the 1950s, but many local professional athletic teams offer community awards (and not necessarily for athletes) as a way to contribute to the cities in which they are based.

> *A Little-Known Secret about Finding Scholarships*
>
> *You can tap into the resources not only of your own high school or college but also of nearby high schools and colleges. Many list scholarships that are applicable to any student in the area. Just take a quick look at the counseling or financial aid sections of their websites.*

**The Hidden Scholarship Application**

Almost all colleges use your application for admission to judge you for scholarships. When applying you are not just trying to get in but to get in with a scholarship.

**Church or religious organizations.** Religious organizations may provide scholarships for members. If you or your parents are members of a religious organization, check with the leaders to see if a scholarship is offered.

**Local government.** Some cities and counties provide scholarships specifically designated for local students. Often, local city council members and state representatives sponsor a scholarship fund. Even if you didn't vote for them, call their offices and ask if they offer a scholarship.

**Local newspaper.** Local newspapers often print announcements about students who win scholarships. Keep a record of the scholarships featured or go to the library or look online at back issues of the newspaper. Check last year's spring issues (between March and June) for announcements of scholarship recipients. Contact the sponsoring organizations to see if you're eligible to enter the next competition.

## Searching Beyond Your Backyard

Once you have exhausted the opportunities in the community, it is time to broaden your search. Although the applicant pool is often larger with national awards, you shouldn't rule them out.

### "Smaller Is Sometimes Better"
### John Chin, Scholarship Winner

I had two friends who were determined to beat each other at winning scholarships. One decided to apply for only the top national scholarships and spent his time crafting a handful of great applications. My other friend, who knew that he would not be able to compete on a national level, concentrated only on local scholarships and applied to as many as he could.

At first it looked like my friend who applied to the big nationwide scholarships would win. He made the semifinals in several competitions and won a couple of $1,000 prizes.

However, his glory was short-lived. My other friend was constantly winning small $250 to $500 prizes. When everything was finally totaled, his collection of small but plentiful loot was $500 more!

When I became a senior guess which strategy I used to win scholarships!

Because many national award programs have marketing budgets, finding these awards may actually be a little easier than the local awards. Most national awards will be advertised and the following places will help you track them down:

**Internet.** The Internet is more than a place to post photos and trade music. (Legally, of course!) One of the benefits of online scholarship directories is that they can be updated at any time. Thus, if you search an online scholarship directory, you can usually find up-to-date information on new scholarships. We recommend that you use as many online scholarship databases as possible as long as they are free. There are enough quality free databases that you should not have to pay for any online search. Here are a few we recommend:

- SuperCollege (www.supercollege.com)
- MoolahSpot (www.moolahspot.com)
- Sallie Mae (www.salliemae.com/scholarships)
- CollegeXpress (www.collegexpress.com/scholarships/search)
- The College Board (https://bigfuture.collegeboard.org/scholarship-search)
- Scholarships.com (www.scholarships.com)
- AdventuresinEducation (www.aie.org)
- CollegeNet (www.collegenet.com)
- Mario Einaudi Center for International Studies (www.einaudi.cornell.edu/funding)

Just remember that while many online databases claim to have billions of dollars in scholarships listed, they represent only a tiny fraction of what is available. We have personally used nearly every free scholarship database on the Internet and know from experience that none of them (including our own at www.supercollege.com) lists every scholarship that you might win. Think of these databases as starting points, that they are not the only places to find awards.

**Professional associations.** There is an association for every profession you can imagine. Whether you want to be a doctor, teacher or helicopter pilot, there are professional organizations that exist not only to advance the profession, but also to encourage students to enter that field by awarding grants and scholarships.

To find these associations, contact people who are already in the profession. If you think you want to become a computer programmer, ask computer programmers about the associations to which they belong. Also look at the trade magazines that exist for the profession since they have advertisements for various professional organizations.

> ### Don't Write Off the Big Competitions
>
> *Don't be discouraged from applying to a scholarship that attracts a lot of students. After all, somebody has to win these awards, and there is no reason that it can't be you.*

Another way to find associations is through books like *The Encyclopedia of Associations.* This multi-volume set found at most college libraries lists nearly every professional association in the United States. Once you find these associations, contact them or visit their websites to see if they offer scholarships.

Professional associations often provide scholarships for upper-level college students, graduate school or advanced training. But even high school students who know what they want to do after college can find money from associations.

**Big business.** If you've never received a personal "thank you" from large companies like Coca-Cola, Tylenol or Microsoft, here it is. A lot of these have charitable foundations that award scholarships. Companies give these awards to give something back to the community (and the positive PR sure doesn't hurt either). When you visit company websites, look for links to their foundations, which often manage the scholarship programs.

Many companies offer similar types of scholarships. What if you're a student film maker? Think about all the companies that make money or sell products to you from cameras to film to tripods. Are you into industrial music? What special software or instruments do you use? How about the makers of audio equipment? Consider the companies that will benefit from more people using their products and services.

Some companies also offer awards to attract future employees. For example, Microsoft, the software company, sponsors a scholarship program for student programmers. Be sure to investigate companies that employ people in your field of study—especially if it is highly competitive—to see if they offer scholarships.

**Colleges.** You may think that checks only travel from your pocket to your college to pay for tuition. But colleges actually give a lot of money to students. Some of this money comes from the college itself while other money is from generous donations of alumni. Every college administers a number of scholarships, some based on financial need and some based on merit. A list of scholarships offered by your college is usually available online. What many students don't know is that often a student's application for admission is also used by the college to determine if he or she may win a scholarship. This is one reason it is worth the submission of any optional essay suggested on a college application. Even if the essay does not impact your admission, it could be used to award you some scholarship dollars.

## Truly Outrageous Scholarships

Believe it or not there are scholarships for students who are left-handed or even skilled at using duct tape. You've probably heard rumors of outrageous scholarships with criteria so specific or outlandish that few students qualify. It may be seductive to think that there might be an award with such specific criteria that only you qualify. But don't spend too much time looking for these types of scholarships. You will win more money if you search for more normal awards that reward your specific range of interests, achievements and background.

Nevertheless, as you search for scholarships, you will discover some strange awards. We certainly did. We want to share a few of these choice awards with you. Keep in mind that the majority of scholarships do not have criteria as outrageous as these. But reading about them is certainly entertaining.

### The Unathletic Scholarship

We have all heard of athletic scholarships. But how about one for those of us who don't participate in any sports? Bucknell University in Lewisburg, Pennsylvania, has an award for those who are unathletic. It was created by a frugal bachelor who left $1 million to create a scholarship for students who don't drink or smoke and, most important, do not participate in any "strenuous" athletics whatsoever. To qualify, you also need to be from certain counties in Pennsylvania.

### The Lefty Award

Lefties put up with a lot of inconveniences—from hard-to-use scissors to smeared ink when writing in notebooks. Now, there is a scholarship that rewards the roughly 10 percent of students who are left-handed. The Mary Francis Beckley scholarship provides up to $1,500 for students at Juniata College in Huntingdon, Pennsylvania. The scholarship is in honor of Mary Francis, a left-hander who met her future husband (also a lefty) while both were attending college.

### Tall Scholarship

As the name suggests, the Tall Club International scholarship program is for tall students--you must be under 21 years old and at least 5'10" if you're female or 6'2" if you're male.

### Little People Scholarship

At the other end of the spectrum, there are also scholarships for those who are short in stature from the Little People of America. You must be no

taller than 4'10" and have a medically diagnosed form of dwarfism.

### The Stuck at Prom Scholarship

The makers of "Duck" brand duct tape sponsor this award. The prize is a $6,000 scholarship for the couple that goes to their high school prom in the most original attire made from—you guessed it—duct tape. This award will give new meaning to the next time you seal a box with the sticky stuff.

### Candy Lovers Scholarship

Are you smitten with Snickers? Hankering for Hershey's kisses? Or gaga for Ghirardelli chocolate? Unfortunately, it's not enough to be a mere candy lover. You must also demonstrate an interest in confectionary technology to win this award from the National Candy Technologists.

### David Letterman Scholarship

He may be most famous for his Top 10 Lists, but David Letterman also has a scholarship for telecommunications students at his alma mater, Ball State University. This scholarship is sometimes nicknamed the C Student Scholarship because its namesake was a C student and the award is based on creativity not grades.

### Quack! Duck Calling Contest

Do you have a talent for duck calling? The Chick and Sophie Major Memorial Contest awards the country's best duck calls.

### Million Dollar Name

Did you know that there is one last name in America that can win you a full-tuition scholarship to Loyola University in Chicago? If you are Catholic and have the following last name you can get a four-year scholarship. Ready? The winning name is Zolp. And to prevent any of you from changing your last name, we should warn you that the school does require that this be the name on your birth certificate.

While these awards are good for a laugh, remember that they are not common, and you should not spend your time trying to find an obscure award that only you can win. Focus instead on creating a list of awards that match your entire range of interests and achievements.

# I Have My Big List of Scholarships. Now What?

Until now, we have focused on places to find scholarships. If you invest time exploring these areas, you should have a fairly long list of potential scholarships. It may be tempting to start cranking out applications. However, this would waste valuable time. Just because you find an award for which you qualify does not mean that you should immediately apply. You want to focus your energies (and limited time) only on those awards that you have the best chance of winning.

# How to Choose Scholarships You Can Win

It would save a lot of time if you knew beforehand which scholarships you'd win and which you wouldn't. With this information, you'd only spend time applying for the scholarships you knew would result in cash in your pocket.

There is no way to be 100 percent certain that you'll win any scholarship. But if you know enough about the scholarship and the organization giving away the money, you can determine if your background, interests and achievements make you a strong contender. By doing the detective work to uncover the purpose of the scholarships on your list, you will be able to focus time on those that fit you best and therefore offer the best chance of winning.

### #1. Heed the Words from the Sponsors

When you're watching television, it's perfectly acceptable to get up and grab a soda or munchies during the commercial breaks. Advertisers certainly don't like it, but there are no negative repercussions for ignoring the sponsors' messages. This is not the case for scholarships.

Scholarships, of course, don't have commercial breaks, but they do have sponsors—the organizations that are providing the money. Nobody, and we mean nobody, gives away money without a reason. Every sponsor has a mission for giving away their hard-earned cash. This mission may be a goal they are trying to achieve or ideology they are trying to promote.

> **Thousands of Scholarships But Only One You**
>
> *It is so important to be selective about which scholarships you apply to. Learning not to apply to a scholarship you won't win is just as important as applying to a scholarship you think you can win.*

For example, a teachers' organization might award a scholarship because its members want to encourage students

**Thinking Like a Judge**

*Train yourself to think from the perspective of the scholarship judges. What are they trying to accomplish by awarding the scholarship? What kind of student are they seeking?  What is the organization's goal and mission?*

to enter the teaching profession. The scholarship fulfills this mission since it helps support students who want to major in education. An environmental group might sponsor a scholarship with the mission of promoting environmental awareness. It might reward students who have done environmental work in school. A local bank might give money to a student who has done a great deal of public service as a way to give back to the community in which it does business.

It is critical that you find the mission of the scholarship since it will tell you exactly what kind of student the selection committee is seeking. Take our example of the teachers' scholarship. By knowing that the organization wants to encourage students to become teachers, you can surmise (if they don't explicitly say so) that they want to give their money to students who are committed to becoming teachers and can show this through qualifications such as being an education major, student teacher or volunteer tutor. You can also guess that when picking a winner, the selection committee will look for students who enjoy interacting with young people and who value education.

The mission of a scholarship is your best clue to what the selection committee wants in a winner. As you go through each award on your list, uncover its mission. In other words, your mission is to find their mission.

## #2. Do the Detective Work

To uncover the mission of a scholarship you need to do some detective work. Begin by carefully reading the description of the scholarship. Sometimes the answer is clearly stated in the award description. Also look at the eligibility requirements to see what kind of questions the scholarship sponsors are asking. Is there a GPA requirement? If there is and it's relatively high, grades are probably important. If the GPA requirement is low, then grades are probably not important. Does the application ask for a list of extracurricular activities? If so, they are probably a significant part of the selection criteria. Do you need to submit an essay on a specific topic or a project to demonstrate proficiency in a field of study? All these requirements are clues about what the scholarship judges think will (and won't) be important.

For example, a public service scholarship may be based only on your philanthropic acts. If that is the case, the entire application will most likely be focused on descriptions of your selfless deeds. On the other hand, a scholarship given by a major corporation may be based on a combination of grades, leadership and personal integrity. The eligibility requirements will provide clues about what criteria the organization will use to judge you and therefore what they consider important.

After you have scanned the application requirements, ask yourself: What is the purpose of the awarding organization? Whether it's helping students who dream of becoming circus performers or rewarding students for their religious fervor, every organization has a reason for its existence. If you're lucky, the goal is clearly stated in the description of the organization, but sometimes you need to look deeper. For example, even if the scholarship description does not directly state it, you can be sure that an award given by an organization that is composed of local physicians will probably prefer that the winner have a connection with medicine or an intention to enter the medical field.

Just as your friends are a reflection of you, most clubs and organizations want to reach students who are similar to their membership. If you don't know much about the organization, contact them to learn background information regarding the history, purpose or contributions of the group. Check out the organization's website to get a sense of their mission and membership. Read their brochures or publications. The more you know about why the organization is giving the award, the better you'll understand how you may or may not fit.

Once you have a sense of whom the scholarship committee is looking for, you can determine if you can make a strong case that you are that person. The only way to do this is to be honest about yourself.

## #3. Be Realistic About How Great You Are

Here's where you need to separate reality in your mom's eyes from the rest of the world's reality. From Mom's perspective, you are the next Bill Gates, Albert Einstein or Amelia Earhart. Mom may be right. But as you are applying for scholarships, take a realistic, un-momlike look at yourself. You know what your strengths are and aren't better than anyone else.

Be careful not to be too hard on yourself. After working with thousands of students, we have learned that students more often underestimate their abilities than overestimate. Try to be realistic, but also don't sell yourself short. Remember that scholarship judges are not looking for the perfect match. There are a lot of factors that will influence their decision, and many of these things like personality or motivation are difficult to measure. However, you do want to find a match between the mission of the scholarship and some of your own interests, goals and achievements.

If you are your school's star journalist, naturally you should apply for journalism scholarships. But if all you have done is write a single letter to the editor, spend your time applying to scholarships that better match what you have accomplished. You can still apply for a journalism scholarship, especially if you only recently realized that you want to become a journalist, but you will be at a disadvantage compared to the other applicants and therefore should place this award below other awards on your to-do list.

As you go through your list of scholarships, move to the bottom those in which you have the weakest matches to the goal of the scholarships. Make those awards that fit you best your highest priority. These are the ones that you want to focus on first.

## #4. Size Up the Competition

Sometimes knowing how tough your competition is will also help you choose which scholarships to select as your focus (and hence your first applications). Your competition can be as broad as every student in America or as limited as the members of your school's Delta Phi Epsilon. As you can guess, the larger your competition, the more outstanding you need to be to win the scholarship. Look at your accomplishments and think about how they compare to others at your school, in your city and in your state.

If you are a pianist and the highest honor you've won is your school's talent show, you probably have a reasonable chance of winning a musical scholarship provided by your school. If your highest honor is winning a state competition, you will want to apply for state and even national-level music scholarships. By understanding how you match up to others who will apply for awards, you can spend your time on scholarships that you have a strong shot to win.

### #5. Remember the Clock Never Stops

Scholarship deadlines are not like tax deadlines, where there is a single day when all forms are due. The deadlines for scholarships vary. Be aware of these crucial dates. Unless you plan carefully, you may miss out on a scholarship simply because you don't have the time to create a decent application. Sandwiched among studying, sleeping and everything else in your busy life, there is limited time to spend on applying for scholarships. If you find a great scholarship that is due next week but requires a yet-to-be-written original composition that would take a month, you should probably pass on the competition. If you know that, given the amount of time available, you won't be able to do an acceptable job, it's better to pass and move on to awards in which you have the time to put together a winning application. Remember, too, that you may be able to apply for the award next year.

> **Balance Quality and Quantity When Choosing Awards**
>
> *When deciding how many scholarships to apply for, create a balance between the quality and quantity of your applications. Don't apply for 75 awards sending in the same application to each. At the same time, don't apply to one or two scholarships and spend four weeks perfecting each application.*

## The Magic Number of Scholarships

The truth is that there is no magic number of scholarships for which you should apply. But you should avoid the extremes. Don't select only a couple of scholarships with the intention of spending countless hours crafting the perfect application. While it is true that to win you need to turn in quality applications, there is also a certain amount of subjective decision making. So even with the perfect application, you may not win. This means that you need to apply to more than a few scholarships. On the other hand, don't apply for 75 awards, sending in the same application to each. You'll just waste your time. You need to strike a balance between quantity and quality.

After you prioritize your scholarships with the ones you feel fit you best at the top of the list, push yourself to apply to as many as you can, working from top to bottom. You probably won't get to the end. This is okay since you have the least chance of winning the awards at the bottom anyway. By prioritizing and working methodically down your list, you will have hedged your bets by making sure that your first applications are for the scholarships that you have the best chance of winning while also not limiting yourself to only a handful of awards.

## Don't Look for Scholarships Alone

Many students treat searching for scholarships like a spy game, where they keep the scholarships that they find top secret. They probably feel that the fewer people who know about the scholarship, the better chance they have of winning.

This is totally counterproductive.

While researching this book, we interviewed hundreds of students and only a small handful actually collaborated with others on their scholarship search. Yet, the students who did work with others found it much easier to find awards and to stay motivated. Ultimately, they won more money than the students who decided to go it alone.

Think about it. You are applying to a scholarship along with thousands of other students from across your state. Does it really matter if your friend applies? Absolutely not. What do you have to gain by working in a group and sharing the awards that you find? Plenty. The students who worked with others discovered that by sharing the awards they found and pooling their resources, they were able to find more scholarships in less time than they would have if they had worked alone. The end result was that these students had more scholarships to apply to and more time to focus on their applications. Hence, they won more money.

Look around you and find others who are also hunting for scholarships. Agree to share awards and even come up with assignments for spreading around the task of searching different sources for scholarships.

You will also find that an additional benefit of being part of a group is that it will keep you motivated. It's easier to stay focused when you have others depending on you. There is no reason why the scholarship process should be one that you embark on alone.

## Chapter 2 Summary: Find Scholarships You Can Win

**Use the two-prong approach to select scholarships.** First, find as many as you can. Then screen and prioritize them based on whether or not you can present yourself as the ideal candidate.

**Find scholarships all around you.** To find scholarships, investigate the surroundings such as your school, community organizations, the Internet, your parents' and your employers, local and state governments and local newspapers and publications. Don't neglect your own backyard.

**Don't count on outrageous awards.** Look at all your talents and interests.

**Choose scholarships you can win.** Some tips: Try to understand what the judges want to achieve by awarding the scholarship and what they are looking for in the winner. Survey your qualifications, and be realistic about how well you fit the awards. Size up the competition both past and present.

**Apply to as many as time allows.** There are two factors that limit the number of scholarships you apply for: the amount of time you have to apply and your fit with the scholarship criteria. Apply for as many appropriate scholarships as you can for which you have the time to develop quality applications.

**Don't go it alone.** Form your own network of scholarship searchers to spread out the work and find more awards.

# Avoid Scholarship Scams

• • • • • • • • • • • • • • • • • • • • • • • •

In this chapter, you'll learn:

- The false promises of scholarship scam artists and how to avoid them

- How to recognize the telltale signs of a scholarship scam

- How one student got taken by an offer that was too good to be true

• • • • • • • • • • • • • • • • • • • • • • • •

## Scholarships That Steal

Now that you know where to find scholarships, you need to be aware of some dangers that may be lurking nearby. While the great majority of scholarship providers and services have philanthropic intentions, not all do. There are some scholarship services and even scholarships themselves that you need to avoid. According to the Federal Trade Commission, in one year there were more than 175,000 cases reported of scholarship scams, costing consumers $22 million. And this is a low estimate since most scholarship scams go unreported!

While we were fortunate to have not been victims of a scholarship scam, we have to admit that the offers we received were tempting. We both received letters in high school and college from companies that promised to help us find and win "unclaimed" scholarships. The pitch was tempting: There is money out there that no one is claiming. All we needed to do was purchase their service to get a list of these awards. Had we done so, we would have been $400 poorer and certainly none the richer.

In this chapter, we will describe some of the common scams that you may encounter. You must avoid these offers, no matter how glamorous they seem.

### The Big Picture

The key to avoiding a scholarship scam is to understand the motivation of the people behind these scams. Those who operate financial aid rip-offs know that paying for college is something that makes you extremely nervous. They also know that most people don't have extensive experience when it comes to scholarships and may therefore believe that there are such things as "hidden" or "unclaimed" scholarships. These charlatans take advantage of your fears and discomfort by offering an easy answer with a price tag that seems small compared to the promised benefits.

Be aware that you are vulnerable to these kinds of inducements. Think about it this way. If you have a weakness for buying clothes, you need to be extra vigilant when you are at the shopping mall. Similarly, because you need money for college, you are more susceptible to tempting scholarship offers. Acknowledging that these fears make you a target of scam artists is the first step to spotting their traps.

## How to Spot a Scholarship Scam

Imagine one day you open your mailbox and find a letter from a very official-sounding organization offering a personalized analysis of your financial aid opportunities and expert recommendations of scholarships you should apply for—all for the low cost of a few hundred dollars. You may think that is not much, considering that the cost of your education could run into six digits. That's exactly what these companies want you to think. The truth is that the information they provide is free public information (like descriptions of various loan programs) and none of it is truly personalized—unless you call typing your name on top of a photocopy personalized.

In most cases there is nothing illegal about these offers, which is why they continue to exist, but they are certainly a waste of money. Our advice is to save your money and invest a little time in researching financial aid opportunities yourself.

The following are some examples of "tempting" offers that you should avoid. Remember while the words may change, the message is still the same: Pay us and you won't have to worry about how to pay for tuition.

**"Pay us $$$ and we will create a personalized financial aid plan for your child. We have a library of hundreds of resources that we will use to create an individualized financial aid plan for you."** What they don't tell you is that the resources they use can easily be found for free on the Internet or in your library. In fact, the scholarships listed in this book are probably their "resources." Save yourself hundreds of dollars and find the scholarships yourself. Plus, you'll do a more thorough job and actually be able to find scholarships that you can win.

**"Pay us $$$ and we will research and identify the 20 scholarships that fit you best. Why spend weeks researching scholarships when our specialized researchers can do it for you? We have scholarship sources that no one else does. Plus, you are guaranteed to win at least one."** You would receive a list of 20 scholarships you could have found on your own for free. Plus, any scholarship that is a "guaranteed" win is a scam as we'll explain later.

**"Each year millions of dollars in scholarships are not awarded. Pay us $$$ and we will locate unclaimed scholarship dollars that your son or daughter can win."** The reality is that there are very few "unclaimed" scholarships. Those that are have such specific eligibility requirements that almost no one can qualify. Plus, you can find thousands of scholarships on your own in books and on the Internet without paying a search fee. You'll also do a much better job.

**"You're a finalist in our scholarship. Pay us $$$ for your registration fee.**

**Avoid All Guarantees**

*You can usually detect a scholarship scam if the promise is too good to be true, if you are "guaranteed" to win or if payment is required.*

**You're guaranteed to win!"** The truth is that you are not guaranteed to win, or if you did win, the prize would be less than the registration fee. Real scholarships never require any fee from applicants.

**"You've won our scholarship, guaranteed! All we need is your credit card number to verify your eligibility."** Instead of winning a "guaranteed" scholarship, you would get some surprise charges on your next credit card bill.

**"You qualify for our exclusive, incredibly low-interest loan program. All you need to do is pay us $$$ to lock in the rate."** The truth is that you would pay the fee but not get the loan. Or you might get the loan, but the interest rate could be much higher than if you shopped around.

**"Come to our very informative financial aid seminar, where you'll learn our secret strategies for scholarships found nowhere else in the world."** Seminars like these may actually be sales pitches for any combination of the above. Not all seminars are scams or rip-offs, so you'll have to use your own judgment. However, one giveaway is if the seminar sounds like a sales pitch or contains promises that sound too good to be true. If you feel like the seminar is just a live version of a late-night infomercial, you are probably looking at a seminar where you will be asked to part with your money for what may be totally worthless information.

In general, the major telltale sign that you are about to be taken by a dubious offer is if you are asked to pay any significant amount of money. Particularly if you are applying for a scholarship, never part with your money. Scholarships are meant to pay *you* money, not the other way around.

## Red Flags That Indicate a Scam

Here are some common red flags to watch for:

- **Registration, entry or administrative fee:** Legitimate scholarship and financial aid programs do not require an upfront fee. Do not pay for anything more than the cost of postage. Remember, real scholarships are about giving you money, not taking funds *from* you.

- **Soliciting your credit card number or bank account:** Never give out this kind of financial information to anyone who contacts you from

## "I Lost $500 from a Scholarship Scam"
### Steven Hecht, Scam Victim

My parents and I attended a free seminar sponsored by a college financial aid service company. During the seminar, the speaker explained how competitive it was to win scholarships and how many dollars aren't awarded each year because students just don't know about the scholarships. He said that his company would use its comprehensive national database to produce a personalized scholarship program for me. Even better, if I didn't win $2,500 in scholarships from their program, they would refund the fee of $495. My parents and I thought that because we could get our money back, there was no risk in trying the program. Along with most of the other families at the seminar, we signed up for the program.

A week later, we received a packet in the mail. It contained some articles about scholarships and financial aid and a one-page document with scholarships listed. I applied for each of the scholarships. Within the next few months, I won none of them.

My parents remembered the guarantee and we wrote a letter requesting our refund of the $495. Were we surprised when our request was refused. The company said we needed to read the small print of the contract we signed. The guarantee was that I would either win $2,500 in scholarships or that the company's program would provide opportunities that could be worth $2,500. In our excitement on the night of the seminar, we never bothered to read the small print. We were out almost $500. We definitely could have used the money toward my tuition instead of toward a bogus scholarship scam.

a scholarship organization. No scholarship needs this information to award you money for college.

- **Refusal to reveal name, address or phone number:** You know that something is wrong when the person on the telephone won't reveal his or her name or contact information.

- **Guarantee:** There is no such thing as a guaranteed scholarship in exchange for a fee. Legitimate scholarships are based on merit or need, not your willingness to pay a registration fee.

If you discover that you have been the victim of one of these scams, don't be embarrassed. This happens to thousands of parents and students every year. Report your experience to the Better Business Bureau and Federal Trade Commission (www.ftc.gov) to help prevent it from happening to others. Also, be sure to

> ### Red Flag
> The biggest tip-off to a scholarship scam is that you must part with your money. Any time that you are asked to open your wallet, be wary.

write us about it in care of SuperCollege, 2713 Newlands Avenue, Belmont, CA 94002. We maintain lists of dishonest and worthless programs and would like to know if you encounter any new ones.

The adage of consumer protection applies to scholarships. If an offer sounds too good to be true, it probably is.

## Chapter 3 Summary: Avoid Scholarship Scams

**Know when a guarantee is not a guarantee.** What is tempting about scholarship scams is that they promise guaranteed money or a money-back guarantee. Read the small print—there is no such thing as a guaranteed scholarship.

**Recognize your weakness.** If you are stressed about paying for col-lege, realize that you are especially susceptible to unrealistic promises to help solve your problem.

**Keep your wallet closed.** Schol-arship services and applications should always be free. If a service sounds too good to be true, it prob-ably is.

# Get Organized and Maximize Your Time

In this chapter, you'll learn:

- How to prioritize the awards you find to focus on your best prospects

- Time-saving tips for creating a library of reusable materials

- How to use class materials to apply to scholarships

## Saving Time and Effort with Scholarships

While there is a seemingly infinite number of scholarships out there, there is only a finite amount of time that you can spend applying to them. That's why you need to get organized. Even if you're the type of person whose room is littered with dirty laundry and crumpled papers, you can still get a handle on your scholarship applications by approaching organization in the right way. Doing so will help you meet all the deadlines, apply to the most number of awards, and, most importantly, save the most money!

In addition to honing your organizations skills, you can also use strategies to maximize your time. By learning how to recycle what you've written and creating a library of reusable materials, you'll be able to apply to more scholarships by not starting over from scratch for each one.

In this chapter you'll learn how to get organized and how to make the most of the limited amount of time that you have.

## The Big Picture

Once you have scholarships to apply to, it's tempting to just start, well, applying. But let's think about this for a moment. You have 10, 20 or maybe even more opportunities in front of you. Unless you plan to make applying for scholarships a full-time job, you probably won't make it through all of them. That's why it's best to spend a little time prioritizing. This will ensure that you apply to the best scholarships first, and if you run out of time, you'll still be okay. Really, it doesn't take that much effort, and it'll save you time in the end.

## Prioritize the Scholarships

In the last chapter, you narrowed down the list of scholarships to probably between a dozen and a couple dozen. Now it's time to figure out which ones to tackle first. There are five measures for determining the scholarships' order:

**Deadline.** This is the greatest factor in ranking the awards. You might have guessed that generally you should apply for the scholarships with the earliest deadlines first. However, this is not always the case, especially when you're running out of time, and there's a scholarship with a later deadline that is a better fit.

**Fit.** How well does the award fit you? If the description from the scholarship organization paints a word-for-word picture of you, then this is one that should jump to the top of the list. Be realistic about how your achievements match up to what the scholarship organization is seeking. For example, if the criteria call for contributions to your school or community, only apply if you've actually made these contributions on an impressive scale. Volunteering once or twice doesn't cut it, but recruiting a group of volunteers to help out does.

**How much work is involved.**  If you are evaluating two scholarships—one for which you can reuse an essay and recommendations you already have, or another for which you need a new essay and recommendations—rank the one that takes less effort higher.

**Competition.**  There's a simple axiom when it comes to scholarships—apply to those that you have the best chances of winning. Numbers do count, and this means that your odds increase with awards with fewer competitors. Of course this doesn't mean that you shouldn't apply for national or statewide scholarships, but it does mean that you should focus your efforts initially on local scholarships that have decent-sized prizes. Generally, the wider the scholarship's net, the more competition there will be. So national awards will draw the most competition, followed by regional, state, county and city awards.

**What else is going on in your life at the time.**  Despite our best efforts, we know that you have more going on in your life than applying for scholarships, so plan for it!  As you're prioritizing, keep in mind the other things going in your life with family, school, friends, etc.

## Schedule Scholarships

Once you've prioritized the scholarships, put them in the order that you'll work on them and create deadlines for yourself. This order may be chronological, or it may be different when you factor in the competition and how much work is involved.

Set up personal deadlines for yourself for when you will:
- Request or download the application form
- Complete the application form
- Request your transcript if required
- Write the essay(s)
- Request recommendation letters if required
- Gather additional materials requested
- Mail or submit the completed application

It helps if you schedule time each week to work on the scholarships. Think of applying for scholarships as a

> ### Why You Need Deadlines
>
> *Because you have so much going on in your life, it's easy to lose track of time when it comes to scholarships. That's why it makes sense to map out what needs to be done and more importantly when it needs to be done.*

> **A Word of Caution about Recycling Your Materials**
> ———
> *While we highly recommend that you reuse materials as often as possible, make sure that the materials still fit. If they don't, edit them or start from scratch.*

part-time job, and schedule "work hours" just as you would for a job. This will help you stay on track and keep scholarships at the top of your mind.

It can also help to make your schedule public. Post a calendar of your deadlines so that you have a daily reminder of what needs to be done and by when. Consider getting your parents involved too. Mom or Dad can be great at reminding you of deadlines, as we're sure you already know, but only do this if their reminders will inspire, not annoy, you.

## Have a Monthly Check-in

Once you have a scholarship schedule and get rolling, it can help to have some regular check-ins on your progress. Each month, reevaluate where you are and what's left to do. Consider any changes in your accomplishments, your schedule outside of applying for scholarships and whether you overestimated or underestimated how quickly you could work. Make any necessary adjustments to the schedule.

## Create a Library of Reusable Materials

The quickest way to write an essay is to not write it. No – we don't mean that you should steal someone else's work, but we do encourage you to steal your own! If done correctly, recycling your own materials can be a significant time saver. There are more details on how to recycle essays in Chapter 10, but we wanted to mention this as a strategy to maximize your time that applies to more than essays.

While you probably won't be able to just copy and paste an entire application, you will be able to reuse data from one application to the next. You can save yourself some time by keeping completed applications handy for your reference. For example, maybe you'll be able to copy and paste a description of one of your accomplishments from one application to another. At the very least, you'll have a list of all of your achievements in one place to refer back to. This is why it's critical to save all of your old applications!

Similarly, save multiple versions of your resume. Depending on the scholarship, you will want to highlight your different strengths. Create one master resume that has all of your accomplishments. Then cut and paste different versions of the resume based on, for example, public service or academic achievement.

Besides essays and applications, your scholarship library should also contain extra copies of all of your recommendation letters, especially the ones that the recommenders allowed you to see. When you ask your recommenders for letters, ask them for extra copies to keep on file. Then you can apply to scholarships with fast-approaching deadlines, and you won't have to bother your recommender each time you apply for an award.

## Take Advantage of Your Classes

When you think about the assignments you've done for them, you might wonder how your classes could possibly help you apply for scholarships. However, if you pull out your old papers, you might just find one that you can use as a scholarship essay. Even if you can't use the whole essay, you may be able to use part of it. Maybe your latest US History paper on the Revolutionary War won't help much for your current application, but you never know when your essay from freshman English about "role models" will. Look back through your files of saved papers. Be open when looking at your old papers, and remember that even though the topic may not be a precise fit, even a slight head start on the writing process will help.

Another option is to be forward-thinking. If you have an assignment coming up, ask your teacher or professor if you can write it on a topic from one of your scholarship applications. If you explain your reason, he or she will likely say yes and you can kill the proverbial two birds with a single stone.

## Think Early about Recommenders

In Chapter 9, we go into great detail on how to select the best recommenders and how to get them to write the best possible letters. We just wanted to mention even before you get to that chapter that it's never too early to start lining up recommenders. Start laying the groundwork now by building your relationship with your teachers, professors, counselors or other people you may ask.

## Make a Checklist for Each Application

Countless students have been disqualified because of incomplete applications. To prevent the same fate, make a quick checklist for each of the applications you'll submit. It may even help to put all of the materials for each application in a separate folder. This way you'll know when you need more copies of a recommendation letter or official transcripts.

While it takes time to get organized, in the long run, you'll save time, be able to apply for more scholarships and have better applications.

## Chapter 4 Summary: Get Organized

**Once you've narrowed down your list of scholarships, it's time to prioritize the awards.** Rank them by deadline, fit, the work that's involved, the competition and what else is going on in your life.

**Schedule when you'll apply for the scholarships by setting personal deadlines.** These may coincide with the actual deadlines but will take into account how you've prioritized the awards.

**Create a library of reusable materials to save time.** It'll help to have old essays and applications at your fingertips for reference and for recycling.

**Take advantage of your classes** by editing old papers and using the scholarship essay topics for future papers.

**Give your recommenders enough time to craft strong letters.** Remember that you aren't the only student who will be asking them to write letters, and now is the time to get on their good side.

**Make a checklist for each application** so you don't forget anything.

# The Packaging of You and Your Personal Theme

• • • • • • • • • • • • • • • • • • • • • • • • • • • •

**In this chapter, you'll learn:**

- How to use information about the scholarships to your advantage

- What a personal theme is and why you need one

• • • • • • • • • • • • • • • • • • • • • • • • • • • •

## Marketing Yourself

When you think of an advertisement, you might think of the latest hip musician to appear in an iPhone commercial or beer bottles playing football during breaks in the Super Bowl. Radio hits and beer may not evoke images of hard work spent applying for scholarships, but understanding the idea behind them and why multi-billion dollar companies put them to use can be helpful in your scholarship application process. In a sense, the scholarship application is an advertisement for you. You are gathering together information about yourself to present to the scholarship judges to convince them that you are the best possible recipient for their award. In a way, you are packaging yourself and your accomplishments through the application.

In this chapter, we'll share with you how to do this in a highly effective but not over-the-top way. You'll learn how to decipher exactly what the scholarship organization is seeking, how to identify your strengths and how they'll match up, and what to do and what not to do for your overall application theme.

## The Big Picture

It might seem strange that you should pick out a "theme" or two for yourself; after all, you're a unique individual, right? But while it is important to let the selection committee know what makes you unique, it is also important to tell your story in a way that forms a lasting impression. Even though you are an individual, you are probably well aware that it is human nature to categorize. Scholarship judges want to see you as the Musician Guy or the Athletic Girl. These classifications help to string your accomplishments together and even strengthen them by providing an easy-to-follow connection among them.

## Learn Why They're Giving Away the Money

Before you can package yourself and figure out your personal theme, you need to understand what kind of package the judges want. In other words, why are they giving away the money? The easiest way to find out is from the scholarship organizations themselves.

Without exception, all scholarship organizations tell you why they are giving the award or the purpose of the scholarship. Just take a look at the descriptions of the awards. Some key words to look for are, "purpose," "based on" "rewards" or "recognize." When you see these words, a green light should go off because they indicate that the mission or purpose of the scholarship is to follow. Using this information, you can craft all of your application materials to demonstrate how you best fit the award. Here are some examples:

**Coca-Cola Scholars Foundation:** Rewards leadership and excellence as exemplified through academic achievement and extracurricular activities, including commitment to community service.

*Purpose: The key words about this scholarship's purpose are, "academic achievement," "extracurricular activities" and "community service." These are the qualities that you should highlight in your application.*

**Burger King Scholars Program:** The purpose of this program is to support students based on their GPA, work experience, extracurricular activities and/or community service.

*Purpose: This program seeks students who achieve both inside and outside of the classroom. It is important to highlight your academic achievements through your grades and the challenging courses you've taken. Non-academic achievements may cover work experience, activities and/or community service so you should focus on how you've excelled in one of these areas.*

**Prudential Spirit of Community Awards:** This community service program rewards students who are "making a positive difference in their towns and neighborhoods."

*Purpose: Naturally, it is essential that you focus on community service, but what is key is that you demonstrate how your work has had a "positive" impact on your community.*

**Most Valuable Student Competition:** Selection is based on scholarship, leadership and financial need.

*Purpose: The winners are selected based on their ratings in academics, leadership and financial need. Since you aren't able to change your financial need, you need to focus on the two other areas that you are able to affect.*

**Bonner Scholars Program:** This program supports students who commit to 10 hours a week of community service during the school year and 280 hours in the summer.

*Purpose: This scholarship gives weight to the popular category of community service, but it's key that you demonstrate how your service has been "meaningful" to the community at large.*

> ### There's No Such Thing As a Free Lunch
>
> *Every scholarship organization has a reason for giving away its money. They may want to encourage a philosophy, promote a career field or even spread the word about their business. Your job is to figure out what this reason is and adapt your application accordingly.*

> ### Putting Yourself in a Box
>
> *It might seem contrary that you'd want to put yourself in a box by picking a personal theme. You have to remember that scholarship judges review hundreds or even thousands of applications. A theme will help them remember yours.*

## Learn What They're Basing Their Decision on

The other key to understanding what you will be judged on is their list of (surprise!) what you will be judged on, or the materials that you are required to submit. These may include an application, an essay, a transcript, recommendation letters and financial information.

Some organizations will spell out how much value the judges will place on each of these items by assigning percentages to each, but most will not. You can get a hint about the relative weight of each element from the breakdown of how much or how many of each item accounts for the complete application. For example, if you are required to submit an essay and three short answer essays (as opposed to just one short essay), you can guess that the essays and short answers play a heavy role. Likewise, if you must submit three recommendation letters (as opposed to one), you know that the opinions of others will be a strong factor.

The point of examining this is so that you know how best to create a cohesive picture of yourself through the most important materials that you will submit.

## Finding Your Theme and What to Do/Not to Do

Once you have a good idea of what the scholarship judges are seeking, you can then figure out how to best present yourself to them. This is where the "themes" come into play. Because we're all about celebrating individuality, it might sound strange that you'd want to pigeonhole yourself by a "theme." True, no two people are exactly the same. (Proof: we'll never understand why people think photos of cats dressed up as people are cute.) But when you start looking at those around you, you'll probably find that there are some traits that tend to be common among students.

You might be thinking, how dare we suggest that all athletes are the same! Of course that is not the case, but what we are saying is that there are some commonalities among student athletes and what you can highlight as a student athlete in your application. We also recognize that you may not fall neatly into a single category. You may be your school's top sprinter-math decathlete. If so, that's great, and you should see the tips that follow for both athletes and academics. However, remember that applications lose their steam when students try to identify themselves with four or even more themes in their applications. It's just too much clutter in a limited amount of space.

Following are some of the most common themes and tips for what to do or not to do for them. You'll see that these themes match up to some of the most popular purposes of scholarships. Note that you don't have to meet all of the criteria listed for each theme but should meet at least one, probably more.

## The Academic Achiever

You are an Academic Achiever if:

- You do well in classes and on standardized tests
- You are one of the top students in your class
- You are involved in academic clubs or activities
- You've won academic awards or honors
- You've attended academic summer programs or taken college courses
- You've done serious academic research

**Do:**

**Explain your academic passion.** Describe why you are so googoo for geography or hyped up on history. In other words, help a non-science person understand why you get so excited about researching autoimmune diseases.

**Cultivate relationships with your teachers or professors, especially in your strong subjects.** This will result in the strongest recommendation letters in the areas that count the most for you.

**If you still have time, go beyond what you do in class.** To really be the highest level Academic Achiever, you need to do more than do well in a class. If chemistry is your thing, you need to eat, drink and breathe chemistry! Okay, not really. But it would help build your theme if in addition to getting an A in the class, you were also an officer in the chemistry club and did some chemistry research in a college lab.

**Try to tie together your academic interests and activities**, if there are connections to be made.

> ### Details Count
>
> *Your accomplishments will be more impressive if you give details. Try to explain what your specific contributions were and what kind of difference your efforts made.*

**Don't:**

**Just count on your numbers to speak for themselves and take you to the top of the pile of applications.** Because you have good stats, it's tempting to just repeat them in places like the essay and recommendation letters. Resist this temptation, and instead use the essay and ask your recommenders to provide more context for your academic achievement.

**Only state that you have attended an academic program or taken college courses.** Explain what you learned.

## The Leader

You are a Leader if:

- You have held an elected or appointed position, the higher level the better
- You've led a significant special project or team

**Do:**

**Describe what you've achieved as a leader.** Throughout your application, it's important to share the specific things that you accomplished while a leader. For example, if you are the president of a service group, you can ask your advisor to write a recommendation letter, list the number of hours you've volunteered and your position in the application and write an essay on how you directed your school's rummage sale to raise funds for needy children.

**Explain what you've learned as a leader.** The more you can take the judges into your mindset the better.

**Don't:**

**Be afraid to take credit for your efforts.** It is common for students to use "we" instead of "I" because they want to make sure to not hog the credit. The truth is that the adult world is an "I" world, and the judges are more interested in what you as an individual achieved than what your group achieved. If you led a project or a group, it's okay to use "I." The judges will know that you are not claiming to have done everything yourself, but they will want to know the role that you as an individual played.

## The Community Servant

You are a Community Servant if:

- You've volunteered a significant number of hours for a cause
- You've led a special project or effort for a cause

**Do:**

> **Provide background for why you are so interested in saving the whales.** Why this cause when there are so many to choose from? What is your inspiration? This is important because it supports the fact that you are involved in your community not because it looks good on your resume but because you really care.

> **Contribute more than time to your cause.** It's good to volunteer a certain number of hours, but it's better to produce a tangible result or lead a group related to the cause. This is because anyone can volunteer as an aid at a hospital, but not anyone can work with the hospital administration to create a toy collection program for hospitalized children.

**Don't:**

> **Give a job description of your volunteer work.** Instead, outline the significance of what you did. Explain the results you saw, the number of people you helped or the funds raised for donation.

## The Artist

You are an Artist if:

- You are involved in the arts including theatre, dance, art, music or writing
- You have won honors or awards for your artistic talent
- You have performed in a school, community or professional setting
- You have had your artwork on display or your writing published

**Do:**

> **Have some validation for your talents besides your own word.** As you can tell from watching "America's Got Talent," there are many talentless people in the world who think that they have talent. Don't let the scholarship judges think that you are one of them! Think about how you can validate your artistic talent through recommendation letters from those who know your level ability or listing honors or awards or performances.

**Include an artistic resume,** if allowed. For actors, list the dates, locations, roles and directors for performances and training. For artists, list awards or honors, displays and art-related jobs or community service. For dancers, note training and performances by type (i.e., ballet, jazz, modern) including locations, dates and directors. For musicians, list honors and awards and performances, including position and dates. For creative writers, note editorial positions, published works and honors and awards.

**Include a portfolio, if allowed.** Work with your teacher or instructor to put together a portfolio that highlights your strongest work and shows the depth of your talent.

**Don't:**

**Overload the scholarship judges with examples of your work.** Part of the challenge of creating a portfolio is not only deciding which works to include but which not to include. The judges have limited time to look at or listen to your work so only include the strongest examples.

### The Athlete

You are an Athlete if:

● You compete in one or more sports at your school or in your community

**Do:**

**Check with NCAA rules to make sure you can receive the funds.** If you are being recruited by colleges, there are limits to the scholarships that you can receive. One of the most important restrictions is that you can't receive a scholarship (besides from the college) that may only be used at a specific institution.

**In addition to describing the physical side of your athletic ability, explain the mental side.** In other words, how does the sport help you grow intellectually? What have you learned from the experience?

**Go beyond the "teamwork" cliché.** Many students will say that they've learned about teamwork from athletics. While this is an admirable trait to learn, it is so often said that it can be boring for the scholarship judges. If you write about teamwork, try to write about it in a way that other student-athletes wouldn't. Or, just choose a different lesson learned from athletics.

**Don't:**

> **Focus only on athletics, especially if the scholarship also considers other factors such as academic performance.** It's important to address all of the qualities that the scholarship committee is seeking.

> **Write about the Big Game.** Or at least not in the same way that everyone else will be writing about the Big Game. It's common for applicants to write about the Big Game in a similar way: describing the sounds and feel of the field, setting up the challenge and then giving the play-by-play of the winning touchdown/basket/score/last few seconds. Try to think of a different topic to write about related to sports or a different aspect of the Big Game. It will make your application stand out.

Until now, the themes have not addressed if you have problem areas or weaknesses. You might think the best thing to do is to hide a flaw. However, there are some weaknesses that are difficult to hide or that should be explained. Here are these kinds of themes:

### The B or C Student or the Extremely Low Test Scorer

You are the B or C Student or the Extremely Low Test Scorer if:

- You have mostly Bs or Cs
- Your test scores are much lower than correlates with your grades

**Do:**

> **Explain briefly why you didn't do as well as you could have.** For grades, you can describe which subject areas or classes have given you problems and why. For exams, this can be an opportunity to outline why tests are not your strength (if that's the case). For either, you can explain the extenuating circumstances for why you didn't have enough time or as much focus as you needed.

> **Target the areas in which you've done well.** It's better to keep your explanations of your weaknesses short so that you can direct more attention to the areas in which you've excelled. Be

> **Focus on the Positive**
>
> It can help to explain your situation if it's less than stellar, but always return to the positive side. Describe what you learned from your circumstances or how you've grown.

### Everyone Has Something to Say

*Even if you weren't the captain of the team or the president of a club, you may have spent your time on an activity outside of school, working or taking care of family members. Scholarship judges are interested in these kinds of activities too.*

prepared to demonstrate through the essay and recommendations where your fortes lie.

**Expand on extenuating circumstances.** Scholarship judges will understand your situation better if they know that you faced extenuating circumstances such as a learning disability, family situation, an ill family member, financial difficulties or other responsibilities you held. This provides support for why you didn't perform as well as you could have.

**Ask your recommenders to validate your circumstances.** It can help to have someone else verify your situation because it will safeguard you from looking like you are simply making excuses.

**Don't:**

**Make excuses.** It's a good thing to let the scholarship committee know extenuating circumstances that may have affected your grades or test scores. It's not a good thing to make excuses. If your reason is that you were too busy going out with your boyfriend or girlfriend or that your dog had the flu, you should probably not offer these up as explanations. Take a step back and ask yourself if your reasons for not doing well are serious and reasonable. If it won't work for your stickler history teacher, chances are it won't work for the scholarship committee!

**Ignore the situation.** It's tempting to just hope that the scholarship judges overlook low grades or test scores. More often than not, if they don't see a reason for them, they'll assume that you just didn't put in the time or effort. This is an assumption you don't want them to make. That's why it's important to quickly address the concern before it's raised.

### The Non-Participant

You are a Non-Participant if:

- You weren't really involved in any school or community activities
- You don't have any hobbies or talents in which you've really excelled
- You were busy with other things such as family responsibilities or a job

**Do:**

**Describe what you did accomplish.** Not everyone chooses to or has the opportunity to participate in activities. There may not have been an organized club or group that matched your interests, or you may not have been drawn to a specific hobby. However, you must have spent your time doing something. If you held a job or took care of your family, explain what you gained from the experience. It's best to focus on the positive.

**Discuss your circumstances.** Let the scholarship judges know if you have special circumstances such as family responsibilities, a parent or sibling that you care for, an ill family member or other constraints. This helps the scholarship judges understand your individual situation and see what obstacles you have faced and overcome.

**Consider asking a recommender to support your situation.** It can help to have the perspective of someone else to support what you are saying.

### Don't:

**Assume you shouldn't apply for scholarships.** A lot of students think that they shouldn't bother applying for scholarships because they aren't involved in a lot of activities. However, scholarship judges value what you've learned from a job or family responsibilities as much as what you've learned from school or community activities.

**Discount your accomplishments.** You may not think it's a big deal to take care of your younger siblings or to hold a job for 20 hours a week, but it is.

In addition to these themes, there are different characteristics you may be asked to exemplify. Here are some suggestions for these characteristics:

### Initiative

**By initiative, the scholarship committee would like to see if you started something, took action or went above and beyond.** Scholarship organizations like to see students who demonstrate initiative because they want to support students who will show initiative and leadership in the future.

**If you started something, it's important to convey the significance of what you started.** What did starting the program involve? What were the results? For example, if you started a Future Business Leaders of America club at your school, you'd want to explain the steps you led such as finding an advisor, getting school approval, organizing a leadership team and recruiting members. You'd also want to share the club's accomplishments under your tutelage such as the events organized or increase in membership. These kinds of details point to the significance of your initiative.

**If you went above and beyond, you should detail how and why.** As an example, if you raised funds for a fellow student who became seriously ill, you could provide details of how you got the word out and encouraged students to participate in the fundraiser.

**As you are thinking of recommenders, think about who can vouch for your initiative and who has seen you go above and beyond and can write about it.**

## Character

**Scholarship organizations are looking for students who exhibit character because this is a universally admired trait.** You may demonstrate character by explaining your values or describing a difficult decision that you made or action that you took to maintain your beliefs.

**It's not enough to say that you have character or to state what your values are.** It's important that they show through in your actions. As you are writing the essay or doing an interview, explain how you have demonstrated character with an illustration. For example, you could describe how you defended a classmate that others were making fun of or how you spoke out against cheating.

**You may also want to ask your recommenders to support your character.** Explain to them that this is one of the characteristics that the scholarship committee is seeking and ask them to address it in their letters of recommendation.

## Tackling Obstacles

**Scholarship judges want to learn about obstacles you've faced to see how you've responded or even excelled in spite of them.** This is important because it's an indication of how you will fare in the future as you face challenges.

**Don't just describe the obstacle, but describe what you learned or gained from the situation.** For example, if you have a learning disability, don't just outline the difficulties that you have faced. Explain how you've worked at learning, how you've managed to balance the extra time that studying requires and how you've progressed. The judges don't want to just know about your problems, they want to understand how you've handled them.

**Try to get feedback on your application as it can be difficult to get perspective when you are very close to the situation.** For example, what you may think makes you sound empowered might come across to someone else as complaining.

As you can tell from this chapter, it's critical to get into the minds of the scholarship judges, understand what they are looking for and showcase your strengths according to your personal theme.

## Chapter 5 Summary: The Packaging of You

**Learn why the organizations are giving away their money.** This will help you package yourself so you best fit the criteria. Look at the purpose of the scholarships and the key words (such as "leadership," "initiative" or "community involvement") that identify exactly what they seek.

**Learn what they're basing their decision on.** Some scholarships are based solely on the essay that you write while others are awarded to students with the strongest grades and test scores. By understanding how the winner is selected, you'll know how to best position yourself.

**As you are completing your applications, it helps to pick a personal theme.** Your theme will help the scholarship judges remember you and immediately see your strengths.

**You are an Academic Achiever** if grades and test scores are your strength. It's important to explain your passion and not rely on your numbers to speak for themselves.

**You are a Leader** if you've held leadership positions or led a special project or team. You should not only state what leadership positions you've held but also describe what you've achieved as a leader and what you've learned.

**You are a Community Servant** if you've been especially involved in volunteering. What counts is not only the number of hours you've racked up but also what you've accomplished during the time and what kind of an impact you've made.

**You are an Artist** if you are involved in the arts including theatre, dance, art, music or creative writing. It's critical to demonstrate how strong your talent is by including a portfolio or artistic resume (if allowed).

**You are an Athlete** if you have competed in sports at your school or in your community. The piece that most Athletes leave out is the mental and intellectual side of being an athlete.

**If you are a B or C Student,** explain why you didn't do as well as you could have without making excuses. Then, focus on the areas in which you've excelled.

**If you are a Non-Participant,** describe what you did accomplish or discuss the circumstances that prevented you from participating in activities.

**To demonstrate initiative,** describe not only what you did but also the significance of your efforts. If you can, quantify what you accomplished.

**To show character,** give an example of how you exemplified character rather than just stating what your values are.

**When describing an obstacle that you've overcome,** detail more than just the obstacle itself. Explain what you did and what you learned from the challenge you faced.

# Scholarship Judge Q&A

In this chapter, you'll learn:

- **How the selection process works**

- **The most common mistakes to avoid**

- **Judges' best tips for the essay**

- **What judges look for when choosing the winners**

# CHAPTER 6

# A Roundtable with Scholarship Judges

You might know a situation or two in which you'd like to be a fly on the wall. When your parents are discussing whether or not to get you a car. When your teacher is deciding what grade to give you on a paper. Or maybe when the object of your affection is discussing you with a friend. Sometimes, inside information can give you the edge when it comes to getting the wheels, scoring the grade, or having your affections returned.

Unfortunately, we can't really help you with any of these situations (unless your parents are holding an essay contest to decide who gets the car, of course). But, we can help you be the fly on one wall–that of the scholarship judging room. It may not be as exciting as learning your romantic fate, but it will help you on your way to getting scholarship dollars.

In this chapter, we'll share with you interviews that we conducted with scholarship judges from a variety of competitions. These competitions cover awards based on essays, art, writing, music, overcoming adversity and college applications. By seeing what the scholarship judges want, in their own words, you'll have an advantage over other scholarship applicants. You'll learn how the selection process works, what made the winners stand out, what mistakes those who didn't win made, and what you can do to position yourself to be a scholarship winner!

## The Big Picture

If you haven't gotten our big message yet, it is this: The more you know about a scholarship competition, the stronger you can make your application. By understanding why an organization is giving away the money and how they give it away, you will be able to use this information to craft your application accordingly.

## A National Scholarship Management Organization

### Scholarship Management Services®
www.scholarshipamerica.org

If you apply for more than a handful of scholarships, it is very likely that for at least one of them you will send your application to Scholarship America®. Through their Scholarship Management Services division, they manage more than 1,200 scholarships nationwide. In this interview, you will see how they handle so many awards and how, despite the fact that they are such a large organization, they evaluate each application on a personal level. You will also see why it is important that you follow instructions carefully when you're applying to a scholarship program that receives many submissions.

## Could you tell us about your scholarship organization?

Scholarship Management Services, a division of Scholarship America, is the nation's premier developer and manager of scholarship, tuition reimbursement and other education assistance programs. More than 1,200 corporations, foundations, associations and individuals, including more than half of Fortune 500 companies, rely on Scholarship Management Services' expertise for easy, streamlined management of their educational needs. In its more than 60 years of operation, Scholarship Management Services has distributed more than $4.2 billion to students. In 2018 alone, more than $225 million was distributed.

A tailored approach is used by Scholarship Management Services to design programs that meet the objectives of the clients, whether that objective is to reach out to children of their employees, students in their community or meet some another educational need.

## How does your selection process work?

The application evaluation method developed and used by Scholarship Management Services identifies the well-rounded student who has the potential to gain admission to college and who will succeed at college. One-half of the evaluation is based on academic performance as measured by grade point average and for high school seniors, rank-in-class and potential as measured by college admissions tests. The other half of the evaluation includes a review of the student's participation and leadership, work experience, a statement of educational plans as they relate to career objectives and future goals, unusual family or personal circumstances and an applicant appraisal completed by a counselor or teacher. The financial need of the student may also be considered.

Selection of recipients for most Scholarship Management Services clients is conducted by a panel of Scholarship America employees. Occasionally, finalists are selected by Scholarship Management Services and the client convenes a committee to select recipients.

### What are some of the most common mistakes that students make?

Two of the most common mistakes students make when completing scholarship applications is waiting until right before the deadline date to start the process and submitting an incomplete application. To avoid rushing at the last minute, Scholarship Management Services recommends students complete their application, set it aside and come back to it another day for review and final edits. Completing the application weeks, instead of days or hours, before the deadline also allows students to secure any transcripts or other documents necessary for a complete application and submit it on time.

Scholarship Management Services recommends students directly and succinctly answer all questions on the application, including all narrative and/or essay sections. Adding additional responses that are not requested usually does not benefit the student.

### Who are the judges for your competitions?

For the majority of the scholarship programs managed by Scholarship Management Services, evaluation specialists (employees of Scholarship America) evaluate the applications. These individuals have educational and career backgrounds in education and business-related fields. Following evaluation, selection of recipients is conducted by an internal selection panel. For a small number of programs, Scholarship Management Services contracts with outside experts to evaluate applications. Examples include programs primarily focused on engineering, art, math and architectural achievements.

### How can applicants best stand out with the application form?

The best tip we can give to students completing a scholarship application is to answer the questions in a complete and concise manner. The biggest mistake we find students make is sending in an incomplete application.

### What are the most common characteristics that you are looking for in applicants? How can students demonstrate these characteristics?

Scholarship Management Services identifies well-rounded students as recipients for most of the programs it manages. Therefore, strong academics is important as is participation in school and community activities, demonstrated leadership, holding a full-time or part-time job and enlisting a teacher or counselor who is able to give a good recommendation. Students should begin thinking about their high school classes in middle school. Getting good grades and taking Honors or AP classes is very important throughout all grades 9-12. Students should also consider running for an office or other lead position in the activities they participate in.

## Do you have any competitions that are based on financial need?

A small number of programs are based entirely on financial need. Since a number of factors are considered in determining need, students should not screen themselves out because they feel their parents' incomes are too high.

## What do you your scholarship evaluators look for in recommendation letters? What is one of the most memorable recommendation letters that you've read?

Scholarship Management Services incorporates an objective Applicant Appraisal section into the application. Therefore, recommendation letters are not requested and do not take the place of a teacher or counselor completing the appraisal section. For a small number of programs that require letters, scholarship evaluators look for specific examples of the student's work that support his/her application. In additional to specific examples, concise responses that directly answer the questions are most beneficial to the student.

One of the most memorable recommendation letters I ever read was from an inner-city high school guidance counselor who worked closely with a young man to help him overcome gang influence in middle school and become a high honors student by his senior year. With very little family support, this young man became the first in his family to attend college. The passion with which the counselor wrote made it very evident that the student had a strong desire to overcome major obstacles in his life and succeed in the next chapter of his life.

## An Art and Writing Competition

**Alliance for Young Artists & Writers**
The Scholastic Art & Writing Awards
www.artandwriting.org

Bryan Doerries
Associate Executive Director, Programs

One of the amazing things about The Scholastic Art & Writing Awards is
that the competition has had the same criteria for the past 94 years. Works
are judged based on their originality, technical skill and emergence of a
personal vision or voice. Understanding the judging criteria is important.
As you'll see, you may submit a piece that is very strong technically, but
if it doesn't show originality or a personal vision, it won't be selected. This
is why it's critical that you study the submission guidelines and adhere to
them closely.

## Please briefly describe your scholarship program and its purpose.

Founded in 1923, The Scholastic Art & Writing Awards is the nation's
longest-running, largest, most prestigious recognition program for creative teenagers. Students who receive our awards qualify for exhibitions,
publication, $120,000 in cash awards and $3.25 million in scholarship
opportunities each year at 100 participating universities, colleges and art
institutes across the country.

## Could you tell us about your selection process?

Creative teenagers in grades 7-12 annually submit 300,000+ works to
81 regional programs of The Scholastic Art & Writing Awards. Of those
students, 30,000 receive regional awards (Gold Keys, Silver Keys and
Honorable Mentions). Works are evaluated blindly by panels of artistic
and literary professionals for their originality, technical skill and emergence of a personal vision or voice. Submissions earning Gold Keys
(approximately 10 percent of submissions), the highest form of regional
recognition, are forwarded to the Alliance for Young Artists & Writers
in New York City for national adjudication, where high-level artistic and
literary professionals evaluate 10,000 national qualifiers. One thousand
national Gold and Silver Medals are bestowed annually in recognition
of the most excellent works of art and writing. Twelve top graduating
seniors are awarded Portfolio Gold Medals and $10,000 cash awards.

## Who are the judges for your competition?

Artists, writers, curators, critics, educators and professionals from the
nation's creative industries—some of whom were recognized through The
Awards as teenagers—participate on the selection panels for The Scholastic

Art & Writing Awards. Notable past and current jurors include Elizabeth Bishop, Judy Blume, Billy Collins, Robert Frost, Frank McCourt, Philip Pearlstein, George Plimpton, Faith Ringgold, Andy Rooney, KiKi Smith, Rick Moody, Francine Prose, Carolyn Forche, Tom Otterness, Mel Bochner and William Saroyan.

## What specific qualities are you looking for in the writing winners? Art winners?

Our three criteria haven't changed for 97 years. Submissions are evaluated for their originality, technical skill and emergence of a personal vision or voice. We are looking for paradigm-shifting young visionaries. We are looking for works or art and writing that go beyond the classroom assignment. We are looking for risk-taking works that express new ideas boldly.

## What is one of the most memorable writing pieces you've read that has won? How about art pieces?

### Writing

The photographer Richard Avedon won an award for a poem he submitted in 1941 entitled "Wanderlust." The poem expresses the young Avedon's desire to set out for adventures in the world. The poem starts out:

You must not think because my glance is quick
To shift from this to that, from here to there
Because I am most usually where
The way is strangest and the wonders thick,
Because when wind is wildest and the bay
Swoops madly upward and the gulls are few
And I am doing as I want to do,
Leaving the town to go my aimless way.

It should come as no surprise, after reading part of the poem, that Avedon dropped out of school that year and joined the Merchant Marines. About winning an award for his poem, Avedon said, "The defining moment of my life was when I was seventeen and was honored by The Awards. Being recognized meant that little pat on the back, that sense of confidence that I could enter a life that I loved. And I had somebody behind me say, 'This is okay.'"

### Art

I shall never forget coming across the work of Art Portfolio Gold winner Ebony Robinson. Her work jumped up and proclaimed its originality and personal vision to the world. This young woman had something burning within her to say, and she was reinventing her chosen medium (painting) in order to say it. All of her paintings were portraits of African American women, and all of her portraits challenged the viewer's notion of what a portrait could be. Each of her subjects intensely stared out from the canvas, burning a hole in the viewer's forehead. About this phenomenon, Ebony wrote: "I think this very direct and blunt gaze makes the viewer want to interact with the subject. I paint this way with the intent of forcing viewers to evaluate themselves with the same unabashed scrutiny with which the subjects of my paintings are evaluating the viewers."

Ebony came from Memphis, TN. She attended a public magnet school for the arts and studied under quite possibly the greatest working art teacher in the country, Dr. Emily "Boo" Ruch. After winning one of our top awards and receiving a $10,000 cash scholarship from the Alliance, Ebony went on to receive a full scholarship at her first choice of colleges: Maryland Institute College of Art.

### What are some of the most common mistakes that students make on their writing or art pieces?

Unfortunately, students sometimes ignore our criteria and submit work that is technically advanced but lacking in originality or personal vision. This is lamentable, as these same students may do very well in other competitions and even receive high marks in school.

### How can you tell if a student's writing is authentic?

The Awards have enjoyed a long, successful track record in discovering authentic young writers. Over the last 86 years, our jurors have been able to spot the emerging voices of celebrated authors like Truman Capote, Bernard Malamud, Joyce Carol Oates, Joyce Maynard, Carolyn Forche, Ned Vizinni and countless others—when they are 14, 15, 16 years old. There is no formula for discovering authentic voices, other than assembling qualified literary professionals to participate in our adjudication process.

### What can students gain from the experience of writing or creating art for the competition even if they don't win?

The submission process is a professionalizing experience for most students. It challenges students to take their work seriously by submitting it for professional review. By participating in our program, students learn important life skills. They learn how to prepare and arrange a portfolio. They are required to follow a complex set of guidelines and meet deadlines. The Awards provide a structure and an impetus for young people to think and act like professional artists and writers.

## Is there anything that students would be surprised to learn about the competition?

It might come as a surprise that well-regarded writers, like Sylvia Plath and Robert Redford, won for painting, or that the photographer Richard Avendon won for poetry. This is because personal vision or voice manifests itself in unexpected ways. Our jurors respect the fact that a poet may go on to be a painter and vice versa. So, when they are looking at work submitted by teenagers, they look for a quality of expression that may in fact transcend the formal constraints of the category or genre they've been asked to judge. That's why originality stands at the center of our program and our process.

### A Music Competition

**LA Music Academy**
www.lamusicacademy.org
Mike Packer
Director of Educational Operations

There are two criteria that carry the most weight for scholarships at the LA Music Academy—students' transcripts and their recorded performances. While it's pretty straight-forward what you need to do for your transcript, it might not be as evident when it comes to submitting a recorded performance. As you'll read, it's important to spend time on the performance, present yourself professionally and perfect it as much as possible.

## Please briefly describe your scholarship program, how much is awarded and its purpose.

The LA Music Academy scholarship program is a merit based program designed to award applicants based on performance, transcripts, essay and letter of recommendation. Awards can range from $1,000 to full tuition.

## Can you tell us about your selection process?

A competitive round of submissions comes in for each start date–there are two start dates per year, fall and spring. Each application is judged by the director of educational operations and then passed along to the president for approval.

## What criteria do you use for selecting the scholarship recipients, and what is the weight of each of the factors you consider?

Each application is divided into three categories: performance, essay and letter of recommendation and transcripts. The performance category is weighted 40 percent, transcript 40 percent and letter of recommendation and essay 20 percent. The scores are totaled and the award given based on the final score. If their scores exceed the minimum requirement, applicants proceed to a final round of judging where the financial award is determined.

## What advice do you have for students preparing their tapes?

Show us what you've got! Only electronic submissions are accepted and should be of good quality. Applications in the past have consisted of live performances and students playing alone with a play a long.

## What are the biggest mistakes that students have made with their taped performances?

The biggest problems we have seen with demo DVD's are simply poor performances and production quality. Applicants need to perform to the best of their ability and portray themselves professionally. I can remember one submission where the student played well enough to win a significant award but was wearing only shorts, no shirt and no shoes. As the old saying goes, no shoes, no shirt no service! He also sneezed before the first count off. Maybe he should have done another take!

## What makes a strong essay answer?

We are looking for students who are talented, hard working and passionate. We want the future leaders of the music industry at the LA Music Academy. The applicants' essays should reflect these traits and portray their personality. Video essays are also welcome.

**One of your essay questions is, "Why do you believe that the LA Music Academy is the best place for you?" What advice do you have for a student answering this question?**

We are looking for the future leaders of the music industry. An applicant's answer should not be passive. Tell us where you see your career going and how you think the LA Music Academy will help prepare you to get there.

## An Essay-Based Competition

### StraightForward Media Scholarships
www.straightforwardmedia.com
Joshua D. Barsch
Chief Executive Officer

Joshua Barsch makes a serious statement about most scholarship essays: "They're terrible." And after having personally read thousands of them, he should know. However, he offers some great tips on how to make your essays better so that they don't end up in the "terrible" pile. A key step—be as specific as possible. Generic answers are not only boring, but they don't tell the scholarship judges enough about you. And, don't have your mom submit a handwritten note saying that you're too busy to write an essay so she's applying on your behalf. (True story.)

**Please briefly describe your scholarship program, how much is awarded and its purpose.**

We run 16 separate scholarship programs, most based on the applicants' field of study. All but one of the 16 programs awards a $500 scholarship once every quarter. We began giving scholarships in 2003 with the Dale E. Fridell Scholarship to honor the memory of my grandfather. We got so many incredible applicants, though, that we decided to expand the programs and eventually to do all of our corporate philanthropy through our scholarship programs.

During that first year of the Fridell Scholarship, we actually had students send in paper applications. And it was a personal, family project, so we had the students send their applications to our home. Big mistake. We had no idea what kind of response we'd get, and we ended up getting thousands of applications. During the month leading up to the deadline, we'd get a couple hundred per day. The mailman would have to leave the big mail crates on our doorstep. He hated us, frankly; we got in a couple of heated arguments about the subject. Trust me, if you don't like your postal carrier and you want to stick it to him, just start a scholarship competition. You'll make his life hell in no time.

Anyway, after that first contest, we switched to online applications only. The last thing we needed was a disgruntled postal worker sticking a rattlesnake in my mailbox.

### Please describe your selection process.

Ours is a little different from others we've heard about. Our committees range from three to five judges. Once the scholarship deadline has passed, we roughly split the essays up equally among the judges. Each judge culls through her pile individually and arrives at two finalists that she will present to the other judges (along with each of the other judges' two finalists) for a total of 10 finalists. Once the 10 finalists are chosen, the judges discuss and vote on who should win the award. That's a process that's almost always virtual–done via email or phone. As I referenced earlier with my mailbox story, due to the surprising logistical challenges of operating a scholarship program, our operation is now virtualized to every possible extent.

There is no numerical scoring of any kind in our judging, and that's not the only way in which our process is unique. Essays that contain typos, misspellings and other basic errors are discarded immediately. It sounds harsh, but if you can't even give your essay the basic attention required to ensure it doesn't have misspellings and typos, then, frankly, your essay isn't worthy of our judges' time. When a judge does find a strong essay that she believes could be a winner, that essay is held as the current "gold standard" against which all further applications in her stack are judged. If subsequent essays are well-written and error-free, yet still aren't judged to be better than the current "gold-standard" essay, then those essays are discarded as well. We informally refer to this as the "king of the mountain" method–if your essay isn't good enough to conquer the reigning king of the mountain, then you're eliminated.

### When you ask about how the scholarship will help students meet their educational and professional goals, what kind of answer are you looking for?

We're looking for something creative, compelling and detailed. The opposite of that would be boring and generic, and you're correct–most of the applications that come in fall into the latter category. Students have to understand that scholarship contests are like any other contest in that the more competition you have, the less room for error you have if you plan to win. If you're competing against a dozen kids from your own school, you might be able to write down some regurgitated, generic drivel and still win. If you're competing against the best in the world, that's not going to work.

If you tell the scholarship committee that you want to be a doctor, that sounds pretty good. If you say that you want to be a doctor who performs research that leads to new drugs to reduce the effects of Alzheimer's or that you want to work to improve dental health among inner-city children or open a practice in the country in order to improve elderly care in under-served rural areas – that sounds exceptional and unique.

### From the tone of your website, it seems that you value essays that show some creativity or humor.

We definitely value creativity. Humor is fine if it's appropriate in the essay, but it's not required and it's rare that we see any. This is about money for the students, and that's a serious matter; consequently, few feel comfortable enough to break the tension and get lighthearted.

### Some of your scholarships also ask what the student's contribution will be to the world. What is the most typical response you get, and why does it work or not work?

A terrible way to answer the questions is to be very generic and basically say what your job is going to be. "I plan to be a doctor" or "I plan to be a teacher," etc. The solution is very simple: be specific, not generic. However, this is a bigger question, and we like to see big dreams and goals from the applicants. I mean, we don't require that you aspire to be a head of state, but we do want to see some concrete examples of things you'd like to achieve. If you tell us that your "contribution to the world" is to be a lawyer; well, that's great, we think, but that's not the most compelling thing to tell the committee. In our more idealistic moments, we hope we're doing more than just packing the professional ranks with 9-to-5 grinders; we're helping kids who want to grow up and give back to the world. Tell us *why* you want what you want and why that's something that a group of individuals should give you money to help you achieve. Remember the committee's perspective here–there are thousands of you asking for this money; you need to convince us why you're the best one to receive it.

### What are some of the most common mistakes that students make when writing their essays? Also, what is one or two of the most egregious errors that you've seen?

We actually put up an entire website, free to everyone, addressing this issue. It's called GiveMeScholarships.com. But I'll touch on some of them:

- Not proofreading their essays.
- Including irrelevant information in their essays.
- Not writing a cohesive essay with a beginning, middle and end.
- Overemphasizing activities that are very, very common among students.
- Not reading the application instructions.
- Putting themselves on a holier-than-thou pedestal among their classmates.
- Preaching about easy solutions to the world's ills.

Gee, it's so hard to choose just one or two of the most egregious. One of the worst things I've ever seen was a lengthy handwritten note from a girl's mother about how good of a student her daughter was and how deserving of our scholarship she was. However, Mom said, she was just too busy with school and activities to write essays for scholarships, so Mom asked for the scholarship on her behalf. I was speechless about that one. Still am. We've had entire essays come in boldface and all-cap type. We've had people send in their essays on the back side of what appears to be a piece of scratch paper. A few applicants have included an insane amount of extraneous information with their application (e.g., their parents' tax returns, their birth certificate, etc.). On the content side, we get a lot of students who insist that their lives may as well be over if they don't get this very scholarship, implying they're destined for the food line without this money. It's also not uncommon for some insistent writers to tell us how absolutely certain they are that no one out there needs the money as badly as they do, and/or that no one has worked as hard for and is more deserving of the award than they are. My answer is always the same: How could you possibly know this? What gives you the right to discount the life and experience of every other applicant?

### Are there any topics that students shouldn't write about?

Yes, two big ones: politics and religion. Some people are surprised at that, but I advise them to consider this very basic truth: the more contentious the issue you choose to write about, the more likely it is that one or more committee members will completely disagree with you. Divisive issues divide, and in all likelihood, you've got no idea who's even judging your scholarship application, let alone the personal and political beliefs of those people. If a judge happens to hold beliefs that run counter to the ones in your essay, should that affect their judgment? In a perfect world, absolutely not. But we don't live in a perfect world. Committee members are people just like you and I are. They try to keep their emotions and personal beliefs out of their decisions, but it doesn't always work. Offend them with the content of your essay and you probably won't win the scholarship. Again–I'm not saying it's right, but that's just how it is. It's real life, it's unfair, and that's how it goes.

## Is there anything that a student might find surprising either about your selection process?

I think there's a great deal they'd find surprising. It's probably nothing like they think. I think they imagine a table full of erudite academics dressed in tweed suits and ascots, sitting at a long antique table and debating the merits of essays while puffing on pipes. It's not really like that at all (not in our case, anyway). Here's something I'm fond of saying: Scholarship judges are normal, busy human beings. In fact, we were quite busy already, before we ever volunteered to be scholarship judges. Judging thousands of essays is an enormous task – a task stacked on top of all the other responsibilities in our lives: our day jobs (and our night jobs, for some of us), spending time with our families, etc.

Ever wonder why the essays you submit are never returned to you? Probably because it's got barbecue stains on it because the judge was reading it over lunch at a restaurant, or it has scribbling all over it because it was accidentally used as a piece of scratch paper during the judging, or it's got a perfect "coffee circle" on it because the judge decided to use it as a coaster. This is the reality of scholarship judging.

## Is there anything else you'd like to add?

Most scholarship essays are terrible. There, I said it. I'm serious about that. You'd weep for the future of America if you saw the drivel that comes in here disguised as students' best efforts.

I'm not going to come out and say that today's students are lazier or less intelligent, because I don't believe that at all (I believe the opposite, actually–I think kids are smarter and more ambitious than ever). Rather, I think schools and parents do a poor job of educating these students about exactly what a scholarship essay must accomplish if they're ever going to win any money. And it's not because the parents and teachers don't care; it's because they themselves don't know.

Writing a "good" essay is nowhere near enough to win money. You have to look at a scholarship contest the same way Tiger Woods looks at a golf tournament. You have to understand that there's only one winner, and it's the person who shows the committee that he/she is the absolute best of the best. That's who wins–no one else, just the best (even if the scholarship contest has 25 winners, approaching the contest this way–that you must be the best of the best–is the wise thing to do. The minute you slip into thinking that your best isn't required, you're toast.)

## A College That Awards Merit-Based Scholarships

### Ohio Wesleyan University
www.owu.edu
Carol J. DelPropost
Assistant Vice President of Admission and Financial Aid

Carol J. DelPropost dispels some common myths about scholarships. The first myth is that you must be the president of your student body in order to show leadership. (You don't–you can show leadership by leading a special project, group or effort.) The second is that you should participate in as many extracurricular activities as possible. (You shouldn't. Quality counts more than quantity.) And the third is that you need to write about an extraordinary experience in the essay. (One of the best essays she read was about the rather ordinary topic of the applicant's father.) A former Advanced Placement English teacher with more than 30 years of experience in college admission, Carol has plenty of experience with essays and shares some of her career highlights and lowlights.

### Please briefly describe your scholarship program.

Ohio Wesleyan University recently awarded more than $14 million in merit scholarships (not including OWU grant aid based on financial need). Awards range from $5,000 to full tuition. These scholarships are renewable if the students maintain the required GPA.

### Please describe the selection process in as much detail as possible, especially how it relates to the admission process.

As admission applications are reviewed, counselors recommend the award that best fits the student's qualifications based on academic profile, strength of high school curriculum, essay and activities, whether service, part-time work, performing arts, etc. If a student qualifies for more than one award, the recommendation is for the award with the highest dollar value. The Community Service award requires a separate application that asks applicants for detailed descriptions of type and length of service, as well as the value of their experiences and their desire to continue service while enrolled at Ohio Wesleyan University. Applications of those who qualify for the Honors awards are reviewed by the faculty, who make written comments. The applications are then sent to the Honors Committee, which consists of faculty members and the vice president for enrollment. There is considerable discussion–and sometimes debate–and comparison of applicants. The committee then determines the award each student will receive.

## How can students demonstrate leadership besides being elected president of the student council? Can you give any examples of creative ways to show leadership?

Students can demonstrate leadership by taking charge of a project, whether for a service organization or church group, a club or a family expedition, or by taking the initiative at their place of work. Some of our scholarship students have demonstrated leadership by stepping forward to organize a GLBT awareness/support group at their school. Some have developed initiatives–study or discussion groups, fundraisers, mission trips  to address world issues like hunger, poverty, homelessness or atrocities against certain groups. Some, who view their work experiences as opportunities for growth, have made suggestions for improvement in the workplace that have been adopted by management.

## What misconceptions do students have about participating in activities and winning scholarships?

Some students (and some parents!) believe that a long list of activities gets noticed. What really gets noticed is the depth of commitment a student makes to a club, organization, athletics or other venture. Putting heart and soul into something you feel passionately about is better for the group–and also for you! Haven't found a passion yet? Skimming the surface of many things won't necessarily help you find it; concentrating on one or two or three endeavors over a longer period of time allows greater, more meaningful experience. It's important to remember the value of work experience, too. Some students work to help with family expenses, to save for college and to gain valuable experience. Their work schedule and academic load may not allow for involvement in other activities. That's OK.

## Are there opportunities to win scholarships from your college for students who don't have the highest grades or test scores?

Ohio Wesleyan University offers the Meek Community Service and Leadership Award for those whose commitment to service and leadership is exceptional. Grades and scores are factors only to the extent that they must be strong enough for admission; otherwise, the level of service and commitment are the primary factors. Additionally, Ohio Wesleyan University values diversity of all kinds and actively recruits a diverse group of applicants.

## Because you often use the admission essay to determine which students will receive scholarships, is there anything that students should do differently to help their chances of being considered for a scholarship?

The essay is an opportunity for the student to reveal who they are–reveal themselves in ways that the rest of the admission process doesn't allow. Writing about an activity is fine if the focus is on the value of the experience, why the experience is important and how it shaped you. The most memorable essays clearly show introspection and in some way move the reader. Write from the heart.

## What are some of the most common mistakes that students make when writing their essays?

Common mistakes include trying to impress the reader with what you think that person wants to read, rather than writing from the heart. Be sincere. Another mistake is being impersonal, submitting an essay that is more like a research paper. This will not be memorable. It's a mistake to write only one draft. Write the essay, then let is "sit" for a few days. When you return to it, you'll see it with a fresh eye and will be able to improve it easily. And it is a big mistake to not proofread several times. Misspellings and poor mechanics are really inexcusable. THE most egregious error–sending to College X an essay that talks about why you want to attend College Y! Again, proofreading is essential.

## What is one or two of the best introductions you remember? What made them so memorable?

One young woman projected into the future and presented herself as president of the United States. In her opening paragraph, she described herself sitting in the Oval Office with heads of state from many countries, discussing policy. She didn't just say she wanted to be president; she actually was president.

Another great essay began with a paragraph so rich in imagery, color and tone that I actually felt myself in the middle of the scene. "Rishikesh smelled of mildewed incense and cattle. The Ganges shimmered, with crowds of women washing clothing to dry under the midday sun. It was cold, the mountains still casting long shadows across the ashram, my hair damp from bathing in the river."

## Can you think of an example or two of when an applicant wrote about an ordinary topic in an extraordinary way?

Many students write about "a most influential person," and often it is a parent. One young man began with, "It took me eighteen years to realize what an extraordinary influence my mother has been on my life." His approach, though, was to paint in vivid detail a picture of his mother's activities, motivations and contributions to family, friends and the world–and then to detail how these specifics influenced his life. He explained how family trips to places far and near–preceded with reading about the destination, the history, the influence on culture and politics–helped broaden his perspective on people, academic work, as well as his plans and dreams for his future.

Another wrote about how her parents influenced her life by challenging her to try new things. Again, a relatively common theme. But this person began with "'I'll give you one whole dollar for each anchovy you eat.' Bait for bait. And I was the catch." She followed with additional and just as colorful examples of challenges her parents encouraged–enticed!–her to accept and how her experiences in meeting the challenges shaped who she is today.

## Are there any topics or approaches to topics that students shouldn't write about?

Unless the treatment of these topics is exceptional, I recommend that students avoid writing about their big moment in their sports–that final play, last 10 seconds, injury, etc. Political and public morality issues also should be avoided because these tend to be written as either research papers or one-sided opinions. Remember, we want to know who you are, not just what you believe. And I really wish one young woman had not written a very vivid descriptive essay about picking her nose!

## A College That Awards Merit-Based Scholarships

### Florida Atlanta University

Dianne M. Reeves, CFRE
Assistant Vice President Advancement, Northern Campuses

Kerry Rosen
Associate Dean and the Director of Admissions

Every student who is admitted to the Wilkes Honors College of Florida Atlantic University and who lives on campus receives a scholarship of up to $15,000 renewable to up to four years. Some students receive scholarships up to full tuition and room and board. It's a generous program and one that surprisingly doesn't even require an essay. (A transcript, test scores, a resume, evaluation letters and a writing sample, however, are required.)

### Could you tell us about your scholarship program and how much is awarded?

Most academic scholarships in the Wilkes Honors College are awarded at the point of admissions and are merit-based. Every student admitted is awarded a minimum of $2,000 per year (renewable for up to four years) if they will be living on campus.

### Please describe the selection process in as much detail as possible, especially how it may or may not relate to the admission process.

The admissions committee makes a holistic evaluation of the admissions file taking into account such factors as high school record, test scores, resume, evaluation letters, writing sample and level of interest and bases the size of the initial scholarship on these criteria. A select number of those students who apply by Dec. 15 each year are invited to campus for Scholars Day in March where they will interview for a number of our more valuable and prestigious scholarships such as the Flagler, Leadership and others. At Scholarship Day, from a pool of 32 or so invited students, we will select the five Flagler Scholars, up to seven IB/AICE Scholars, up to five Leadership Scholars and a number of Founder Scholars.

## What do you look for in recommendation letters?

Recommendation letters should give us information about the student that is not available from other sources (i.e. transcripts and resumes). They should address such things as the student's personal characteristics, sense of integrity, their relationship to the world of ideas and scholarship, as well as the way they interact with others and their communities. It is helpful to give examples and anecdotes rather than merely describe qualities.

## Who are the best people for students to ask for recommendations from? How detrimental is a recommendation letter that is not positive?

Students should request these letters from those who know them well and have interacted with them in a significant way at their schools, place of employment or community organization.

Even letters that mention "negative" qualities are not necessarily something that would result in a denial of admission. In fact, that may even validate the sincerity of the writer and give us more confidence in those "positive" aspects that are also mentioned.

## What would you say to students who think that it's not worth the time or effort to apply for scholarships?

It is always worthwhile to apply for scholarships for which one is qualified.

## Is there anything students are surprised to learn about your scholarships?

I think students are surprised that we do not require an essay. We require our applicants to submit a graded writing sample, a piece of academic work they have submitted as a class assignment. We find this to be a very useful tool in assessing the student's readiness for work at our very challenging institution.

They are also sometimes surprised that high test scores are not sufficient for some of our more valuable scholarships such as the Flagler. I think it is important that students realize that top-quality affordable education is available at public institutions, especially in honors programs and colleges. The WHC is a perfect example of this, providing generous academic scholarships to all its students, thus enabling everyone regardless of their socioeconomic status to receive an outstanding education.

## Supporting Students at Women's Colleges

**The Sunflower Initiative**
https://www.thesunflowerinitiative.com/scholarship/
Margaret McKean
Harriet Fitzgerald Scholarship Committee Chair

Founded by women, the Sunflower Initiative is a non-profit organization that supports women who attend women's colleges. The volunteer selection committee and board of directors review up to 450 applications in two series of evaluation.

## Could you tell us about your scholarship organization?

The Sunflower Initiative awards the Harriet Fitzgerald Scholarship of $10,000 (with the possibility of renewal) to a woman attending a women's college. Only those about to enter their first year of college are eligible. Our purpose is to contribute to enabling women to attend college in a supportive environment that encourages them to discover all of their talents. Given the superior record of women who have graduated from women's colleges (compared to women who have gone to coed schools), it is clear that attending a women's college does indeed empower women to achieve great things.

## Could you tell us about your selection process?

The Harriet Fitzgerald Scholarship receives between 80 and 450 applications per year. Our committee of three to five readers, all volunteers with backgrounds in higher education and women's colleges, uses a scoring system to evaluate the various components of the applications. We narrow submissions to about 50, and then on the basis of re-reading, narrow to a group of about 12 to 20 semi-finalists. Re-reading and considerable discussion allow us to narrow further to a group of about five or six finalists whom we interview. On the basis of further discussion, we arrive at a ranking of the finalists and submit this recommendation, along with full application materials, to our board of directors. After considerable additional discussion and reading of files and notes, the board and the committee then settle on a final ranking.

## What are some of the most common mistakes that students make?

The most egregious mistakes we have seen in applications are queries and submissions indicating that the applicant has not read our web page, requirements, and purpose carefully or even at all, leading us to urge first and foremost that applicants read about the scholarship they are applying for very carefully. A sloppy inquiry is not worth our time, but in addition, it is not worth the applicant's time either. In fact, it creates a bad impression that could affect a resubmission. We strongly recommend that students preparing applications for special-purpose scholarships do a bit of research on the scholarship before sending in a question. Some aggregator websites provide only our email address and not our scholarship web site. Students should look up our web site and read it before asking us for a personalized description of the scholarship as a substitute for doing a bit of homework in advance.

Within the essays themselves, the most common mistake is for students to write an essay that simply repeats factual information about their accomplishments that we can read elsewhere in the application. We, at least, process applications very carefully and read them thoroughly, so we do not need to read the same thing two or three times. Instead, we want the essay to tell us something that no other part of the application can provide—about the applicant's motivation, values, and personal experiences. We expect a good essay to help us get to know the applicant as a fully complex human being, we want to know what the applicant cares about in life, and we want specific answers to our essay question too. We look favorably on an essay written for our scholarship rather than a generic essay written for other purposes or for the basic application for admission to college.

Our readers have expertise in literature and writing and years of experience grading papers, so we are particularly sensitive to errors in grammar and usage, yet at the same time we might wonder about an essay that is too perfect. We strongly recommend proofreading. Our readers vary on reactions to the heavy use of "I"—we prefer active voice, so in an essay about oneself the pronoun "I" has to occur. But beginning every sentence with "I" is a bad idea, because it is repetitive and boring.

## How can you tell if a student's essay is authentic? What is an example of an essay that you thought was not authentic?

We may not have ever received an essay that was obviously inauthentic but we have sometimes read essays that were clearly written from a template offering suggestions (when three essays in the same year both begin with almost the same introductory sentence about the student's messy room or an inspiring sign or picture that the student sees on the wall, readers get suspicious!).

## What are examples of the best introductions you remember?

One particularly memorable essay was written as a personal letter to Adolf Hitler; the essay was sometimes naïve but was thoroughly moving. Several others used a difficult personal experience (death of a parent, a birth defect, criticism from others, an election defeat or a problem on debate or crew team) to explain the student's motivations in life. In these cases, either the technique or the content of the experience made the essay memorable. Of course, we do not recommend fabricating experiences in order to use them in an essay—the essay needs to be authentic and convincing.

## Can you think of an example of when an applicant wrote about an ordinary topic in an extraordinary way?

One essay conveyed a parent-child relationship in the third person. Another conveyed her love of history by writing about historical figures as friends, a method that managed to convey both what the applicant loves to study but also how the student thinks while learning. The essays we read are filled with accounts of experiences, which is all to the good, but authenticity is probably more important than cleverness. An essay written in flowery language in a misguided attempt to seem elegant will fall flat—language should be a vehicle for conveying content and should never overwhelm the content.

## Are there any topics that students shouldn't write about?

We probably have not encountered inappropriate topics, but we like to see essays that come from the student and her experience and that manage to get to the issue of what the student wants to study and to end up doing in life. Essays that end in the present, by reciting accomplishments to date without conveying any plans, goals or ambitions for the future, are very unsatisfying.

## Do you recommend that students ask someone else to read their essay and give feedback?

We have rarely seen an essay that has been heavily worked over by someone other than the scholarship applicant. Feedback from a casual helper who cannot or will not try to imagine the process that readers of applications go through may not give adequate or appropriate advice at all. Such feedback would actually be dangerous. However, feedback from someone who has read applications and essays before (so can put herself in the shoes of readers of the applications we get) might be quite valuable as a source of general advice. Above all, the essay has to be authentic and believable to succeed.

## Do you have any advice for letters of recommendation?

The best letters are the ones that go into great detail, and our guess is that people who have to read letters of recommendation for other purposes and also take them very seriously are the ones who know how much detail we want. The letters we find most helpful go beyond listing the applicant's attributes to tell us stories about the student. Such detail helps not only to show us that the letter-writer really does know the student, but also adds fuller material to the detailed picture of the student that we are already building from the student's essay. We know it is difficult for students to know who will be able to write letters that really strengthen their applications, but we would suggest being wary of asking for letters from family friends or employers who do not know much about selection processes or the kinds of material we evaluate in these applications. Our applicants might find it valuable to explain to letter-writers that we look for detailed accounts with supporting evidence.

## Is there anything that a student might find surprising about what you are looking for in the winners?

Our web page should provide adequate explanation as to what we are looking for

## Why is it important to support students to be able to attend a women's college?

Women's colleges do something special for the women who attend them that a coeducational setting cannot provide. At a women's college, everything has to be done by women—there are no men in the classes or the clubs or the student government who take over leadership roles. The women have to build stage sets for dramatic productions, they have to organize anything that's to be organized, they have to fill all the offices of student government, and they take primary roles in discussions and presentations in their classes. The fact that the women have to do everything also means that the women CAN do everything they might want to choose to do. There is no glass ceiling, there are no habits of deference or subordination to suppress effort—the sky is the limit.

# Create Stunning Scholarship Applications

**CHAPTER 7**

· · · · · · · · · · · · · · · · · · · · · · · ·

In this chapter, you'll learn:

- To create a plan of attack

- How to present your achievements to captivate the attention of the judges

- Which accomplishments to highlight and which to hide

- Top 10 scholarship application do's and don'ts

· · · · · · · · · · · · · · · · · · · · · · · ·

## Scholarship Applications: Your Entry Ticket

At first glance, scholarship applications look easy—most are only a single page in length. Piece of cake, right? Don't let their diminutive size fool you. The application is a vital part of winning any scholarship. Scholarship judges must sift through hundreds or even thousands of applications, and the application form is what they use to determine which applicants continue to the next stage. It's crucial that you ace your application to make this first cut.

In this chapter, we'll look at strategies you can use to transform an ordinary scholarship application form into a screaming testament of why you deserve to win free cash for college. Along the way, you'll meet students just like you who have used well-crafted applications to win incredible amounts of money. We'll also introduce you to a few who made fatal application blunders that you'll want to avoid.

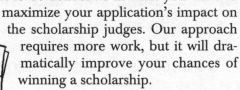

## The Big Picture

Our strategy for the application form is simple. Although you can't control the questions that are asked or even the activities and achievements you already have, you can control how you describe each accomplishment, whether to include or omit information and the order in which you present each item. In short, you control how you portray yourself on paper.

This is why the application form is deceptively simple. Most students rush through the application since they believe it's an unimportant part of the scholarship process. They don't spend the time to consider which activities, honors and awards to list and how each contributes to conveying who they are to the judges. Big mistake! Even though there is limited space on applications, you want to be deliberate in what you write to maximize your application's impact on the scholarship judges. Our approach requires more work, but it will dramatically improve your chances of winning a scholarship.

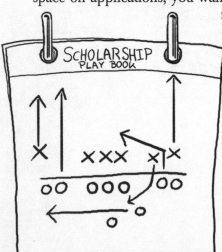

## Create Your Plan of Attack

With thousands of scholarships available and only one you, it makes sense to develop an overall strategy before you begin tackling scholarship applications. So, let's start with some high level planning.

**Prioritize the scholarships to which you think you are a match.** In Chapter 2, you learned how to select scholarships that best match your background and experience. Be sure you have your list of scholarship opportunities prioritized so that you know in which order to apply. If time runs out and you can't get to all the awards on your list, at least you have applied to those you have the best chance of winning.

**Build a timeline.** After you have a prioritized list of scholarships, look at their deadlines and create a schedule for applying. Set deadlines for when you will have the application forms completed, essays written and recommendations, if required, submitted. Post this schedule where you can see it every day. We also recommend that you share it with your parents. Moms and dads are great at nagging (we mean reminding) you to meet deadlines so you might as well use their nagging (we mean motivating) skills to your advantage.

> ### Don't Underestimate the Application Form
>
> *Don't take the application form lightly. It may be short, but it is critical that you ace it if you want to advance to the next round. Most scholarship judges use the application form to separate those who will advance from those who will receive the "Sorry, try again later" letters.*

**Look for recycling opportunities.** The first scholarship for which you apply will take the most time and it will no doubt be the most difficult. But with each application you complete, it will get easier. This is because for each successive application, you can draw on the materials you developed for the previous one. To complete your first application, you need to think about your activities and recall achievements that you have forgotten. If there is an essay component, you will need to find a topic and craft an articulate essay. When you work on your second application, you can benefit from the work you've already done for the first. As you're building your timeline, look for scholarships in which you can recycle information from one application to another. Recycling will save you time. In addition, you can improve on your work each time that you use it. For example, the second time you answer a question about your plans after graduation, you can craft your response more effectively than the first. As you recycle information, don't just reuse it, improve it!

Once you have your prioritized list of scholarships and a schedule that takes advantage of "parental motivation" you are ready to start. Keep recycling opportunities in the back of your mind and you'll save even more time, which will help you apply to more scholarships.

## General Rules for Completing the Application

### Fill in as Many Blanks as Possible

*Blank spaces can bring out the agoraphobia in you—the open space can be frightening. While you want to fill in each space, you don't want to stretch something to the point of looking ridiculous. So if you absolutely don't have anything worthwhile to list, don't stress and just leave the space blank.*

Before you fire up your computer, here are a few basic application rules to keep in mind:

**Make application form triplets.** If you receive a paper copy of the application, the first thing to do when you receive it is to make three photocopies. Why do you need three copies? Your goal is to craft the perfect application. As unlikely as it seems, you probably won't achieve perfection the first time around. A spare copy is your insurance should you make a mistake. It's not uncommon to discover that only four out of your five most important life accomplishments fit within the two-inch space on the form. Regardless of how many copies you make, never use your last clean copy of the application form. Trust us—and every student who has ruined their original at 2 a.m. on the day their application was due. It's well worth your time to have plenty of extra copies.

**Be a neat freak.** You may have dirty laundry strewn across your room and a pile of papers large enough to be classified as its own life form, but you don't want the scholarship judges to know that. When it comes to applications, neatness does count.

We would not ordinarily be neatness zealots—we admit to having our own mountains of life-imbibed papers—but submitting an application with globs of correction fluid, scratched out words or illegible hieroglyphics will severely diminish your message. Think how much less impressive the Mona Lisa would be if da Vinci had painted it on a dirty old bed sheet. You may have the most incredible thoughts to convey in your applications, but if your form is filled with errors, none of it will matter. In a sea of hundreds and even thousands of other applications, you don't want yours to be penalized by sloppy presentation.

**Know when to leave a space blank.** An official mom rule from childhood is this: "If you don't have anything nice to say, don't say it." While this is a good lesson on self-restraint, it does not always hold true for scholarship applications. In general, it is not a good idea to leave any area blank. You don't need to fill the entire space, but you should make an effort to list something in every section. However, before you try to explain how the handmade certificate that your mom presented you for being *Offspring of the Year* qualifies as an "award," realize that there are limits. If you've never held a job, don't list anything under work experience. If, however, you painted your grandmother's house one summer and got paid for it, consider listing it if you don't have any other options.

Use your judgment and common sense when trying to decide whether or not to leave an area blank. Ask yourself if what you are including will strengthen or weaken your application. Think like a judge. Is the information relevant? Or does it seem like a stretch? If you cannot convince yourself that what you are listing is justified, it will certainly not go over well with the judges. Remember your mom's advice; leave it blank and move on to the sections where you have something great to say.

**Nip and tuck every sentence.** Succinct and terse, scholarship application forms bear the well-earned reputation for having less space than you need. Often offering only a page or less, scholarship applications leave little room for much more than just the facts. As you are completing your applications, remember to abbreviate where appropriate and keep your sentences short. Often judges are scanning the application form. If they want an essay, they will ask for one.

**Instructions do not have to be taken literally.** If the instructions say to limit your essay to one page, you do need to follow the directions literally. However, if the instructions say to list your awards, you can add explanation if you need to. If you have three great awards, it is better to use your space to list those three with short explanations rather than cram in all 15 awards that you've won in your life. (No argument can be made for the timeliness of your *Perfect Attendance Award* from kindergarten.) You are trying to present the most relevant information that shows the scholarship judges why you deserve their money. Use the space to explain how each award, job or activity relates to the scholarship.

Also, feel free to interpret some instructions. Work experience does not have to be limited to traditional jobs. Maybe you started your own freelance design business or cut lawns on the weekends. The same goes for leadership positions. Who said that leadership has to be an elected position within an organization? Just be sure to explain the entry if the relationship is not totally clear. Here's an example:

> Volunteer Wilderness Guide. Led clients through seven-day trek in Catskills. Responsible for all aspects of the trip including group safety.

> **Spin but Don't Lie**
>
> *You can't change the facts about your accomplishments, but you can change how you describe them. Employ a different spin for each scholarship. Remember, you can spin, but NEVER lie.*

## "How My Support of Legalizing Marijuana Cost Me"
## Mike Porter, Scholarship Applicant

I went to high school in what I thought was a liberal-minded city. Our school principal seemed to be a hippy, straight out of the 1960s, with long hair and even wearing tie-dyed shirts on Fridays. The mayor of our city was constantly in the newspaper for his liberal stands on everything from funding for the homeless to gay rights.

In my senior year I applied for a scholarship for students in my high school. When asked about my leadership in extracurricular activities, I thought nothing of putting down that I was president of our school's Advocate Club. Our club promoted political activism, and we had made local headlines for rallies we held for increasing funding for education, keeping large chain corporations out of our downtown and legalizing the medicinal use of marijuana. There was a photo of me in the local newspaper holding a marijuana plant at a sit-in.

My friends told me they thought I had a really good chance of winning because I had the highest grades in our class and I was one of a handful of students admitted to Berkeley. I hate to brag, but my teachers really liked me because I took the time to get to know them, and they wrote great recommendation letters. I wrote an essay about my experiences with the Advocate Club and my fight to legalize marijuana.

When the winners were announced at our senior banquet, I was disappointed that I did not win any of the three prizes. I was pretty cocky and thought I should have been a shoo-in. I was so distraught that the next day at school I spoke with my counselor, who was one of the judges, and asked her why she thought I didn't win.

At first she was hesitant to give me any information about what happened behind closed doors. After reassuring her that I wasn't going to tell anyone and that I only wanted to know so I could improve my applications in the future, she let me in on the judges' thoughts. She said that everyone knew that I was qualified, but there were three judges who voted against me because while they admired my devotion to causes, they disagreed with my lobbying for the legalization of medicinal uses for marijuana. I couldn't believe what I was hearing—that my political views prevented me from winning.

After I found out who the judges were, it was easy to understand why they voted against me. They were members of our local government who were very conservative compared to the rest of the city's political leaders. The ironic thing was that I could have found out who the judges were before turning in my application. If I had, I might have given less attention to my most controversial belief.

***Moral of the Story:*** *Understanding the awarding organization and who is likely to read your application can give you insight into what to focus on and what to avoid. If Mike had asked some basic questions about the judges, he probably would have won.*

**Always remember that the application is you.** A scholarship application is more than a piece of paper. In the eyes of the scholarship judges, it is you. It may not be fair, but in many cases the application is the only thing that the judges will have as a measurement standard. The last thing you want to be is a dry list of academic and extracurricular achievements. You are a living, breathing person. Throughout the application, take every opportunity—no matter how small—to show the judges who you really are. Use descriptions and vocabulary that reveal your passion and commitment. Always remember that the application is a reflection of you.

## The Five Steps to Crafting a Winning Application

We have reduced the process for completing your application to five distinct steps. As you read each step think of how you can apply it to the specific applications that you are working on.

### Step 1: Use a Little "Spin" to "Wow" Your Audience

Politicians are notorious for telling their constituents what they want to hear. Good politicians never lie, but they do put a flattering "spin" on their words depending on whom they're addressing. While you must never lie on your application forms, you do want to present yourself in the best possible way and appeal to your audience. In other words, employ a little spin.

We know that some politicians have a difficult time distinguishing between lying and spinning. You shouldn't. Let's say you are applying for a scholarship that rewards students who are interested in promoting literacy. You have been a volunteer at your local library where each week one of your responsibilities is to read stories to a dozen children. Here are three ways you could describe this activity on your application:

**Non-spin description:**

Library volunteer.

**Lie:**

Library reading program founder. Started a national program that reaches thousands of children every day to promote literacy.

**Spin:**

Library volunteer. Promoted literacy among children through weekly after-school reading program at public library.

> ### Know Your Audience
>
> *You would never give a speech without knowing who your audience is, right? So don't start your applications until you know who will read them.*

> ### Find Out Why They Are Giving Away Their Money
>
> *Nobody gives away money without a reason. Behind every organization's philanthropic actions lies a motive. Your job is to uncover what this motive is and spin your application accordingly.*

At one extreme, you can see that a lie exaggerates well beyond the truth. At the other extreme, the non-spin description is not very impressive because it does not explain how the activity relates to the purpose of the scholarship. The spin version does not stretch the truth, but it does make clear how this activity fits within the context of the goal of the scholarship. It focuses on what is important to the judges while at the same time it ignores other aspects of your job that are not relevant—such as shelving books.

To take this example one step further, let's say that now you are applying for a scholarship that rewards student leaders. One of your other responsibilities as a library volunteer is to maintain the schedule for volunteers and help with the recruitment of new volunteers. Your description for this scholarship might read:

> Library volunteer. Coordinated volunteer schedule and recruited new members for after-school reading program.

Notice how you have "spun" your activity so that it highlights a different aspect of what you did and better shows the judges how you fit their criteria. In the application you should use the opportunity to spin your accomplishments to match the goal of the award.

To be able to spin effectively you need to know your audience. When you prioritized your scholarships earlier, you should have discovered the purposes of the scholarships. Remember that in most cases the scholarship judges want to give their money to students who are the best reflections of themselves. For example, the Future Teachers of America judges will want to fund students who seem the most committed to pursuing a teaching career. The American Congress of Surveying and Mapping judges, on the other hand, want to give their money to students who have the strongest interest in cartography.

To determine your audience, ask the following questions. Use your answers to guide your decisions on how much detail to provide, what to include or omit and how to prioritize your achievements. You'll find that just thinking about these questions and putting yourself into the mindset of the judges will enable you to craft a better application.

 **What is the mission of the organization giving away the scholarship? Why do they want to give free money to students?**

Organizations don't give away scholarships and expect nothing in return. Behind their philanthropic motives lies an ulterior motive—to promote their organization's vision. To find this vision, visit the organization's website, call its offices to ask for

more information or request materials to read. If it's a local group, meet some of its members or attend a meeting. Once you know what the organization is all about, you can better decide which of your achievements would make the biggest impression on the scholarship application.

Let's imagine that you are applying for an award given by an organization of professional journalists. In visiting their website you learn that print and broadcast journalists join this group because they are passionate about the profession of journalism and want to encourage public awareness about the importance of a free press. Immediately, you know that you need to highlight those experiences that demonstrate your zeal for journalism and, if possible, your belief in the value of a free press. Among your activities and accomplishments are the following:

> Columnist for your high school newspaper
> Vice President of the Writers' Club
> English essay contest winner
> Summer internship at a radio station

As you look at this list, you remember that in the Writers' Club you participated in a workshop that helped a local elementary school start its own newspaper. Since this achievement almost perfectly matches the mission of our hypothetical journalism organization, use your limited space in the application to list it first and to add an explanation.

You might write something like this:

> Writers' Club, Vice President, organized "Writing Counts" workshop at Whitman Elementary School, which resulted in the launch of the school's first student-run newspaper.

Think of the impact this would have on the scholarship judges. "Look here, Fred" one journalist on the judging committee would say. "This student does what we do! Definitely someone we should interview!"

Before you can even begin to evaluate which activities to list and how to describe them, you need to know as much as you can about the organization sponsoring the scholarship. By understanding the purpose of the

### Stand Out

*To stand out from the competition you need to predict who will enter and imagine what will be on their applications.*

### How to Brag Without Being Conceited

*Bragging without sounding conceited is an art. The key is to cite facts and figures to support your statements.*

organization, you can select achievements and spin them in ways that will be sure to attract the attention of the judges.

**Q** **Who is going to read your scholarship application? What kind of people make up the organization that is giving away the money?**

Let's imagine for a moment that you need to give a speech to two groups of people. Without knowing who your audience is, you would have a difficult time composing a speech that would appeal to them, right?

It would make a big difference in your presentation were one a group of mathematicians and the other a group of fashion designers. To grab the attention of each of these audiences, you'd need to adjust your speech accordingly. References to mathematical theorems would hardly go over well with the designers, just as the mathematicians probably could not care less about how black the new black really is.

It's not always possible to know who your audience is, but you should try to find out who is likely to be on the judging committee. In some instances you may actually know the people by name—such as an administrator at your school, a local congressman or business leader. Often you will have a sense of what kind of people will most likely be judging. Most groups have identifiable traits among their membership. The Veterans of Foreign Wars and American Civil Liberties Union, for example, have members with identifiable beliefs.

In the same way that understanding the mission of an organization helps you to decide how to present certain information, so too does knowing the composition of the judging panel. For example, if you know that members of the community who are committed to public service are on the judging committee, then stress your contributions in that area.

Be sure to avoid things that might be offensive to the organization's members. Just imagine what would happen if you thoughtlessly mentioned that you were the author of an economics project entitled "How Labor Unions Make the U.S. Unable to Compete and Lowers Our Standard of Living" to judges who are members of the International Brotherhood of Teamsters.

It should also be clear to you why you can't use the same list of activities and accomplishments for every scholarship. Take the time to craft a unique list that matches what each of the scholarships is intended to reward.

## Step 2: Stand Out from the Competition

Think of the scholarship competition as a reverse police lineup where you want to stand out and be picked by the people behind the one-way mirror. You want the judge to say without hesitation, "That's the one!" The only way this will happen is if your application is noticed and doesn't get lost in the crowd. One of the best ways to accomplish this is to know what you're up against—in other words, think about who else will be in the lineup with you.

Try to anticipate your competition—even if it's just an educated guess. Depending on to whom the scholarship is offered, you may have a limited or broad pool of competitors. If the award is confined to your school, you may know everyone who will enter on a first-name basis. If it's national, all you may know for a medical scholarship, for instance, is that the applicants are students interested in becoming doctors.

More important than the scope of the competition is the type of students who will apply. One of the biggest challenges in any competition is to break away from the pack. If 500 pre-med students are applying for a $10,000 scholarship from a medical association, you need to make sure that your application stands out from those of the 499 other applicants. If you are lucky, you may have done something that few have done. (Inventing a new vaccine in your spare time would certainly set you apart!) Unfortunately, most of us will have to distinguish ourselves in more subtle ways, such as through the explanation of activities and accomplishments.

Say you are applying for a scholarship given by a national medical association that seeks to promote the medical sciences. It just so happens that you are considering a pre-med major and you have interned at a local hospital. If you hadn't read this book, you might have listed under activities:

Summer Internship at Beth Israel Children's Hospital

But you did read this book! So you know that this is a great activity to elaborate on since it demonstrates your commitment to medicine and shows that you truly are interested in entering the medical field. You also know that you need to stand out from the competition and as great as this activity is, you know that a lot of other applicants will also have volunteered at hospitals. So instead of simply listing the internship, you add detail to make the experience more unique. You could write:

Summer Internship at Beth Israel Children's Hospital, assisted with clinical trial of new allergy medication.

This description is much more unique and memorable. By providing details, you can illustrate to the judges how your volunteer work is different from that of other students. Remember that you can add short descriptions in most applications even if the instructions do not explicitly ask for them.

Let's look at another example. If you know that many applicants for a local public service scholarship have participated in your school's annual canned food drive, you need to highlight contributions that go beyond this program. You'd probably want to highlight the other public service activities you did besides the canned food drive because you know that the food drive alone will not set you apart from the others.

If you can anticipate who your competition will be and what they might write in their applications, you will be able to find a way to go one step further to distinguish yourself from the crowd. Even the simple act of adding a one-sentence description to an activity can make the difference between standing out and getting lost.

## Step 3: List Important Accomplishments First

In movies, the most dare-devilish car chase, the most harrowing showdown and the most poignant romantic revelations are usually saved until the end. While this works for Hollywood, it does not for scholarship applications. Since scholarship judges review so many applications and the space on the form is limited, you need to highlight your most impressive points first.

If you have listed four extracurricular activities, assume that some judges won't read beyond the first two. This doesn't mean that all judges will be this rushed, but there are always some who are. It's extremely important that you prioritize the information that you present and rank your accomplishments according to the following—which should not come as too much of a surprise.

> ### Always Describe an Award
>
> Don't expect the judges to know the ins and outs of the honors or awards you've won. Provide descriptions that illustrate how prestigious the honor is and how it fits with the purpose of the scholarship.

**Fit.** The most important factor in prioritizing your achievements is how they fit with the goal of the scholarship. This is, after all, why these kind people want to hand you some free dough. Emphasize accomplishments that match the purpose of the scholarship. If you are applying for an award that rewards athleticism, stress how well you've done in a particular sport before listing your volunteer activities.

**Scope.** Prioritize your accomplishments by their scope, or how much of an impact they have made. How many people have been affected by your work? To what extent has your accomplishment affected your community? Did your contribution produce measurable results? In simple terms, put the big stuff before the small stuff.

**Uniqueness.** Since your application will be compared to those of perhaps thousands of others, include accomplishments that are uncommon. Give priority to those that are unique or difficult to win. Being on your school's honor roll is certainly an achievement, but it is an honor that many others have received. Try to select honors that fewer students have received. Remember the reverse police lineup idea—you want to stand out in order to be selected.

**Timeliness.** This is the least-important criterion, but if you get stuck and aren't sure how to arrange some of your accomplishments, put the more recent achievements first. Having won an election in the past year is more relevant than having won one three years ago. Some students ask us if they should list junior high or even elementary school achievements. Generally, stick to accomplishments from high school if you're a high school student and to college if you're a college student. An exception is if your accomplishment is extremely impressive and relevant—such as publishing your own book in the eighth grade. Of course, if you run out of recent achievements and there is still space on the form, go ahead and reach back to the past—but try to limit yourself to one or two items.

You want your application to be as unforgettable as the best Hollywood movies. The only difference between your work and Spielberg's—besides the millions of dollars—is that you need to place the grand finale first.

## Step 4: Write to Impress

The inspiring words of Martin Luther King Jr.'s "I have a dream" speech were punctuated with his dramatic, emotion-filled voice, hopeful expression and confident presence. His delivery would not have been as forceful had he spoken in a drab, monotone with hands stuffed into his pockets and eyes lowered to avoid contact with the audience. Nor would his dramatic presentation have been as effective had his message been unimportant. The lesson? Both content and delivery count.

While you don't have the opportunity for person-to-person delivery with your scholarship applications, you can and should present information in a compelling way. Here are some time-tested writing strategies for creating a positive impression through your applications:

**Showcase Your Smarts.** There's a reason why your parents wanted you to study and do well in school. In addition to the correlation between studying and success in college, almost all scholarships (even those that are athletic in nature) require some level of academic achievement. College is, after all, about learning (at least that's what you want your parents to believe).

As you are completing your applications, keep in mind that while you may be applying for a public service scholarship, you should also include at least a few academic achievements. For example, it does not hurt to list on an athletic scholarship form that you also came in second place at the science fair. This should not be the first thing you list, but it should be included somewhere to show the committee that you have brains in addition to brawn.

When you describe your intellectual activities, explain how they match the scholarship's goal most closely. For example, if you are applying for a science scholarship, focus on the awards you've won at science fairs and the advanced courses you've taken in the sciences rather than writing awards or advanced literature courses. Use your academic achievements to illustrate why you see your future in the sciences. Scholarship judges ideally want to see that your academic talents are in line with the scholarship's purpose.

**Extracurricular Activities and Hobbies Show Your Passion.** If your only activity were studying, your life would be severely lacking in excitement. Scholarship organizers recognize this and thus the criteria for many scholarships include extracurricular activities or hobbies. Scholarship committees want evidence that you do more than read textbooks, take exams and watch television. They want to know that you have other interests. This makes you a more well-rounded person.

**(Don't do this!)**

As always, when completing your applications, select extracurricular activities and hobbies that fit with the scholarship's mission. If you are applying for a music scholarship, describe how you've been involved in your school's orchestra or how you've taken violin lessons. By showing that you not only have taken classes in music theory but have also been involved with music outside of your studies, the scholarship committee will get a more complete picture of your love for music. Remember to use your activities and hobbies to illustrate your passion for a subject.

**Leadership Is Always Better Than Membership.** If you've ever tried to motivate a group of peers to do anything without taking the easy way out–bribery–you know that it takes courage, intelligence and creativity to be a leader. Because of this, many scholarships give extra points to reward leadership. Scholarship judges want to know that the dollars will be awarded to someone who will not only make a difference in the future but who will also be a leader and motivate others to do the same. Think of it this way: If you were a successful businessperson trying to encourage entrepreneurship, wouldn't you want to give your money to a young

---

### "My Midnight Scholarship Application"
### Charlene Davis, Scholarship Applicant

I've always considered myself a fast person. I speak, walk and move quickly. That's why I didn't think it was out of the question to complete my scholarship application the night before it was due. It was a one-page document with about a dozen questions on it. How difficult could it be?

At about 9 p.m., I whipped out the application. It was a scholarship given by my department, which was sociology. The questions seemed easy enough. They asked about the classes I had taken, my involvement in activities on campus and what I planned to do after graduation.

Boy, did I underestimate the amount of time it would take to answer those dozen questions. I didn't anticipate spending two hours searching for my transcript because I couldn't remember the exact classes and grades that I received in the two previous years. By 11 p.m., I found a copy of my transcript in the very back of a file box I kept in the corner of my closet.

I also didn't think I would make so many errors completing the application and thinking about my answers. I spent hours writing and re-writing my responses.

By 6 a.m., I finished completing the application. Full of poorly worded sentences, it certainly wasn't one of my best pieces of work. I hand-delivered the completed application to the assistant in my department at 9 a.m. She took one look at me and asked, "Pulled an all-nighter, eh?" I nodded lethargically. After crashing, I awoke in the afternoon to look at a copy of what I submitted. There were mistakes everywhere including incomplete sentences and incoherent thoughts.

As expected, I didn't win the scholarship. I knew I would have had a decent chance if I had spent some quality time on the application. My advice: Don't wait until the night before. You may think you can do it, but I am proof that you can't.

**Remind Yourself
That the
Application Is You**

*Above everything
else remember that
the application form
is you. Through
this sheet of paper
you are showing
the scholarship
judges why they
should choose you.
If you keep this and
the mission of the
award in mind, you
will create a solid
application.*

person who is not only an entrepreneur but who also motivates others to become entrepreneurs? Scholarship providers believe the return on their investment will be higher when they put their money behind leaders rather than followers.

Describing leadership in your activities or hobbies will also help set you apart from the other applicants. Many students are involved with environmental groups, but what if you are the only one to actually help increase recycling on your campus? Wouldn't that make your application a standout?

To show scholarship judges that you are a leader, list any activities in which you held an office. Describe leadership positions you've had and what your responsibilities were. Use active verbs when describing your work:

Organized band fundraiser to purchase new instruments
Led a weeklong nature tour in Yosemite
Founded first website to list volunteer activities
Directed independent musical performance

Remember that you don't need to be an elected officer to be a leader. Many students have organized special projects, led teams or helped run events. Even if you didn't have an official title, you can include these experiences. Here's an example:

Environmental Action Committee Member. Spearheaded committee on reducing waste and increasing recycling on campus.

When describing your leadership, include both formal and informal ways you have led groups. This shows the scholarship committee that you are a worthy investment.

**Honors and Awards Validate Your Strengths.** There's a reason why all trophies are gold and gaudy. They shout to the world in a deafening roar, "Yes, this glittery gold miniature figure means I am the best!" For applications that ask for your honors and awards, impart some of that victorious roar and attitude. In no way are we recommending that you ship your golden statuettes off with your applications. We are saying that you should highlight honors and awards in a way that gets the scholarship committee to pay attention to your application.

What makes an award impressive is scope. Not a minty mouthwash, scope in this case is the impact and influence of the award. You worked for the award and earned every golden inch of it. Show the committee that they don't just hand these statuettes out to anybody. One way to do this is to point out how many awards are given:

English Achievement Award. Presented to two outstanding juniors
each year.

By itself, the English Achievement Award does not tell the scholarship committee
very much. Maybe half the people in your class were given the award. By revealing the scope of the award (particularly if it was given to only a few) it becomes
much more impressive.

In competitions that reach beyond your school, it is important to qualify your
awards. For example, while everyone at your school may know that the Left
Brain Achievement Award is given to creative art students, the rest of the world
does not.

**Don't write**:

Left Brain Achievement Award.

**Do write**:

Left Brain Achievement Award. Recognized as an outstanding
creative talent in art as conferred upon by vote of art department
faculty.

You've worked hard to earn the honors and awards that you have received, and
you should not hesitate to use them in your applications to help you win scholarships.

## Step 5: Make Sure the Application Fits

You'd never buy a pair of pants without trying them on. Treat your applications
the same way. You have limited space in which to cram a lot of information. You
will need to do quite a bit of editing and may even have to omit some accomplishments. Of course by now you know which ones to include and which can be
safely omitted. To make sure that everything fits, start
completing one of the photocopies that you made of
the application. Here's where you'll appreciate having
those backup practice forms.

As you fill out the application, you may find that you
are trying to squeeze in too many details or that you
have more room and can expand on your most impressive achievements. Don't forget to adjust font sizes and
line spacing if necessary—just don't sacrifice readability
(i.e., don't go below 10-point fonts).

Only by trying on your application will you know if
what you have in mind will fit. Now that you know

> ### Make Sure Everything Fits
>
> *What you want to write and what you have room to write may be two different things. Use a practice application before the real one to see what fits.*

the five steps to insure that your application is a winner, here is our Top Ten list of application form do's and don'ts which will serve as a final reminder of how to create that stunning application!

## Top Ten Application Do's and Don'ts

With money on the table, it's much better to learn from others' successes and mistakes before you risk your own fortunes. From interviews with students and scholarship judges and firsthand experience reviewing scholarship applications, we've developed our Top Ten list of scholarship application do's and don'ts. Let's shed the negative energy first and start with the don'ts.

### Don'ts

**1. DON'T prioritize quantity over quality.** It's not the quantity of your accomplishments that's important. It's the quality of your contributions.

**2. DON'T stretch the truth.** Tall tales are prohibited.

**3. DON'T squeeze to the point of illegibility.** Scholarship applications afford minimal space. It's impossible to fit in everything that you want to say. Don't try by sacrificing legibility.

**4. DON'T write when you have nothing to say.** If you don't have something meaningful to present, leave it blank.

**5. DON'T think you're on your own.** Ask your counselor, teacher or parent for feedback as you're completing the applications.

**6. DON'T procrastinate.** Don't think you can finish your applications the night before they're due.

**7. DON'T settle for less than perfect.** You can have imperfections. Just don't let the selection committee know.

**8. DON'T miss deadlines.** No matter the reason, if you miss the deadline, you won't win the scholarship.

**9. DON'T turn in incomplete applications.** Make sure your application is finished before sending it.

**10. DON'T underestimate what you can convey.** Scholarship applications may appear to be short and simple. Don't undervalue them. In a small space, you can create a powerful story of why you should win.

And now the good stuff.

## Do's

**1. DO understand the scholarship's mission.** Know why they're giving out the dough.

**2. DO remember who your audience is.** You need to address animal rights activists and retired dentists differently.

**3. DO show how you fit with the scholarship's mission.** You're not going to win unless you have what the selection committee wants.

**4. DO be proud of your accomplishments.** Don't be afraid to brag.

**5. DO focus on leadership and contributions.** Make your contributions known.

**6. DO make your application stand out.**

**7. DO practice to make sure everything fits.** Use your spare copies of the application for trial and error.

**8. DO get editors.** They'll help you create the best, error free applications you can.

**9. DO include a resume.** Whether they ask for it or not, make sure you include a tailored scholarship resume. See the next chapter for how to create a great resume.

**10. DO make copies of your finished applications for reference.** Save them for next year when you do this all over again.

## Finishing Touches

Once you've completed your applications, check and double-check for accuracy. Look at every line and every question to make sure you've filled out all the information that is requested on the form. Make sure you have someone else take a look at your application. They will catch mistakes that you invariably will miss. Remember that presentation affects how scholarship judges view applications. You want to convey that you are serious about winning the scholarship by submitting an application that is complete and error-free.

Finally, before submitting, save a copy of everything. If for some reason your scholarship form is lost, you have a copy you can resend. Plus, you will have a great starting place for when you apply for scholarships next year.

## Chapter 7 Summary: Create Stunning Applications

**Create an application plan of attack.** Prioritize the scholarships to which you'd like to apply, build a timeline and schedule for applying and determine recycling opportunities.

**Do application pre-work.** Before you start, make three copies of the scholarship forms for practice, remember to be neat and realize that the application is a reflection of you.

**Give them what they want to hear.** Don't lie, but present the truth in a way that matches the mission of the award. Keep in mind why the organization is providing the award and who your audience is as you are completing your applications.

**Spin.** Use words deliberately to highlight how each accomplishment fits the mission of the award.

**Go for the gusto quickly.** This means don't bury your main point. Concentrate on how your accomplishments match the scholarship's goal and the scope, uniqueness and timeliness of your achievements.

**Write to impress.** Focus on academics, leadership, extracurricular achievements, honors and awards.

**Make sure the application fits.** Get the most important information in your application forms.

**Put on those finishing touches.** Every question should be answered, and all information requested should be provided.

# The Scholarship Resume

· · · · · · · · · · · · · · · · · · · · · · · · · · · · · · · · · ·

In this chapter, you'll learn:

- What goes into a scholarship resume

- How to write a resume that stands out

- What an actual scholarship resume looks like

· · · · · · · · · · · · · · · · · · · · · · · · · · · · · · · · · ·

# Scholarship Resumes: One-Page Autobiographies

If your life were a book, then your scholarship resume would be the Cliffs Notes. A scholarship resume is your opportunity to tout your greatest achievements and life's accomplishments. The only catch is that you are limited to one page. Some scholarships require resumes to get a quick overview of your achievements. Others don't, but including a resume will always enhance your application.

A scholarship resume is not the same as one that you would use to get a job. It's unlikely that your work experience (if you have any) will be the focus. However, the principles and format are the same. A good resume that scores you a job shows employers that you have the right combination of work experience and skills to be their next hire. Similarly, your scholarship resume should show the committee why you are the most qualified student to win their award.

## The Big Picture

Think of the scholarship resume as a "cheat sheet" that you give to the judges. By looking at your resume the judges get a quick overview of your achievements and interests. The resume is not an exhaustive list of everything you have done. It only highlights and summarizes the most impressive and relevant achievements.

To make sure that it really focuses on the crème de la crème, your resume should fit on a single sheet of paper. This is sometimes harder than it sounds.

Here is the information you need for a scholarship resume:

**Contact information.** Your vital statistics, including name, address, phone number and email.

**Objective.** Purpose of the resume.

**Education.** Schools you've attended beginning with high school, expected or actual graduation dates.

**Academic achievements.** Relevant coursework, awards and honors received.

**Extracurricular experience.** Relevant extracurricular activities, locations and dates of participation, leadership positions, responsibilities and accomplishments.

**Work experience.** Where and when you've worked, job titles, responsibilities and accomplishments on the job.

**Skills and interests.** Additional relevant technical, lingual or other skills or talents that do not fit in the categories above.

There are many good ways to format a resume. Most important, your resume should be easy to skim and be organized in a logical manner.

On the next page you will find an example of a well-written scholarship resume. Remember that there are other equally good formats in which to present this information.

Your resume should be descriptive enough for the judges to understand each item but not so wordy that they can't find what they need. It should be neatly organized and easy to follow. Having reviewed hundreds of resumes, here are some simple strategies we've developed:

**Don't worry if your resume presents the same information that's in the application form.** Some judges will read only the application or your resume, so it's important your key points are in both. However, in the resume, try to expand on areas that you were not able to cover fully in the application.

**Include only the important information.** Remember to incorporate only the most relevant items and use what you know about the scholarship organization to guide how you prioritize what you share in your resume. For each piece of information, ask yourself: Will including this aid the selection committee in seeing that I am a match for the award? Is this information necessary to convince them that I should receive the award? Only include things that support your fit with the scholarship's mission.

**Focus on responsibilities and achievements.** In describing your experiences in work and activities, focus on the responsibilities you held and highlight measurable or unique successes. Successes could include starting a project, reaching goals or implementing one of your ideas. For example, if you were the treasurer of the Literary Club, you would want to include that you were responsible for managing a $10,000 annual budget.

**Demonstrate in your resume how you showed leadership.** Leadership could include leading a project or team, instructing others or mentoring your peers. What's more important than your

> **Your Resume**
> ───────
>
> *A scholarship resume is a one-page overview of your most important achievements. It shows the judges why you are the most qualified student to win their scholarship, and it does so in just one page.*

**Melissa Lee**
1000 University Drive
San Francisco, CA 94134
(415) 555-5555

**Objective**
To obtain funding for college through the SuperCollege.com Scholarship.

**Education**
University of San Francisco                            San Francisco, CA
B.A. candidate in sociology. Expected graduation in 2024. Honor roll.

Lowell High School                                     San Francisco, CA
Graduated in 2020 with highest honors. Principal's Honor Roll, 4 years.

**Activities and Awards**
SF Educational Project                                 San Francisco, CA
Program Assistant. Recruit and train 120 students for various community service projects in semester-long program. Manage and evaluate student journals, lesson plans and program participation. 2018-present.

Lowell High School Newspaper                           San Francisco, CA
Editor-In-Chief. Recruited and managed staff of 50. Oversaw all editorial and business functions. Newspaper was a finalist for the prestigious Examiner Award for excellence in student journalism. 2016-2020.

Evangelical Church                                     San Francisco, CA
Teacher. Prepared and taught weekly lessons for third grade Sunday School class. Received dedication to service award from congregation. 2016-2020.

Asian Dance Troupe                                     San Francisco, CA
Member. Perform at community functions and special events. 2018-present.

**Employment**
Palo Alto Daily News                                   Palo Alto, CA
Editorial Assistant. Researched and wrote eight feature articles on such topics as education reform, teen suicide and summer fashion. Led series of teen reader response panels. Summer 2020.

Russian Hill Public Library                            San Francisco, CA
Library Page. Received "Page of the Month" Award for outstanding performance. Summers 2018-2019.

**Interests**
Fluent in Mandarin and HTML. Interests include journal writing, creative writing, photography, swimming and aerobics.

Some points to note about this resume:

- Notice how this resume is concise and very easy to read. By limiting herself to a single page, Melissa makes sure that even if you just scan her resume you will pick up her key strengths.

- See how each description includes examples of leadership as well as awards or special recognition.

- Melissa conveys the impact of her work by pointing out concrete results.

- Notice how her description of summer jobs highlights some of her key accomplishments.

- The final section adds a nice balance by describing some of her other hobbies and interests.

title or where you worked is the quality of your involvement. Explaining your successes and your role as a leader will provide concrete evidence of your contribution.

**Be proud.** Your resume is your time to shine. Don't be afraid to draw attention to all that you've accomplished. If you played a key role in a project, say so. If you exceeded your goals, advertise it. No one else is going to do your bragging for you.

**Use active verbs.** When you are describing your achievements, use active verbs such as: *founded, organized, achieved, created, developed, directed* and, our personal favorite, *initiated*.

**Don't tell tall stories.** On the flip side of being proud is being untruthful. It's important that you describe yourself in the most glowing way possible, but stay connected with the truth. If you developed a new filing system at your job, don't claim that you single-handedly led a corporate revolution. With your complete scholarship application, selection committees can see through a resume that is exaggerated and doesn't match the rest of the application, essay and recommendations.

**Get editors.** After the hundredth time reading your resume, you'll probably not notice an error that someone reading it for the first time will catch. Get others to read and edit your resume. Editors can let you know if something doesn't make sense, offer you alternative wording and help correct your boo-boos. Some good choices for editors may be

**Give Your Resume to Your Recommenders**

---

*Besides including your scholarship resume in your application you may also give it to your recommenders so that they have a cheat sheet to your accomplishments and can include them in their recommendations.*

teachers or professors, work supervisors or parents. Work supervisors may be especially helpful since part of their job is to review resumes of job applicants. Your school may also offer resume help in the counseling department or career services office.

**Avoid an eye test.** In trying to squeeze all the information onto a single page, don't make your font size so small that the words are illegible. Try to leave space between paragraphs. The judges may have tired, weary eyes from reading all those applications. Don't strain them even more.

**Strive for perfection.** It's a given that your resume should be error-free. There's no excuse for mistakes on a one-page document that is meant to exemplify your life's work.

## Chapter 8 Summary: The Scholarship Resume

**Your one-page autobiography.** A resume presents the main highlights of your education and achievements in an easy-to-read format and provides scholarship judges with a brief overview of you.

**Remember that your resume is a summary and highlight of your accomplishments.** The biggest mistake in writing a resume is to try to be comprehensive and list everything you have done in great detail.

**Force yourself to use one page.** Without resorting to micro-sized fonts and spacing, force yourself to fit everything onto one page. That will ensure that you only include the most important and relevant information.

**Focus on achievements.** If possible, quantify your accomplishments.

**Use active verbs.** Don't be afraid to brag by using active verbs.

**Get editors.** The best way to make sure your resume is clear and concise is to get feedback from others.

# Get the Right Recommendations

. . . . . . . . . . . . . . . . . . . . . . . . . .

In this chapter, you'll learn:

- How to get recommendations that make an impact

- Who makes the best recommenders

- Essential information you must provide to guarantee great recommendations

- How to ensure your recommenders meet the deadlines

. . . . . . . . . . . . . . . . . . . . . . . . . .

## Getting the Praise of Others

If you need a reason to kiss up to your teachers or professors, here's one—recommendations. Scholarships sometime require that you submit recommendations from teachers, professors, school administrators, employers or others who can vouch for your accomplishments. Scholarship judges use recommendations to get another perspective of your character and accomplishments. Viewed together with your application and essay, the recommendation helps the judges get a more complete picture of who you are. Plus, it's always impressive when someone else extols your virtues.

Many students believe that they have no control over the recommendation. This isn't true. You actually have a lot of control over the letter that your recommenders write. In this chapter we will explore several ways—all perfectly ethical—to ensure that you get great recommendations.

## The Big Picture

A recommendation is an important opportunity for someone else to tell scholarship judges why you deserve to win. You may assume that because others do the actual writing, recommendations are completely out of your control. Banish that thought. The secret is to not only pick the right people but to also provide them with all of the information they need to turn out a great letter of recommendation. Many applicants overlook this fact. But not you, right? Armed with superb recommendations, your scholarship application is sure to rise to the top.

## Finding People to Say Nice Things about You

### Find Someone Who Knows You

*As a rule, select recommenders who can speak meaningfully about both your academic abilities and your character.*

Your first task is to find recommenders. Unfortunately, mom, dad and anyone else related to you are excluded. So, how do you get those recommendations without familial ties to sing your praises?

First, think about all the people in your life who can speak meaningfully about you and your accomplishments. Your list may include teachers, professors, advisors, school administrators, employers, religious leaders, coaches or leaders of organizations and activities in which you are involved. While some scholarships require recommendations from specific people (like a teacher or professor), most are pretty liberal and allow you to select anyone who knows you.

Second, once you have a list of potential recommenders, analyze which of these people could present information about you that best matches the goals of the scholarships. If you apply for an academic scholarship, you'll want at least one teacher or professor to write a recommendation. If you apply for an athletic scholarship, a coach would be a good choice. Select people who are able to write about the things that are most important to the scholarship judges. A good exercise is to imagine what your potential recommender would write and whether or not this would enhance your case for winning the scholarship.

> *Don't Only Pick Teachers Who Gave You A's in Class*
> ___
> *Be careful about asking teachers or professors who gave you an A in their class but don't really know you. Some professors will use form letters for students whom they have not had a meaningful conversation with but did well in their classes.*

After considering these two questions, you should be left with only a few people from which to choose. If you can't decide between two equally qualified people, choose the one who knows you the best as a person. For example, if you got A's in three classes and are trying to decide which professor to ask for a recommendation, pick the one who can write more than a testament to your academic ability. This is important because a recommendation that contains comments on your character is extremely memorable. Maybe one of the professors knows you well enough to include a few sentences on your drive to succeed or your family background. Ideally, your recommender is able to describe not only your performance in the classroom but also the values and character traits that make you special.

## Give Your Recommender the Chance to Say "No"

Once you've selected whom you'd like to write your recommendations, ask them to do so—early. A general rule is to allow at least three weeks before the recommendation is due. Explain that you are applying for scholarships and are required to submit recommendations from people who know you and who can comment on some of your achievements.

It's important to ask the person a question like this: "Do you feel comfortable writing a recommendation letter for me?" This allows the person the opportunity to decline your request if he or she doesn't feel comfortable or doesn't have the time. If you get a negative or hesitant response, don't assume that it's because he or she has a low opinion of you. It could simply be that the person doesn't know you well enough or is too busy to write a thoughtful recommendation. It's much better to have the recommender decline to write a letter than to get one that is rushed or

> ### Don't Become Star Struck
>
> *What's more important than the name recognition of your recommenders is how well they know you. If they can't write a personalized letter, don't ask them.*

not entirely positive. In most cases, however, potential recommenders are flattered and happy to oblige.

## Don't Play the Name Game

From being recognized by strangers to getting preferential reservations at the hottest restaurants, there are a lot of perks to being famous. You might think that this special treatment carries over to recommendations, and that scholarship judges will be star-struck by a letter from someone with a fancy title. However, don't assume that just because you ask someone well known to write your recommendations that you are a shoo-in for the scholarship. In fact, you might be surprised to learn that doing so could actually hurt your chances of winning.

So the question is this: "Should I try to find someone famous to write a letter of recommendation for me?" The answer comes down to the principles outlined above. How well does the person know you, and can he or she write about you in a way that presents you as a viable candidate for the scholarship? If the answer is "yes," then by all means ask the person to help you. However, if you don't know the person very well or if what he or she will write could lack a connection to the qualities that the scholarship committee is looking for, it's better to forgo the value of high name recognition and ask someone who can address what's most important in a letter of recommendation.

For example, if you work as a summer intern for your state senator, you may think that a letter from such a political luminary would give your application the star power to set it apart from others with recommendations from mere mortals. However, if you spent more time photocopying or stuffing envelopes than you did developing keen political strategies and saw the senator as many times as you have fingers on your left hand, chances are that he or she would have very few meaningful things to say about your performance. "A skilled photocopier" and "brewed a mean cup of coffee" are not compliments you want sent to the scholarship judges.

If you ask someone well known to write your recommendations, make sure that he or she really knows you and can speak about your accomplishments personally and meaningfully. The quality of what is said in the recommendations is much more important than whose signature is on the bottom of the page.

## Do the Grunt Work for Your Recommenders

Once you've selected your recommenders, give them everything they need to get the job done. Since they are doing you a favor, make the process as easy as possible for them. This is also where you can most influence what they write and actually direct what accomplishments they highlight. But before we delve into the specifics, here is an overview of what you need to provide each recommender:

**Cover letter.** This describes the scholarships you are applying for. In the letter, you should list deadlines and give the recommenders direct guidance on what to write. More on this in a bit.

**Resume.** A resume provides a quick overview of your most important achievements in an easy to follow one-page format. It is also what your recommenders will use as they cite your important achievements. (See Chapter 8 for details on creating a scholarship resume.)

**Recommendation form.** Some scholarships provide an actual form that your recommenders need to complete. Fill in the parts that you can, such as your name and address.

**Pre-addressed, stamped envelopes.** Read the application materials to find out if you need to submit your recommendations separately or with the rest of your application. For letters that are to be mailed separately, provide your recommenders with envelopes that are stamped and have the scholarship's mailing address on them. If you are supposed to submit the letters with your application, provide your recommenders with envelopes on which you have written your name.

Many recommenders prefer to write letters that are confidential and that you don't get to read.

Once you have everything, place it in a folder or envelope and label it with your recommender's name.

## Give Your Recommenders a Script

Because you know yourself better than anyone else, you would probably receive the best recommendations if you sat down and wrote them yourself. Unfortunately, this practice is frowned upon by scholarship judges. Short of writing your own recommendations, you can influence how they turn out by providing your recommenders with detailed descriptions of your accomplishments that can help them decide which

> ### The Cover Letter Is Key
>
> *A well-written cover letter is a powerful tool. It allows you to suggest what to write and provides guidance for your recommenders. Craft your cover letters carefully and include everything that you would like your recommenders to mention in their letters.*

aspects of you to highlight in their letters. This is best done through the cover letter that you send to the prospective recommender.

This letter provides your recommenders with all the information they need to write your letters, including details about the scholarships and suggestions for what you'd like the recommendations to address. Since the cover letter also includes other essentials like deadlines, mailing instructions and a thank you, you will not sound as if you are giving orders but rather that you are providing helpful assistance. In fact, your recommenders will appreciate your reminding them what's important and what they should include.

Here are the elements to include in your cover letter:

**Details on the scholarships.** List the scholarships for which you will use their letters. Give a brief one-paragraph description of the mission of each of the awards and what qualities the scholarship committee seeks. This information will help your recommenders understand which of your qualities are important to convey and who will read the letters.

**How you fit the scholarship.** This is the most important part of your cover letter because it's your chance to remind your recommenders of your accomplishments and to offer suggestions for what to write. Make sure that you highlight how you match the goals of the scholarships. For example, if you are applying for a scholarship for future teachers, include information about your student teaching experience and the coursework you've taken in education. Leave out the fact that you were on the tennis team.

**Deadlines.** Inform your recommenders of how long they have to compose the letters. If time permits, ask them to mail the letters a week before the actual deadlines.

**What to do with the letters when they're done.** Give your recommenders instructions about what to do with the completed letters.

**Thank you.** Recommendations may take several hours to complete, and your recommenders are very busy people. Don't forget to say thank you in advance for writing you a great letter of recommendation.

To illustrate the power of a good cover letter, read the example on the following page as if you were a recommender. Remember that this is only one example and your cover letter will naturally be different. However, regardless of your individual writing style, your cover letter should include the same points as the following example.

Dear Dr. Louis,

Thank you again for writing my scholarship recommendations. These awards are very important for my family and me to be able to pay for my education. Here are the scholarships I am applying for:

SuperCollege.com Scholarship                    Deadline: August 31

This is a national scholarship based on academic and non-academic achievement, including extracurricular activities and honors. I believe I'm a match for this scholarship because of my commitment to academics (I currently have a 3.85 grade point average) and because of the volunteer work I do with the Youth Literacy Project and the PLUS program.

Quill & Scroll Scholarship                    Deadline: April 20

This scholarship is for students who want to pursue a career in journalism. Journalism is the field I want to enter after graduation. As you know, I am an editor for our school newspaper, contributing a column each week on issues that affect our student body.

Community Scholarship                    Deadline: May 5

This scholarship is for students who have given back to their communities through public service. I have always been committed to public service. Outside of class, I not only formed the Youth Literacy Project but have also volunteered with the PLUS program.

To help you with your recommendation, I've enclosed a resume. Also, here are some highlights of specific accomplishments that I was hoping you might comment on in your letter:

* The essay I wrote for your class that won the Young Hemingway competition

* How I formed the Youth Literacy Project with you as the project's advisor

* My three years of volunteer work with the PLUS program

* The weekly column I've written for the newspaper on school issues

After you've finished, please return the recommendations to me in the envelopes I've enclosed. If you have any questions, please feel free to contact me at 555-5555 or email@email.com. Again, thank you very much for taking the time to help me.


Sincerely,
Beth

---

Some notes about this cover letter:

- Beth describes each scholarship she is applying for, its goal and deadline and why she feels she is a fit with the award.

- The heart of the cover letter is here, where Beth gives a quick summary of information she suggests her professor include in the letter.

- Beth provides instructions about what to do with the letters when completed.

- This is a well-written cover letter that is brief and easy to understand.

## Tie a String Around Your Recommenders' Fingers

All recommenders have one thing in common: Too much to do and not enough time. It's important that you check with your recommender a couple of weeks before the letters are due. You need to monitor the progress of your recommendations. You may find that they're complete and already submitted. A more common discovery is that they won't have been touched. Be polite yet diligent when you ask about the progress. It's crucial that you work with your recommenders to get the letters in on time.

## The "You Can't Spell Success Without U" Mug

You now have everything you need to ask for and receive stellar recommendations. It's important to remember that even if it is a part of their job description, your recommenders are spending their time to help you. Remember this as you ask others to write recommendation letters and be sure to let them know that you appreciate their efforts.

Sometimes, a thank you gift is appropriate. Every time my (Kelly) mother wants to say thank you to a friend or acquaintance, she writes a note and gives a small token gift. My favorite is the "You Can't Spell Success Without U" mug because of its campy play on words.

Whether or not you select an equally campy token of appreciation, it's important that you thank your recommenders. After all, they are dedicating their free time to help you win funds for college.

## "Follow Up or Fall Down"
## Marla Sabin, Scholarship Applicant

Last year I applied for a scholarship for women who are planning to go into business. In addition to the application, I needed to get three recommendation letters from previous employers and professors. An obvious choice was my manager from the previous summer. I had interned in the product development department of a national software company. For the other two recommendations, I asked a professor and advisor at school.

I did everything right, providing all three with my resume, pre-addressed envelopes and information on the scholarship and its deadline. I let them know that they were supposed to send the letters directly to the organization. In the meantime, I worked on my part of the application, writing an essay about my summer internship and getting my transcript and other materials together. Amazingly, I completed the application a few days before the deadline and sent it off early. I was feeling pretty good about myself for being so put together. I had to admit that even I felt it was a pretty strong application.

A couple of months later, I received a letter from the women's organiza-

tion. It said that while I had a very high-quality application, regretfully because my application was incomplete, the organization was unable to award me a scholarship and instead offered the non-paying distinction of honorable mention. I racked my brain trying to think of what was missing. Over and over I replayed my trip to the post office and knew that I hadn't left anything out.

The next day I contacted the organization to find out what was missing. I was able to speak with someone who was on the selection committee. She looked up my file and said that I only had two recommendations on file, one from my professor and the other from my advisor. My previous manager had not submitted my third recommendation! She said that had all my materials been submitted, I probably would have won an award.

I learned my lesson. I had assumed that the three people I asked would be responsible enough to remember to submit the recommendation letters, but I was wrong. Two out of three is not good enough. Had I just reminded them, I probably would have won the scholarship.

## Chapter 9 Summary: Get the Right Recommendations

**You have more influence than you think.** You can affect what your recommenders write by whom you select, what materials you provide and how you follow up.

**Familiar faces.** Select people who can write meaningfully about your abilities and experience and who can convey how you fit the mission of the award. Try to choose teachers, professors or others who know you beyond how well you perform on tests.

**Do the grunt work.** Provide everything the recommenders need to get the job done including cover letter, resume, recommendation paperwork and pre-addressed, stamped envelopes.

**A script.** You can't write your own recommendation letters, but you can offer reminders to assist your recommenders as they are writing the letters. Include descriptions of the awards, information about accomplishments that they may want to mention and what they should do once they have completed the letters.

**Be a watchdog.** It's your job to make sure that the letters are submitted on time. Check in with your recommenders and make sure they meet the deadlines.

**Say thank you.** After all, your recommenders are trying to help you win money!

# Secrets to Writing Winning Essays

In this chapter, you'll learn:

- The real question being asked by every scholarship essay question

- Six steps to writing a winning scholarship essay

- How to choose the right topic

- Tips to overcome writer's block

- Strategies for introductions and conclusions

- The seven most important essay writing don'ts

- How to recycle your essays

# The Scholarship Essay: Your Ticket to the Finals

Here's a situation repeated a million times each year. A student receives a scholarship application and quickly glances over the form. It looks pretty straightforward, so it's tossed into the "to do" pile. The day before it's due, the student finally gets around to filling it out. Breezing through the application form, the student is about to celebrate finishing when he or she encounters the final requirement. It reads as follows:

> In 1894 Donald VonLudwig came to America with 10 cents in his pocket and within a decade built an empire. Write an 800-word essay on how you would incorporate the lessons of VonLudwig's success into your life.

Uh, oh. Life just got harder. Meet the dreaded scholarship essay. And the hypothetical student described above—the one we are poking fun at—was one of us! After a few experiences like this one, (which were usually accompanied by all night writing sessions), we learned to work on the essay first and never underestimate how much time it requires.

For most scholarship competitions it is the essay (not the application or recommendations) that will make or break your chances of winning. Why? Because the essay offers you the best chance to show the scholarship judges why you deserve to win. While your application form will get you to the semifinals, it is the essay that will carry you into the winner's circle.

Since the essay is so important, you must not assume that you can crank out a quality essay the night before it's due. A quality essay will take both time and effort. In this chapter we will take you step by step through the process of crafting a winning essay—don't worry, it's easier than you may have imagined. Plus, you will read examples of essays that won thousands of dollars in scholarships. From these, you can see firsthand how the strategies presented in this chapter are actually put to use in real life.

## The Big Picture

Regardless of the specific wording, the underlying question for almost all essay questions is the same: "Why do you deserve to win?" (Your answer should not be, "Because I need the money!")

Think about these questions: The Future Teachers of America scholarship asks you to write about the "future of education." The Veterans of Foreign Wars asks you to define "patriotism." The National Sculpture Society asks you to "describe your extracurricular passions." Believe it or not, all these seemingly different questions are asking for the same answer: Why do you deserve to win our money?

Your answers to each must address this underlying question. When writing the Future Teachers of America essay, you can discuss the general state of education and quote a few facts and figures, but you'd better be sure to include how you personally fit into the future of education. If you are planning to be a teacher, you might elaborate on how you will contribute to shaping students' lives. Similarly, use the topic of patriotism to impress the VFW judges with not only what you perceive patriotism to be but also how you have actually acted upon those beliefs. And if you answer the National Sculpture Society question with an essay on how much you love to play the guitar, then you really don't deserve to win!

Our approach is to use the essay to prove to the scholarship committee that you are the worthiest applicant for the award. Often the question will lead you in the right direction. (Would it surprise you to learn that the Amelia Earhart award asks about your interest in aerospace?) But even if the question is not obvious or is general in nature, you should still answer the same question ("Why do you deserve to win?") in every essay.

## Six Steps to Writing a Winning Scholarship Essay

By now you should be tired of hearing us repeat our mantra of knowing the mission of the scholarship. You have used this to guide your selection of those scholarships you are most likely to win and how to complete the application form for them. So it shouldn't surprise you that you must also use it to guide your essay. Remember, when you are writing about why you deserve to win, the answer and all the examples that you use should show how you fulfill that mission of the scholarship. With this in mind, let's begin our six steps to writing a winning scholarship essay.

### Step 1: Find the Right Topic and Approach

You will encounter two types of essay questions. The first asks you to write about a specific topic. For example, "Why is it important to protect our natural environment?" The second type of question gives you a very broad topic such as, "Tell us about yourself." In the first case you don't need to

### Pick a Topic You Care About

*Finding a good topic can take time. However, the key to writing a good essay is to be passionate about your subject. If you invest the time to pick a good topic, you will find that it is much easier to write the essay.*

think about a topic, but you do need to develop an approach to answering the question. In the latter you need to come up with both a topic and an approach. Let's look at how this is done, starting with the more difficult task of finding a topic.

## Finding a Topic

Let's imagine that you are applying for a scholarship that presents an essay question so broad that you can essentially choose your own topic. To get the ideas flowing, you should use that idea-generating technique you learned in fifth grade—brainstorming. Take out a notebook or start a new file on your computer and just start listing possible topics and themes. Ask yourself questions like these:

- What was a significant event in my life?
- What teacher, relative, friend or other person has influenced who I am?
- What have I learned from my experiences?
- What are my goals for the future?
- Where will I be 10 years from now?
- What motivates me to achieve my goals?

When brainstorming, don't be critical of the topics you unearth—just let the creativity flow. Ask parents and friends for suggestions.

Once you have a list of topics, you can start to eliminate those that don't help you answer the question of why you deserve to win. For example, if you apply to a scholarship that rewards public service, you would not want to write about the time you got lost in the woods for three days and had to survive on a single candy bar and wild roots. While that might make an interesting and exciting essay, it does not show the scholarship judges why you are the epitome of public service. This topic, however, may come in handy when you need to write an essay for a scholarship based on character or leadership or why you love Snickers bars.

After you whittle down your list to a few topics that will help show why you deserve to win this particular scholarship, choose the topic that is the most interesting to you or that you care about the most. It seems self-evident, but surprisingly many students do not select topics that excite them. Why is it important to pick a topic that you are passionate about? Because if you truly like your topic, you will write a better essay. In fact, your enthusiasm and excitement will naturally permeate your writing, which will make it interesting and memorable. It's so much easier to stay motivated writing about something you enjoy rather than something you find boring.

**Developing a Unique Approach**

Whether you have to think of a topic yourself or one is given to you, the next task is to figure out how you are going to approach it. For any given topic there are probably a hundred ways you could address the subject matter in an essay. Most topics are also way too large to completely cover in an 800- to 1,000-word essay, so you are going to have to narrow it down and only share a small part of the larger story. All this involves coming up with an approach to what you will present in your essay—an approach that must convince the judges that you deserve to win their money.

Let's take a look at writing about the traumatic experience of being lost in the woods for three days. You choose this topic since the scholarship wants to reward students with strong character and leadership and this is an experience that you believe shows both. But how do you write about it? If you just retell the story of the ordeal, it will not help the judges see why such an experience reveals the quality of your character or leadership. You need to dig deeper and think about how this experience revealed your strengths. To do this, ask yourself questions like these:

- What does this topic reveal about me?
- How has my life been changed by this experience?
- Why did I do what I did?
- What is the lesson that I learned from this experience?
- What aspect of this topic is most important to making my point?
- How would I describe my life philosophy?
- What meaningful things have I done during summers?
- What academic class, project or teacher has really influenced me?
- What are my greatest strengths?
- What are my hobbies, and what do they say about me?
- What five words best describe me and why?

## "How I Beat Writer's Block"
## Kevin Meyers, Scholarship Winner

When I first started writing my scholarship essay it was like a scene from TV, where I looked at a single sentence on a piece of paper, didn't like what I saw, crumpled the paper and tossed it into the trash can. I repeated this process many times until the crumpled paper started overflowing and I wanted to stop.

Finally, I told myself that I should just start writing and not stop until I had a complete page. It really worked. It wasn't a masterpiece I didn't come up with the final version of my essay in a single sitting. But I did get two whole pages written at one time and, more important, I got over my writer's block.

From then on it was much easier because I had something to work with instead of crumpled pieces of paper.

In thinking about your experience alone in the woods, you may realize that on the second day you came close to breaking down and losing all hope of being rescued. This was the critical point where you had to make a decision to give up or push forward. You decide to focus your essay only on this small sliver of time, what went through your mind and how you decided that you were not going to give up. The details of how you got lost and of your eventual rescue would be unimportant and may be mentioned in only a sentence or two. Focusing your essay on just the second day–and more particularly on how you were able to conquer your fears and not lose hope–would clearly demonstrate to the judges that even under extreme pressure, your true character was revealed. Since you also need to address the leadership aspect, you decide to focus on how you took charge of your fears on the second day. To do this, your essay will describe specific actions you took to lead yourself successfully through this ordeal.

Finding the right approach is just as important as finding the right topic. This is especially true if you answer a question that provides a specific topic. With every scholarship applicant writing about the same topic, you need to be sure that your approach persuasively shows the judges why you deserve to win more than anyone else.

## Step 2: Ensure That Your Topic and Approach are Original by Sharing a Slice of Your Life

Now that you have a topic and an idea of your approach, you need to decide how you are going to convey your message on paper. Keep in mind that scholarship judges are going to read hundreds if not thousands of essays. Often the essays will be on similar topics, particularly if the topic was given in the scholarship application. Therefore, you need to make sure that your writing is original.

The best way to do this is to share a "slice of your life" in the essay. Imagine that you are writing about your summer trip to Europe. Travel is a very common topic. If you decide to write about how your trip made your realize people from around the world are really quite similar, then you run the real risk of sounding just like every other travel essay. The same would be true for writing about sports. If you tell the story of how your team rallied and came from behind to win the game, you can be sure that it will sound like many other essays about sports. To make sure your essay is original, you need to share a "slice of life." Find one incident that happened during your travels or pick one particular moment in the game and use that to make your point. By focusing on a single day, hour or moment, you greatly reduce your chances of having an essay that sounds like everyone else's. Plus, essays that share a slice of life are usually a lot more interesting and memorable.

> ### It's All About You
>
> The essay is about you—your opinions, experiences and thoughts. For every scholarship essay that you write, remember to tie it in some way, directly or indirectly, to yourself.

Let's look at an example. What if you choose to write about how your mom has been your role model? Moms are one of the most popular role models for essays (and they should be, considering the pain of childbirth). How do you make your mom distinct from all the other applicants writing about their moms? Go ahead and take a moment to think about your mom. Be very specific. Can you find one character trait or incident that really influenced you? Let's say your mom has an obsession with collecting porcelain figurines and this passion led to you becoming interested in collecting baseball cards. Because of this, you are now considering a career in sports management. Now we have something! Imagine that first day when you realized how much your mom loved collecting figurines. Maybe you even bought her one as a present and now she cherishes it above all others. Perhaps it was that moment that jump-started your love for baseball cards, which has now developed into a full blown obsession with sports to the point where you intend to make it a career. You've just succeeded in turning a very popular topic—Mom—into an entirely original essay by finding that slice of life. No two people share the exact same slice of life, so by finding one to share, you are almost always guaranteed to have an original essay.

Want another example? Let's set the stage. Imagine that you are applying to a scholarship for students who major in psychology. The question posed on the application is this: "Tell us about an influential person who inspired you to pursue psychology." As you brainstorm, you list the authors of books you've read and some professors whose classes you have enjoyed. But how many students will be writing about these same people? You would even wager money that every other essay will be about Freud!

As you brainstorm, you recall the worst fight you have ever had with your best friend Susan. As you think about this fight that nearly destroyed a 10-year friendship, you realize that it was one of the first times you applied classroom knowledge to a real-life experience. In analyzing the fight, you realize that those psychology principles you studied have practical applications beyond the textbook. So for your essay you decide to write about the fight and how it made you even more committed than ever to become a psychology major.

You don't have to look far to find originality. We all have experiences that are unique to us. Even common experiences can be made original, depending on how you approach them. So don't exclude a topic just because it is common. By spending some time thinking about how you will write about it, you may be surprised at how original it could be.

# Step 3: It's Time to Start Writing

The most challenging part of writing a scholarship essay is getting started. Our advice: Just start writing. The first words you put down on paper may not be brilliant literature, but don't worry. You can always return to edit your work. It's easier to edit words you've already written than words that don't exist.

Do you think you have a bad case of writer's block? If so, the cure may surprise you. The best cure for writer's block is to just start writing!

We all have different writing styles, but certain points should be kept in mind as you are writing something that is focused on winning over a scholarship committee. Think about these things as you craft that winning essay:

### Write for the Scholarship Judges

Let's pretend you're a stand-up comedian who has two performances booked: one at the trendiest club in town where all cool college students congregate and the other at a retirement home. As a skilled comedian, you would prepare different material aimed at the different audiences. The college crowd would be able to relate to jokes about relationships and dating, while your jokes about dentures and arthritis would probably—and this is a hunch—go over better with the senior citizens.

The same goes for writing your essays. Since many are given by specialized organizations or for specific purposes, you need to write an essay that is appropriate for the audience. Think about who is going to read your essay. Is your audience natural science professors, circus performers or used car salesmen? Write your essay so it appeals to that audience. This should guide not only your selection of topics but also your word choice, language and tone.

### Be Yourself

While you want to present yourself in a way that attracts the attention of the scholarship judges, you don't want to portray yourself as someone you are not. It's okay to present selected highlights from your life that fit with the award, but it's not ethical to exaggerate or outright lie. If you apply for a scholarship to promote the protection of animals, don't write about your deep compassion for helping animals when you've never ventured closer than 10 feet to one because of your allergies. Feel comfortable about everything you write, and don't go overboard trying to mold yourself into being the student you think the scholarship judges want to read about. If you've done your job of picking scholarships that match you best, you already know that you are a good fit. Your task in the essay is to demonstrate this to the judges.

## Talk Your Essay Out

If you have writer's block or just prefer talking over writing, it may help to talk your essay out. Many students find that it's easier to say your thoughts instead of write them. You can use your phone to record your thoughts. Then, transcribe your words. In just a few minutes you can finish a first draft of your essay.

## Personalize Your Essay

Think of the scholarship judges as an audience who has come to see your Broadway show. You are the star. To keep them satisfied, give them what they want. In other words, the scholarship judges want to know about your life and experiences. When you write your essay, write about what has happened to you *personally* or about how you *personally* have been affected by something. If you are writing about drug abuse for an essay about a problem that faces college students today, do more than recite the latest national drug use statistics and the benefits of drug rehabilitation programs. Otherwise, your essay may be informative, but it won't be interesting. Instead, write about how a friend nearly overdosed on drugs, how others tried to pressure you into trying drugs or about your volunteer work at a rehabilitation clinic. Instantly, your essay will be more interesting and memorable. Plus, the judges really do want to learn more about you, and the only way for them to do this is if you share something about yourself in your essay.

## Make Sure You Have a Point

Try this exercise: See if you can encapsulate the point of your essay into a single sentence. If you can't, you don't have a main point. So, you'd better get one!

You may think this is obvious, but many students' essays don't have a main point. Use that most basic lesson from *Composition 101*: Have a thesis statement that states the main point of your essay. Let's say you are writing about growing up in the country. You might structure your essay around the idea that growing up in the country gave you a strong work ethic. This is the essay's main point. You can describe all the flat land and brush you like, but unless these descriptions help to support your point, you don't have a quality essay.

### Positive Is Better Than Negative

*Being positive does not mean you have to break out the pompoms, but you should strive to give your essay—whatever the subject—a positive tone and outlook.*

## Support Your Statement

Once you put your main point out there, you can't abandon it. Like a baby learning to walk, you have to support your thesis statement because it can't stand on its own. This means you have to provide reasons why your statement is true. You can do this by giving detailed and vivid examples from your personal experiences and accomplishments.

## Use Examples and Illustrations

When a reader can visualize what you are writing about, it helps to make an impression. Anecdotes and stories accomplish this very effectively. Examples and illustrations also make your ideas clearer. If you want to be a doctor, explain how you became interested in becoming one. You might describe the impact of getting a stethoscope from your father when you were a child. Or maybe you can write about your first day volunteering at the hospital. Examples help readers picture what you are saying and even relate to your experiences. The scholarship judge may have never volunteered at a hospital, but by reading your example that judge can easily understand how such an experience could be so influential.

The one danger of examples is that you need to be sure to keep them concise. It is often too easy to write a long and detailed example when only a few sentences are sufficient. Remember, in an example you are not retelling an entire story but just pulling out a few highlights to illustrate the point you are trying to make.

## Show Activity

> ### Use Common Sense When Picking a Topic
>
> *While no topic is totally taboo, use common sense and avoid topics that are too radical or risque. The scholarship judges might admire your openness or conviction, but if your essay makes them feel uncomfortable they will probably not select you as the winner.*

If you were forced to sit in an empty room with nothing but a bare wall to stare at, you would probably get bored pretty quickly. The same goes for an essay. Don't force the scholarship judges to read an essay that does nothing. Your essay needs activity and movement to bring it to life. This may consist of dialogue, action, stories and thoughts. The last thing you want to do is bore your readers. With action, you won't have to worry about that!

## Highlight Your Growth

You may not have grown an inch since seventh grade, but scholarship judges will look for your growth in other ways. They want to see evidence of emotional and intellectual growth, what your strengths are and how you have developed them. Strengths may include—but certainly aren't limited to—mastery of an academic course, musical talent, helping others, athletic ability, leading a group and more. Overcoming adversity or facing a challenge may also demonstrate your growth.

## Be Positive

You don't need to break out the pompoms and do a cheer, but you need to convey a positive attitude in your essay. Scholarship committees want to see optimism, excitement and confidence. They prefer not to read essays that are overly pessimistic, antagonistic or critical. This doesn't mean that you have to put a happy spin on every word written or that you can't write about a serious topic or problem. For example, if you were a judge reading the following essays about the very serious topic of teen pregnancy, to which author's education fund would you rather make a contribution?

> **Put Your Modesty On Hold**
>
> *Some students find it hard to brag in their essays. Part of the reason is that they have been taught to be modest. It's time to put modesty aside and be proud of your accomplishments.*

Thesis 1: We could reduce the number of pregnant teens by one-half if we shifted our efforts away from scare tactics to providing responsible sex education combined with frank discussions on the responsibilities of caring for a child.

Thesis 2: Teen pregnancy is incurable. Teenagers will always act irresponsibly and it would be futile for us to believe that we can control this behavior.

Scholarship committees favor authors who not only recognize problems but also present potential solutions. Leave being pessimistic to adults. You are young, with your entire future ahead of you. Your optimism is what makes you so exciting and why organizations want to give you money to pursue your passion for changing the world. Don't shy away from this opportunity.

## Be Concise

The scholarship essay may not have the strict limits of a college admission essay, but that does not give you a license to be verbose. Keep your essay tight, focused and within the recommended length of the scholarship guidelines. If no parameters are given, one or two pages should suffice. You certainly want the readers to get through the entirety of your masterpiece. Remember that most scholarship selection committees are composed of volunteers who are under no obligation to read your entire essay. Make your main points quickly and keep your essay as brief and to the point as possible.

# Step 4: Perfect Your Introduction and Conclusion

Studies have found that the most important parts of a speech are the first and last minutes. In between, listeners fade in and out of paying attention. It is the introduction and conclusion that leave a lasting impact. This holds true for scholarship essays as well. You need to have a memorable introduction and conclusion. If you don't, the readers may not make it past your introductory paragraph or they may discount your quality essay after reading a lackluster ending. Spend extra time making sure these two parts deliver the message you want. Here are some tips to create knockout introductions and conclusions:

### Introductions

**Create action or movement.** Think of the introduction as the high-speed car chase at the beginning of a movie that catches the audience's attention.

**Pose a question.** Questions draw attention because the readers think about how they would answer them and are curious to see how you will answer them in your essay.

**Describe.** If you can create a vivid image for readers, they will be more likely to want to read on.

### Conclusions

**Be thoughtful.** Your conclusion should make the second most powerful statement in your essay because this is what your readers will remember. (The most powerful statement should be in your introduction.)

**Leave a parting thought.** The scholarship committee members have already read your essay (we hope), so you don't need to rehash what you have already said. It's okay to summarize in one sentence, but do more than just summarizing by adding a parting thought. This could be one last observation or idea that ties into the main point of your essay.

**Don't be too quick to end.** Too many students tack on a meaningless conclusion or even worse, don't have one at all. Have a decent conclusion that goes with the rest of your essay and that doesn't consist of two words, "The End."

## Step 5: Find Essay Editors

Despite what you may think, you're not infallible. Stop gasping—it's true. This means it's important to get someone else to edit your work. Roommates, friends, family members, teachers, professors or advisors make great editors. When you get another person to read your essay, he or she will find errors that eluded you, as well as parts that are unclear to someone reading your essay for the first time. Ask your editors to make sure your ideas are clear, that you answer the question appropriately and that your essay is interesting. Take their suggestions seriously. The more input you get from others and the more times you rewrite your work, the better.

You want your essay to be like silk—smooth and elegant. When you read your work, make sure the connections between ideas are logical and the flow of your essay is understandable. (This is where editors can be extremely helpful.) Also check that you have not included any unnecessary details that might obscure the main point of your essay. Be careful to include any information that is vital to your thesis. Your goal is to produce an essay with clear points and supporting examples that logically flow together.

You also want to make sure that your spelling and grammar are perfect. Again, the best way to do this is to have someone else read your work. If you don't have time to ask someone, then do it yourself—but do it carefully. Read your essay at least once with the sole purpose of looking for spelling and grammatical mistakes. (Your computer's spell check is not 100 percent reliable and won't catch when you accidentally describe how you bake bread with one cup of "flower" instead of "flour.") Try reading your work out loud to listen for grammatical mistakes.

## Step 6: Recycle Your Essays

This has no relation to aluminum cans or newspapers. In this case recycling means reusing essays you have written for college applications, classes or even other scholarships. Because colleges and scholarship committees usually ask very broad questions, this is generally doable and saves you a tremendous amount of time.

Later in this chapter you will read an example essay. You may be surprised to learn that the author recycled her essay with minimal changes to answer such differing questions as these: "Tell us about one of your dreams," "What is something you believe in strongly?" and "What past experience continues to influence you today?"

However, be careful not to recycle an essay when it just doesn't fit. It's better to spend the

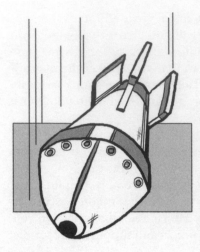

extra time to write an appropriate essay than to submit one that doesn't match the scholarship or answer the question.

## Seven Sins of the Scholarship Essay

Instead of writing an essay, one student placed the sheet of paper on the floor and tap danced on it. She then wrote that she hoped the scuff marks on the paper were evidence of her enthusiasm. In the judges' eyes, this was a silly stunt and, of course, her application was sent to the rejection pile. While you may not make such an egregious error, there are common mistakes that you need to avoid. Most of these lessons were learned the hard way—through actual experience.

### 1. DON'T Write a Sob Story

Everyone who applies for a scholarship needs money. Many have overcome obstacles and personal hardships. However, few scholarships are designed to reward students based on the "quantity" of hardships. Scholarship judges are not looking to give their money to those who have suffered the most. On the contrary they want to give money to students who came up with a plan to succeed *despite* an obstacle. Therefore, if you are writing about the hardships you have faced, be sure that you spend as much time, if not more, describing how you have overcome or plan to rise above those challenges.

### 2. DON'T Use the Shotgun Approach

A common mistake is to write one essay and submit it without any changes to dozens of scholarships—hoping that maybe one will be a winner. While we do recommend that you recycle your essays, you should not just photocopy your essays and blast them out to every scholarship committee. This simply does not work. Unless the scholarships have identical questions, missions and goals, your essay cannot be reused verbatim. Spend the time to craft an essay for each scholarship, and you will win more than if you write just one and blindly send it off to many awards.

### 3. DON'T Be Afraid to Get Words on Paper

One common cause of writer's block is the fear of beginning. When you sit down to write, don't be afraid to write a draft, or even ideas for a draft, that are not perfect. You will have time to revise your work. What you want to do is get words on paper. They can be wonderfully intelligent words or they can be vague concepts. The point is that you should just write. Too many students wait until the last minute and get stuck at the starting line.

### 4. DON'T Try to Be Someone Else

Since you want to be the one the scholarship judges are seeking to reward with money, you need to highlight achievements and strengths that match the criteria of the scholarship. But you don't want to lie about yourself or try to be someone you are not. Besides being dishonest, the scholarship judges will probably pick up on your affectation and hold it against you.

### 5. DON'T Try to Impress with Feats of Literary Gymnastics

By this, we mean you won't get any bonus points for overusing clichés, quotes or words you don't understand. Too many students think that quotes and clichés will impress scholarship judges. Unless they are used sparingly and appropriately, they will win you no favors. (Remember that quotes and clichés are not your words and are therefore not original.) The same goes for overusing the thesaurus. Do experiment with words that are less familiar to you, but do not make the thesaurus your co-author. It's better to use simple words correctly than to make blunders with complicated ones.

### 6. DON'T Stray Too Far from the Topic

A mistake that many students make is that they don't actually answer the question. This is especially true with recycled essays. Make sure that your essays, whether written from scratch or recycled from others, address the question asked.

> ### Get Good Editors
>
> *The best way to improve your essay is to find good editors. Good editors provide a different perspective, help you see your work in a fresh light and enhance the message of your writing. Parents, teachers, professors and friends make convenient editors.*

### 7. DON'T Write Your Stats

A common mistake is to repeat your statistics from your application form. Often these essays begin with "My name is" and go on to list classes, GPAs and extracurricular activities. All this information is found in your application. On top of that, it's boring. If you are going to write about a class or activity, make it interesting by focusing on a *specific* class or activity.

## Putting What You Learned into Practice

Now that you have learned how to write a winning scholarship essay, it's time to put what you learned into practice. Before you head off to write, however, we recommend that you read the essays in the Appendix. These essays were used by students to win tens of thousands of dollars in scholarships. While each essay is unique to the writer, you will be able to see many of the strategies outlined in this chapter being put to use. Once you have read the example essays, you are ready to write your own scholarship essay that will help you get some free cash for college.

---

### "Essays in No Time Mean No Money"
### Stan Rollins, Scholarship Applicant

I have first-hand experience with the importance of starting early and editing your scholarship essay. I found five scholarships that asked virtually the same question so I procrastinated on writing my essay until a few days before. Then to make matters worse, I quickly wrote the essay while watching *The Simpsons* and sent it to the five scholarship committees. I sent the same exact essay to each one of the scholarships.

I also applied for one other scholarship where I could use an essay that I wrote in my AP English class. I had spent a lot of time and effort on this essay since it was for class. I had asked my teacher for feedback and carefully edited the essay. So it was a good essay and I was lucky that I could also use it for the scholarship application.

Well you can guess what happened. I lost the five scholarships and only won the one where I had used my AP English essay. But what really killed me was that the five I lost were all for awards over $1,000 while the one I won was for a measly 50 bucks!

## Chapter 10 Summary: Secrets to Winning Essays

**The real question.** There are many questions you may be presented as a topic for a scholarship essay. Whatever it is, remember that you need in some way to convey in your answer why you should win the award.

**Choose a topic you care about.** You'll write the best essay when it is about something meaningful to you.

**Be an original.** Don't write about what you think every other student will write about. Or, if you do, take an original approach to the topic. Scholarship essays offer the opportunity for you to set yourself apart from the other applicants.

**Write for your audience.** Keep in mind who is likely to read your essay and what viewpoint or information you can share to convince each judge that you are a fit with the award.

**Your essay is you.** Show who you are through your essay by describing an experience, opinion, accomplishment or goal. Paint a more complete portrait of yourself that expands beyond the facts and figures of your application.

**It's alive!** Use examples, illustrations, dialogue and description to inject life into your essay. Create a narration and develop sights, sounds and emotions that the judges can relate to and envision. Draw them into your work.

**Show your strengths and growth.** Demonstrate to the selection committee that you have developed the intellectual maturity to take on college and the real world. Describe experiences or traits that show personal growth.

**The big two.** The two most important paragraphs are the introduction and conclusion. Open with something that will catch the attention of the judges, and close with what you want them to take away from your essay.

**Get editors.** The best way to enhance your work is to have others read it, and then help you improve it. They can suggest content, structural and technical improvements.

**Recycle.** Whenever possible, save time and sanity by reusing an essay that you've written before. Remember to modify it to fit the new topic.

**Learn by example.** Get inspired by the essays that others have written to win scholarships.

# Ace the Interviews

In this chapter, you'll learn:

- The importance of interviews

- What homework you must do before every interview

- The best way to prepare for the interview

- How to remain calm during a stressful interview

- What to wear and how to speak

- Secrets of creating interactive interviews

- The most common interview questions

- Strategies for phone or group interviews

CHAPTER 11

# The Face-to-Face Encounter

A judge for a nationally-recognized service organization shared with us the following true story. For the last phase of the scholarship competition for his region, the finalists met with the selection committee for an interview. The interview was very important and was the final step in determining who would win the $25,000 scholarship.

One finalist was an Ivy League student who flew across the country for the interview. Within the first five minutes, it was painfully clear to all the judges that the applicant didn't have the foggiest idea what the club stood for. It's as if the applicant thought that his resume and Ivy League pedigree would make him a winner.

As you can guess, this applicant had a very disappointing flight back to his college. Lesson number one for the scholarship interview: At the very least know what the organization stands for.

Many students dread the interview. If your heart beats faster or your palms moisten when you think about the prospect of sitting face to face with the judges, you are not alone. While the other parts of the scholarship application take time and effort, they can be done in the privacy of your home. Interviews, on the other hand, require interaction with–gasp–a real live human.

The good news is that the interview is usually the final step in the scholarship application process and if you make it that far, you're a serious contender. In this chapter, we show you what most scholarship committees are looking for and how you should prepare to deliver a winning interview. We also show you how to make the most of your nervousness and how to turn it into an asset rather than a liability.

## The Big Picture

There are two secrets for doing well in scholarship interviews. The first is: Remind yourself over and over again that scholarship interviewers are real people. Repeat it until you believe it. As such, your goal is to have as normal a conversation as possible, despite the fact that thousands of dollars may hang in the balance. It's essential that you treat interviewers as real people, interact with them and ask them questions.

The second secret is just as important: The best way to have successful interviews is to train for them. The more you practice interviewing, the more comfortable you'll be during the real thing. In this chapter, we'll tell you what kinds of questions to expect and how to perfect your interviewing skills.

## Why Human Interaction Is Needed

The first step to delivering a knockout interview is to understand why some scholarships require interviews in the first place. With the popularity of technology like e-mail and instant messaging, there seems to be less need for human interaction. (Believe it or not, there was a time when telephones were answered by a person instead of a maze of touchtone options.)

For some scholarship committees, a few pieces of paper with scores and autobiographical writing are not enough to get a full picture of who the applicants really are. They are giving away a lot of cash and the judges are responsible for making sure they are giving it to the most deserving students possible.

Scholarship judges use interviews as a way to learn how you compare in person versus on paper. Having been on both sides of the interview table, we can attest to the fact that the person you expect based on the written application is not always the person you meet at the interview.

It's important to know that the purpose of interviews is not to interrogate you, but rather for the scholarship committee to get to know you better and probe deeper into the reason why you deserve their money.

## Interviewers Are Real People Too

If you've ever met a celebrity, you've probably realized that while their face may grace the covers of magazines and they have houses big enough to merit their own ZIP code, they eat, drink and sleep and have likes and dislikes just like any other person. The same thing holds true for interviewers.

Interviewers can be high-profile professors or high-powered businesspeople, but they are all passionate about some topics and bored with others. They enjoy speaking about themselves and getting to know more about you. Acknowledging this will help keep your nerves under control. Throughout the interview, remind yourself that your interviewer is human, and strive to make the interview a conversation, not an interrogation.

## Interview Homework

You'd never walk into a test and expect to do well without studying the material. The same is true for interviews. Don't attempt them without doing your homework. There is basic information you need to know before starting your interviews so that you appear informed and knowledgeable. It's not difficult information to obtain, and it goes a long way in demonstrating that you care enough about winning to

### Try to Relax

*You don't have to picture your interviewers in their underwear to relax. Just keep reminding yourself that they are real people. They may be well known in their field or leaders in the community, but they are still just people.*

have put in some effort. Here are some things you should know before any interview:

**Purpose of the scholarship.** What is the organization hoping to accomplish by awarding the scholarship? Whether it's promoting students to enter a certain career area, encouraging a hobby or interest or rewarding students for leadership, every scholarship has a mission.

**Criteria for selecting the winner.** From the scholarship materials, you can get information about what the judges are hoping to find in a winner. From the kinds of information they request in the application to the topic of the essay question, each piece is a clue about what is important to the judges. Scholarships can be based on academic achievement, nonacademic achievement or leadership to name a few criteria. Understand what kind of student the organization is seeking and stress that side of yourself during the interview.

**Background of the awarding organization.** Do a little digging on the organization itself. Check out its website or publications. Attend a meeting or speak with someone who's a member. From this detective work, you will get a better idea of who the organization's members are and what they are trying to achieve. It can also be a great topic of conversation during the interview.

**Background of your interviewer.** If possible, find out as much as you can about who will be interviewing you. In many cases, you may know little more than their name and occupation, but if you can, find out more. You already have one piece of important information about your interviewers: You know that they are passionate about the organization and its mission. They wouldn't be volunteering their time to interview if they weren't.

In addition to learning about the scholarship organization and the reason why it's giving away the award, here is some more homework to do before the interview:

**Review your application and essay.** It's important to know what you wrote in your own application and essay because your interviewer may refer to these. Since you may have written them weeks or months ago, take a few minutes to review what you submitted.

**Prepare a portfolio if necessary.** This is especially true if you are applying for a scholarship in which you need to share visuals such as an art scholarship. However, you may also want to prepare a portfolio even if you aren't applying for this type of scholarship. In a binder, you can put together a very brief collection of photos, articles or awards that highlight your greatest accomplishments. Keep the pieces limited to 10 or fewer. It may help your interviewer to have a visual to go along with your conversation.

## Use Your Detective Work to Create an Advantage

Once you've done your detective work on the above topics, it's time to *use* the information you've uncovered. For example, if you are in front of a group of doctors and they ask you about your activities, you would be better off discussing your work at the local hospital than your success on the baseball diamond. As much as possible, focus the conversation on areas where your activities, goals, interests and achievements match the goal of the awarding organization. By discussing what matters most to the scholarship judges, you will insure that this will be a memorable conversation—one that will set you apart from the other applicants that are interviewed.

By knowing something about your interviewers beforehand, you can think of topics and questions that will be interesting for them. Most interviewers allow some time for you to ask questions. Here again your detective work will come in handy since you can ask them more about the organization or their background. By asking intelligent questions (i.e., not the ones that can be answered by simply reading the group's mission statement) you will demonstrate that you've done your homework. You'll also give interviewers something interesting to talk about—either themselves or their organization.

The more information you can get before the interview, the better you will perform. Having this background material will also allow you to answer unexpected questions better and come up with thoughtful questions for the judges if you are put on the spot.

## You Are Not the Center of the Universe

Despite what Mom or Dad says, the Earth revolves around the sun, not you. It helps to remember this in your interviews. Your life may be the most

## "The Only Thing in Life that Matters Is Calculus"
### Kelly Tanabe, Author and Scholarship Judge

*Following is the experience that I had interviewing an applicant for a scholarship based on academic achievement and contributions to extracurricular activities. Mark, the college sophomore I interviewed, is mathematically gifted but lacked in his presentation an attempt to keep the conversation interactive. Learn from his mistakes.—Kelly Tanabe*

The student is sitting at the table with his hands covering his face. His mop of stringy, brown hair dangles around his face. I greet him with a cheery, "Hi. How are you?" Absent of enthusiasm, he mumbles under his breath with his hands still partially covering his face, "Fine." He resists making eye contact of any kind and tilts his head even further down. My intuition tells me that this is going to be one very long hour.

With that promising start, I notice what Mark is wearing. I can't help it. I'm human. He is wearing jeans with an orange sweater over a faded green T-shirt. His sweater even has a few holes in it. I have nothing against his holey sweater. I, too, have been known to wear clothes with extra ventilation in the privacy of my home. The thing that bothers me is: Why did he choose to wear mismatching, worn clothes to such an important interview? I'm giving up five hours on a Saturday to interview finalists for this scholarship, and Mark can't even find a decent shirt to wear?

Our conversation is hardly better than his color coordination. When I ask him a question, he replies with short and mumbled single-sentence answers. What gets him mildly excited is calculus. Pretty much everything he says relates back to the subject of calculus. His father is a calculus professor. He tutors other students in calculus. He even named his twin Golden Retrievers Sine and Cosine. His knowledge and the graduate-level coursework he has taken impress me.

After he finishes listing all the calculus classes he has taken and calculus awards he has won, I try to direct the conversation in a different route. I want to find out what more there is to him. I ask him about what he likes to do outside of schoolwork. He continues to tell me how to prove a calculus theory and how he dreams of calculus formulas in his sleep. His calculus barrage is unrelenting.

To again try to get him to change the subject I mention that I was a sociology major, which, by the way, is about the furthest removed from calculus as possible. It has been several years since I've done a calculus problem. I understand that he is very talented in mathematics, but why don't we talk about something else he enjoys? After all, this is not a scholarship for mathematical achievement. It's a scholarship for overall academic and extracurricular achievement.

He doesn't get the hint and continues to carry on about calculus. As I tune out his math lesson, I can't get over the fact that he never makes eye contact, speaks under his breath whenever he talks and never puts together more than two sentences at a time. Getting him to speak about anything other than calculus is virtually impossible. When I ask him what his greatest strength and greatest weakness are, he tells me his strength is (surprise, surprise) his mathematical ability and his weakness is his social skills. At least he is honest!

In the end I give up trying to direct the conversation beyond calculus. My overall impression of him is that he may be a mathematical wizard, but he lacks the ability to hold a normal conversation. At the end of an hour,

he has not smiled, made eye contact or asked a single question. As we end the interview I thank Mark for coming in. He does not reply and shuffles out of the room. His head hangs low, and again his stringy, brown hair drapes his hidden face.

In spite of his mathematical talents, I find the other applicants to be much more interesting even if they cannot prove a complex theorem as quickly as Mark. The other interviewers agree, and we award the scholarship to a student who is not only academically strong but can also communicate effectively.

interesting ever lived, but this is still no excuse for speaking only about you for the duration of the interview.

The secret to successful interviews is simply this: They should be interactive. The surest way to bore your interviewers is to spend the entire time speaking only about yourself. You may have had the unfortunate experience of being on the receiving end of a conversation like this if you have a friend who speaks nonstop about herself and who never seems to be interested in your life or what you have to say. Don't you just hate this kind of conversation? So will your scholarship interviewers.

To prevent a self-centered monologue, constantly look for ways to interact with your interviewers. In addition to answering questions, ask some yourself. Ask about their experiences in school or with the organization. Inquire about their thoughts on some of the questions they pose to you. Take time to learn about your interviewers' experiences and perspectives.

Also, speak about topics that interest your interviewers. You can tell which topics intrigue them by their reactions and body language. From the detective work you've done, you also have an idea of what they are passionate about.

Try to make your interviews a two-way conversation instead of a one-way monologue. Engage your interviewers and keep them interested. If you do this, they will remember your interview as a great conversation and you as a wonderful, intelligent person deserving of their award.

**Make Your Interview a Two-Way Conversation**

*Strive for interactive interviews. Do not do all the talking. Pose questions, ask for advice and have fun.*

## Look and Sound the Part

Studies have shown that in speeches what's more important than what you say is how you sound and how you look when you say it. It's important that you make a good visual presentation. Here are some tips to make sure that you look and sound your best, an important complement to what you actually say to the judges:

**Dress appropriately.** A backward-turned baseball cap and baggy jeans slung down to your thighs may be standard fare for the mall (at least they were last season), but they are not appropriate for interviews. You probably don't have to wear a suit, unless you find out through your research that the organization is very conservative, but you should dress appropriately. No-no's include the following: hats, bare midriffs, short skirts or shorts and iron-free wrinkles. Think about covering obtrusive tattoos or removing extra ear/nose/tongue/eyebrow rings. Don't dress so formally that you feel uncomfortable, but dress nicely. It may not seem fair, but your dress will affect the impression you make and influence the decision of the judges. Save making a statement of your individuality for a time when money is not in question.

**Sit up straight.** During interviews, do not slouch. Sitting up straight conveys confidence, leadership and intelligence. It communicates that you are interested in the conversation. Plus, it makes you look taller.

**Speak in a positive tone of voice.** One thing that keeps interviewers engaged is your tone. Make sure to speak in a positive one. This will not only maintain your interviewers' interest but will also suggest that you have an optimistic outlook. Of course, don't try so hard that you sound fake.

**Don't be monotonous.** If you've ever had a teacher or professor who speaks at the same rate and tone without variation, you know that this is the surest reason for a nap. Don't give your interviewers heavy eyelids. Tape record yourself and pay attention to your tone of voice. There should be natural variation in your timbre.

**Speak at a natural pace.** If you're like most people, the more nervous you are, the faster you speak. Be aware of this so that you don't speed talk through your interview.

**Make natural gestures.** Let your hands and face convey action and emotions. Use them as tools to illustrate anecdotes and punctuate important points.

**Make eye contact.** Eye contact engages interviewers and conveys self-assurance and honesty. If it is a group interview, make eye contact with all your interviewers—don't just focus on one. Maintaining good eye contact can be difficult, but just imagine little dollar signs in your interviewers' eyes and you shouldn't have any trouble. Ka-ching!

**Smile.** There's nothing more depressing than having a conversation with someone who never smiles. Don't smile nonstop, but show some teeth at least once in a while.

If you use these tips, you will have a flawless look and sound to match what you're saying. All these attributes together create a powerful portrait of who you are. Unfortunately, not all these things come naturally, and you'll need to practice before they become unconscious actions.

## The Practice Interview

One of the best ways to prepare for an interview is to do a dress rehearsal. This allows you to run through answering questions you might be asked and to practice honing your demeanor and style. You will feel more comfortable when it comes time for the actual interview. If anything will help you deliver a winning interview, it's practice. It may be difficult, but force yourself to set aside some time to run through a practice session at least once. Here's how:

**Find a mock interviewer.** Bribe or coerce a friend or family member to be your mock interviewer. Parents or teachers often make the best interviewers because they are closest in age and perspective to most actual scholarship interviewers.

**Prep your mock interviewer.** Share with your interviewer highlights from this chapter such as the purpose of scholarship interviews, what skills you want to practice and typical interview questions, which are described in the next section. If you're having trouble with eye contact, for example, ask them to take special notice of where you are looking when you speak and to make suggestions for correcting this.

**Set up to video.** Set up your phone or camera to tape yourself so that you can review your mock

> **Dress for Success**
>
> No one has ever been penalized for being overdressed. If you have questions about what's appropriate, err on the side of being conservative.

## "Don't Hate Me Because I'm Beautiful and Faultless"
### Kelly Tanabe, Author and Scholarship Judge

*One student I interviewed was a better fit for a beauty pageant than a scholarship competition. —Kelly Tanabe*

From my first impression, she seems promising. I say "Hello," and she responds with a smile, eye contact and a friendly "Hello" in return. I notice she is fashionably dressed in a blue color-coordinated pantsuit. She is strikingly beautiful, with long blond hair and deep blue eyes. Her makeup is perfectly in place.

Maria tells me that her dream is to travel the world. Why? She finds other cultures "interesting." A generic answer. At this point, I envision her on stage in a Miss America pageant. I ask her to explain. Miss California comes out of the soundproof room dressed in her blue-sequined evening gown. It's her turn to answer the question that will show the judges her ability to demonstrate grace and composure while being beautiful and holding up under the pressure.

She says, "I think it's so neat to be able to learn about other cultures. We are so different. I just want to learn about cultures around the world." The judges wince. Nine points for composure, zero for substance.

Miss California, er Maria, tells me she is an aspiring model. "It was so incredible. I was sitting at a cafe when a woman came up to me and gave me her business card. She told me she wanted me to model." That explains the perfect makeup. I can almost hear the singing, "Here she comes, Miss America."

At this point I admit to myself that I am a little envious of this freshman who has spent her life turning the heads of the opposite sex. To make up for my bias, however, I purposely give her the benefit of the doubt. I think that there must be more to her than her good looks and Miss America answers. Throughout the remainder of the interview, however, I find no evidence of this. I ask her what leadership experience she has. She says she is the leader among her friends. Because of her they all now aspire to become models. Ugh. Just what the world needs—another slew of teenage girls starving themselves with noble aspirations of appearing on magazine covers.

I resort to an easy question. What are her grade point average and test scores? She says she can't remember. I wonder if she is telling the truth or if they are so bad she doesn't want me to know.

I ask a standard job interview question. What are your greatest strength and weakness? She replies, "My greatest strength is my ability to get along with my friends. I am good at getting along with pretty much anyone." Her greatest strength is that she is popular?!? "My weakness. Hmm. Well. Um. I can't think of a weakness." What kind of answer is this? Everyone has a weakness! I try to coach her, "Isn't there something that is more challenging for you or that you want to work on?" She answers, " Well, I can't really think of anything I want to work on. If something is more challenging I just work harder." Ladies and gentlemen, not only is Maria perfect looking, but in her mind she is also perfect.

I am tempted to ask something tougher, what recruiters from those high-paying consulting and investment banking firms ask to understand candidates' thought process and to see how they hold up under pressure. If you have a stack of quarters as high as the Empire State Building, how many quarters will you have? How would you figure out how many psychiatrists there are in the Chicago area? I envision the serious look on her perfectly matted face and the furrow of her delicately plucked eyebrows in thought. Then, her head slowly bloats into an oversized, perfectly blond beach ball, and KABOOM! an explosion from brain overexertion.

I return to reality and end the interview asking if she has any questions. Usually students ask at least one. For many, this is one of their best opportunities to learn about the organization that is awarding the scholarship. Maria has none. Not only is she beautiful, folks, but she has all the answers. The host places the sparkling crown on her head. The newly crowned Miss America starts crying the requisite tears and waves to the cheering audience.

I bid farewell to Maria. I wonder if the outcome would have been different had she had a male interviewer. One flash of her pearly toothed smile may have won.

interview afterward. Position the camera behind your interviewer so you can observe how you appear from their perspective.

**Do the dress rehearsal.** Grab two chairs and go for it. Answer questions and interact with your mock interviewer as if you were at the real thing.

**Get feedback.** After you are finished, get constructive criticism from your mock interviewer. Find out what you did well and what you need to work on. What were the best parts of the interview? Which of your answers were strong, and which were weak? When did you capture or lose your mock interviewer's attention? Was your conversation one-way or two-way?

**Review the video.** Evaluate your performance. If you can, watch or listen to the video with your mock interviewer so you can get additional feedback. Listen carefully to how you answer questions so you can improve on them. Pay attention to your tone of voice. Watch your body language to see what you are unconsciously communicating.

> ### Practice, Practice, Practice
>
> Practice does make perfect when it comes to interviews. Even if you have to sit in front of a mirror and interview yourself, doing even one mock interview will really boost your performance on the real thing.

**Do it again.** If you have the time and your mock interviewer has the energy or you can find another mock interviewer, do a second interview. If you can't find anyone, do it solo. Practice your answers, and focus on making some of the weaker ones more interesting.

The bottom line is the more you practice, the better you'll do.

## Answers to the Most Common Interview Questions

The best way to ace an exam would be to know the questions beforehand. The same is true for interview questions. From interviewing dozens of judges and applicants as well as having judged dozens of scholarship competitions ourselves, we've developed a list of commonly asked questions along with suggestions for answering them. This list is by no means comprehensive. There is no way to predict every question you will be asked, and in your actual interviews, the questions may not be worded in exactly the same way. However, the answer that interviewers are seeking is often the same.

Before your interviews, take the time to review this list. Add more questions particular to the specific scholarship to which you are applying. Practice answering these questions to yourself and in your mock interviews with friends and family.

You will find that the answers you prepare to these questions will be invaluable during your real interviews. Even though the questions you are asked may be different, the thought that you put in now will help you formulate better answers. To the interviewer, you will sound incredibly articulate and thoughtful. Let's take a look at those questions.

> ### Ask Your Own Questions
>
> *An interview should not be an interrogation, with the interviewer firing all the questions and you answering. Ask some questions to make the interview interactive. It will be more interesting for both of you.*

### Why did you choose your major?

● For major-based scholarships and even for general scholarships, interviewers want to know what motivated you to select the major, and they want a sense of how dedicated you are to that area of study. Make sure you have reasons for your decision. Keep in mind that an anecdote will provide color to your answer.

● If you are still in high school, you will probably be asked about your intended major. Make sure you also have reasons why you are considering this major.

## Why do you want to enter this career field?

- For scholarships that promote a specific career field, interviewers want to know your inspiration for entering the field and how committed you are to it. You will need to articulate the reasons and experiences that prompted your interest in this career and also anything you have done to prepare yourself for associated studies in this area.

- Be prepared to discuss your plans for after graduation, i.e. how will you use your education in the field you have chosen. You may be asked what kind of job you plan to have and why you would like it.

- Know something about the news in the field associated with the scholarship. For example, if you are applying for an information technology award, read up on the trends in the IT industry. There may be some major changes occurring that you will be asked to comment on.

## What are your plans after graduation?

- You are not expected to know precisely what you'll do after graduation, but you need to be able to respond to this common question. Speak about what you are thinking about doing once you have that diploma in hand. The more specific you can be the better.

- Provide reasons for your plans. Explain the process in which you developed your plans and what your motivation is.

- It's okay to discuss a couple of possible paths you may take, but don't bring up six very different options. Even if you are deciding among investment banking, the Peace Corps, banana farming and seminary, don't say so. The interviewer will think that you don't have a clear direction of what you want to do. This may very well be true, but it's not something you want to share. Select the one or two possible paths that you are most likely to take.

### Role of the Interview

*Interviews play an important role in the scholarship selection process. Judges use interviews to see who you are beyond what you write in your application and essay and to select a winner among highly qualified finalists.*

## Why do you think you should win this scholarship?

● Focus your answer on characteristics and achievements that match the mission of the scholarship. For example, if the scholarship is for biology majors, discuss your accomplishments in the field of biology. Your answer may include personal qualities as well as specific accomplishments.

● Be confident but not arrogant. For this type of question, be careful about balancing pride and modesty in your answer. You want to be confident enough to have reasons why you should win the scholarship, but you don't want to sound overly boastful. To avoid sounding pompous, don't say that you are better than all the other applicants or put down your competition. Instead, focus on your strengths independent of the other people who are applying.

● Have three reasons. Three is the magic number that is not too many or too few. To answer this question just right, offer three explanations for why you fulfill the mission of the scholarship.

## Tell me about times when you've been a leader.

● Interviewers ask this type of question (although sometimes worded a little differently) to gauge your leadership ability and your accomplishments as a leader. They want to award scholarships to students who will be leaders in the future. When you answer, try to discuss leadership that you've shown that matches what the scholarship is meant to achieve.

● Don't just rattle off the leadership positions you've held. Instead, give qualitative descriptions of what you accomplished as a leader. Did your group meet its goals? Did you start something new? How did you shape the morale of the group you led? For this kind of question, anecdotes and short stories are a good way to illustrate how you've been effective.

● Remember that leadership doesn't have to be a formally elected position. You can describe how you've informally led a special project or group. You could even define how you are a leader among your siblings.

● Be prepared to discuss what *kind* of leader you are. Your interviewer may ask about your approach to leadership or your philosophy on being a good leader. Have examples to explain how you like to lead. For example, do you lead by example? Do you focus on motivating others and getting their buy-in?

## What are your strengths? Weaknesses?

- As you are applying for jobs, you will answer this question more times than you will shake hands. It is a common job interview question that you may also get asked in scholarship interviews. Be prepared with three strengths and three weaknesses. Be honest about your weaknesses.

- Your strengths should match the mission of the scholarship and should highlight skills and accomplishments that match the characteristics the judges are seeking.

- You should be able to put a positive spin on your weaknesses. (And you'd better say you have some!) For example, your perfectionism could make you frustrated when things don't go the way you plan but could also make you a very motivated person. Your love of sports could detract from your studies but could provide a needed break and be representative of your belief in balance in your life. Just make sure that the spin you put on your weakness is appropriate and that your weakness is really a weakness.

## Where do you see yourself in 10 years?

- We know that nobody knows exactly what he or she is going to be doing in 10 years. The interviewers don't need specific details. They just want a general idea of what your long-term goals are and what you aspire to become. If you have several possibilities, at least one should be in line with the goals of the scholarship.

- Try to be as specific as possible without sounding unrealistic. For example, you can say that you would like to be working at a high-tech company in marketing, but leave out that you plan to have a daughter Rita, son Tom and dog Skip. Too much detail will make your dreams sound too naive.

## Tell me about yourself. Or, is there anything you want to add?

- The most difficult questions are often the most open-ended. You have the freedom to say anything. For these kinds of questions, go back to the

mission of the scholarship and shape your answer to reflect the characteristics that the judges are seeking in the winner. Practice answering this question several times because it is the one that stumps applicants the most.

● Have three things to say about yourself that match the goal of the scholarship. For example, you could discuss three personal traits you have, such as motivation, leadership skills and interpersonal skills. Or, you could discuss three skills applicable to academics, such as analytical skills, problem-solving skills and your love of a good challenge.

● The alternative, "Is there anything you want to add?" is typically asked at the end of the interview. In this case, make your response brief but meaningful. Highlight the most important thing you want your interviewer to remember.

## Other Questions

In addition to these, here are some more common questions:

● What do you think you personally can contribute to this field?
● How do you plan to use what you have studied after graduation?
● Do you plan to continue your studies in graduate school?
● What do you want to specifically focus on within this field of study?
● Do you plan to do a thesis or senior project?
● Who are your role models in the field?
● What do you see as the future of this field?
● How do you see yourself growing in your career?
● What can you add to this field?
● What do you think are the most challenging aspects of this field?
● What is your ideal job after graduating from college?
● Tell me about a time that you've overcome adversity.
● What are your opinions about (fill in political or field-related issue)?
● Tell me about your family.
● What do you hope to gain from college?
● Who is a role model for you?
● What is your favorite book? Why?
● What is the most challenging thing you have done?

Remember that with all these questions your goal is to demonstrate that you are the best fit for the scholarship. Be sure to practice these with your mock interviewer. The more comfortable and confident you feel answering these questions, the better you'll do in your interviews.

## Questions for the Questioner

There is a huge difference between an interview and an interrogation. In an interview, you also ask questions. Make certain that your interview does not become an interrogation by asking questions throughout the conversation. Remember that you want to keep the conversation two-way.

Toward the end of your interview, you will probably have the opportunity to ask additional questions. Take this opportunity. If you don't ask any questions, it will appear that you are uninterested in the conversation or haven't put much thought into your interview. Take time before the interview to develop a list of questions you may want to ask. Of course you don't have to ask all your questions, but you need to be prepared to ask a few.

To get you started, we've developed some suggestions. Adapt these questions to the specific scholarship you are applying for and personalize them.

- How did you get involved with this organization?
- How did you enter this field? What was your motivation?
- Who do you see as your mentors in this field?
- What do you think are the most exciting things about your career?
- What advice do you have for someone starting out?
- What do you see as the greatest challenges for this field?
- What do you think will be the greatest advancements in 10 years?
- What effect do you think technology will have on this field?
- I read that there is a (insert trend) in this field. What do you think?

The best questions are those that come from your detective work. Let's say that in researching an organization you discover that they recently launched a new program to research a cure for diabetes. Inquiring about this new program would be a perfect question to ask. It not only shows that you have done your homework, but it is also a subject about which the organization is deeply concerned.

> ### Don't Be Afraid to Be Animated
>
> *When you speak, be animated, using gestures and making eye contact. These visual cues tell your interviewer that you are confident, charismatic and interested in the conversation.*

## Use Time to Your Advantage

The best time to ask Mom or Dad for something is when they're in a good mood. It's all about timing. Timing is also important in interviews. If you have more than one scholarship interview, time them strategically. Schedule less important and less demanding interviews first. This will allow you the opportunity to practice before your more difficult interviews. You will improve your skills as you do more interviews. It makes sense to hone your skills on the less important ones first.

If you are one of a series of applicants who will be interviewed, choose the order that fits you best. If you like to get things over with, try to be interviewed in the beginning. If you need more time to prepare yourself mentally, select a time near the end. We recommend that you don't choose to go first because the judges will use your interview as a benchmark for the rest. They may not recognize you as the best applicant even though it turns out to be true.

## The Long-Distance Interview

If you've ever been in a long-distance relationship, you know there's a reason why most don't last. You simply can't communicate over the telephone in the same way you can in person. Scholarship interviews are the same. You may find that an interview will not be face-to-face but over the telephone instead. If this happens, here are some strategies to help bridge the distance:

**Find a quiet place to do the interview where you won't be interrupted.** You need to be able to give your full attention to the conversation you are having.

**Know who's on the other end of the line.** You may interview with a panel of people. Write down each of their names and positions when they first introduce themselves to you. They will be impressed when you are able to respond to them individually and thank each of them by name.

**Use notes from your practice interviews.** One of the advantages of doing an interview over the telephone is that you can refer to notes without your interviewers knowing. Take advantage of this.

**Look and sound like you would in person.** Pretend that your interviewers are in the room with you, and use the same gestures and facial expressions that you would if you were meeting in person. It may sound strange, but your interviewers will actually be able to hear through your voice when you are smiling, when you are paying attention and when you are enthusiastic about what you're saying. Don't do your interview lying down in your bed or slouched back in a recliner.

**Avoid speaker phone and seek good reception.** Speaker phones often echo and pick up distracting surrounding noise. Make sure you have strong reception if you use your cell phone.

**Turn off call waiting.** Nothing is more annoying than hearing the call waiting beep while you are trying to focus and deliver an important thought. (And, this may sound obvious, never click over to take a second call.)

**Use the techniques of regular interviews.** You'd be surprised how much is translated over the telephone. Don't neglect good speaking and delivery points just because the interviewers can't see you!

## The Group Interview

So it's you on one side of the table and a panel of six on the other side. It's certainly not the most natural way to have a conversation. How do you stay calm when you are interviewed by a council of judges?

**Think of the group as individuals.** Instead of thinking it's you versus the team, think of each of the interviewers as an individual. Try to connect with each person separately.

**Try to get everyone's name if you can.** Have a piece of paper handy that you can use to jot down everyone's name and role so that you can refer to them in the conversation. You want to be able to target your answers to each of the constituents. If you are interviewing with a panel of employees from a company and you know that Ms. Sweeny works in accounting while Mr. Duff works in human resources, you can speak about your analytical skills to appeal to Ms. Sweeny and your people skills to appeal to Mr. Duff.

**Make eye contact.** Look into the eyes of each of the panelists. Don't stare, but show them that you are confident. Be careful not to focus on only one panelist.

**Respect the hierarchy.** You may find that there is a leader in the group like the scholarship chair or the CEO of the company. Pay a little more attention to stroke the ego of the person in charge. They are used to it, they expect it and a little kissing up never hurt anyone.

**Include everyone.** In any group situation, there are usually one or two more vocal members who take the lead. Don't focus all your attention only on the loud ones. Spread your attention among the panelists as evenly as possible.

## The Disaster Interview

Even if you do your interview homework and diligently practice mock interviewing, you may still find that you and your interviewer just don't connect or that you just don't seem to have the right answers. For students who spend some time preparing, this is a very rare occurrence. Interviewers are not trying to trick you or make you feel bad. They are simply trying to find out more about you and your fit with the award. Still, if you think that you've bombed, here are some things to keep in mind:

**Avoid should have, would have, could have.** Don't replay the interview in your head again and again, thinking of all the things you should have said. It's too easy to look back and have the best answers. Instead, use what you've learned to avoid making the same mistakes in your next interview.

**There are no right answers.** Remember that in reality there really are no right answers. Your answers may not have been perfect, but that doesn't mean that they were wrong. There are countless ways to answer the same question.

**The toughest judge is you.** Realize that you are your own greatest critic. While you may think that you completely bombed an interview, your interviewer will most likely not have as harsh an opinion.

## The Post-Interview

After you complete your interviews, follow up with a thank you note. Remember that interviewers are typically volunteers and have made the time to meet with you. If you feel that there is very important information that you forgot to share in your interview, mention it briefly in your thank you note. If not, a simple note will suffice. You will leave a polite, lasting impression on your interviewer.

# For More Help

Because the interview is often the last stage in scholarship competitions, it is one of the most important factors. In this chapter, we have shared strategies that should help you to ace interviews. If you would like more help, refer to our book *How to Write a Winning Scholarship Essay*. In addition to providing essay help, this book has advice from scholarship judges about interviews and more than 20 example scholarship interview questions and answers.

## Chapter 11 Summary: Ace the Interviews

**Scholarship interviewers are real people.** Remember to think of your interview as a conversation with an adult who is interested in your life. This will serve to calm your nerves and to help you relax and be yourself.

**Do your interview homework.** Before the big day, know the purpose of the scholarship, the criteria for selection, the background of the awarding organization and the background of your interviewer.

**Appearances count.** Look and act the part by dressing appropriately, sitting up straight and speaking with interest in your voice.

**Do a mock interview.** The best way to prepare for scholarship interviews is to practice for them. Get a friend or family member to practice interviewing you. The more practice you get, the more you'll know what to expect and the more comfortable you'll be in the real situation.

**Get familiar with the questions that you are most likely to be asked.** Practice answering these questions. (See the section in this chapter on the answers to the most common interview questions.)

**Don't just react. Interact!** Create a two-way conversation with your interviewer so that you are not just answering questions but asking them too.

**Because of distance, some interviews may not be face-to-face.** For telephone interviews, use the same strategies you use for in-person interviews. The person on the other end of the line can't see you but can hear interest in your voice.

**Some interviews may be group sessions with you and have more than one interviewer.** Remember to direct attention to everyone in the group and try to connect by addressing each person individually and making eye contact.

**If you feel like you've blown an interview, remember that you are your toughest judge.** Understand that the other pieces of your application count and you probably did better than you think.

# Strategies for Specific Scholarships

• • • • • • • • • • • • • • • • • • • • • • • • • • • • • • •

In this chapter, you'll learn strategies to apply for scholarships based on:

- Major or academic field

- Career goal

- Leadership

- Athletics

- Community service

- Ethnic background

- Rellgious background

- Hobbies

- Parents' employer

- Financial need

• • • • • • • • • • • • • • • • • • • • • • • • • • • • • • •

## College Cash from Your Hobbies and Pastimes

Scholarships provide the perfect opportunity for reaping financial gain as a result of your delight in dogs or your gusto for golf. From automobile aficionados to zephyr zealots, there exists an organization for the love of almost anything you can imagine. Where there are enthusiast organizations, there are often scholarships to promote that interest.

Add to this list organizations that want to promote academic fields, industries, sports, public service, religions, political agendas and education, and you get a large number of scholarships with very specific goals and objectives. This means that the majority of scholarships available to you will reward students with specific backgrounds, skills or achievements. To take the same approach when applying to these scholarships, which have disparate aims, would be a fatal mistake. Each has its own requirements, judging criteria and competition. Each demands an individualized, well-developed plan of attack.

In this chapter, we provide strategies for specific types of scholarships. Depending on the scholarship, there are different twists you can give your application to ensure that it fits the goals of the award and has the best chance of winning.

### The Big Picture

When you start searching, you will find scholarships for nearly every talent, hobby and interest imaginable. There are scholarships for linguistic majors, soccer players and future museum curators. It is tempting to use the same application and essay to apply to all these scholarships. However, if you look carefully, you will notice that while there may be many commonalities among scholarships, each is focused on a specific quality that you need to have in your application. If you hope to win, don't take any shortcuts. Spend the time to tune your applications for each scholarship and you will be rewarded with lots of free cash for college.

## Awards Based on Your Current or Future Major

Whether you're majoring in Taisho-period Japanese history or computer science, there are scholarships open to you. Scholarships based on an academic major or concentration of study are some of the most commonly available. Colleges, foundations and associations provide the scholarships to encourage study in these academic areas. The difficult question is this: How do you make your application

stand out from those of other students who by definition have similar goals and training as you? Here are
some strategies to help you set your application apart
from others in your academic field:

**Emphasize your passion for the field.** Show the
scholarship judges that you are not only a good student
of Asian history, for example, but that it is a passion
and source of intellectual curiosity that you will pursue for the rest of your life. This does not mean that
you need to become a professor of history after you
graduate. However, finding some way to tie the skills
of the discipline with your future career is essential. In
all elements—the application, essay, recommendations
and interview—demonstrate your commitment to your
major and how it will influence the rest of your life.

> ### Show Your Commitment
>
> *For scholarships based on major, the judges want to see evidence of your commitment to your field and your potential for contributing to it while you are in college and afterward.*

**To prevent essays from being a list of coursework, one possible approach
is to focus on your inspiration for selecting the major.** Again, reveal a passion
for the subject that goes beyond the fact (true as it may be) that you picked the
major because your roommates did too! Ask yourself questions like these: What
motivated you to select this field of study? Do you have an interesting anecdote to
illustrate how you made your decision? This is something that differs from student
to student and that will help personalize your application. Think about how you
plan to use the skills from this major in your future. Do you plan to make this
major a career? What contributions to the field have you made or are you planning to make? Remember, the goal is to show your commitment to this area of
study or career field.

**For the essay, do not just reiterate your
qualifications as listed in your application or resume.** Use the space to add color
to your application and to illustrate in a
creative way your commitment to the academic field. Think about describing your
first interaction with something or someone
related to this area of study, a mentor who
has influenced your decision or your vision
of the future of the field. Anecdotes go a
long way since most essays focus solely on
the academic pursuits of their authors.

**Although your focus throughout the
application should be on academics,
you can also discuss how you have developed skills or interests outside the
classroom that relate to the field.** For
example, if you are studying the sciences,

maybe you also volunteer with an organization that helps encourage females to pursue careers in science. Weaving in nonacademic experiences that support your academic goals is very powerful and shows your dedication to the field beyond the classroom.

**In interviews, don't just list off the facts that are in your application.** Try to add a personal dimension to your academic interests. Explain how you selected your major and what your plans are for utilizing your knowledge. Describe in detail your passion for the field and why it is important to you. Ask your interviewer about his or her commitment and thoughts on its future. Asking a roomful of professors about the state of their field and where it's headed is sure to generate a stimulating conversation. You already know that this is an area of great interest for your interviewers. Use the topic to relate to them.

**Recommendations should be from teachers or professors who can vouch for your dedication.** Select those who have worked with you in your studies or in developing skills needed in the field. If you apply for a history-related scholarship, you could ask your history teacher or professor for a recommendation. You could also ask a librarian with whom you've worked closely on research, since this is a highly desirable skill for the study of history.

**Overall, remember that there will be many other students who have taken similar coursework and received similar grades.** Be sure that your application presents your qualifications, your devotion to the field and your plans for contributing to its advancement. This is how you can differentiate yourself from the other applicants.

## Scholarships for Your Future Career

In most everything, there are the "usual" and the "unusual." It is no different with scholarships. There are the usual scholarships for future accountants, doctors and business-people. Then, there are the unusual scholarships for those who want to seek answers about the existence of aliens or work underwater. But one thing is for sure: In nearly every career field you can imagine—both the expected and unexpected—there are scholarships available.

Companies and professional organizations award career-based scholarships to encourage talented young people to enter their fields. They want to create a relationship with the most promising future leaders in their industries. Your challenge is this: How do you convince the judges that you are the applicant with the most promise? Since these scholarships attract others interested in the industry, you can bet that many will have similar backgrounds as yours. Also, many will say that they intend to enter this career after graduation. These two facts alone will not guarantee a win. You need to distinguish yourself from the pack. Read on to learn how.

> ### Give Examples
>
> *It's not enough for you to say that you are a leader or committed to XYZ cause. You need to be able to back up your statements with actual actions and results.*

**As you are completing your applications, keep in mind that you want to show how much promise you have for succeeding in the career field.** Describe related work experience, coursework and honors or awards. Relate experiences in which you've developed the skills needed in the career. Even if you aren't absolutely certain that you will enter the field, it's okay to apply for scholarships. Nobody expects you to sign away your life at this point.

**Concentrate on what contributions you plan to make within the industry.** If you plan to be a graphic designer, what kind of design do you plan to do? What kind of innovative projects would you like to tackle? The more thoughtful your responses are the better. Sharing this will make your future contributions to the field more real.

**To differentiate your application from the others, discuss how your interest in the career started.** Did you have a mentor who piqued your curiosity? Did your studies influence your interest? Your background will be different from that of other students.

**Essays offer you the opportunity to share your personal or emotional dedication to the career.** Utilize the space to illustrate your commitment with an anecdote or example. Share your personal motivations, i.e. what attracts you to the field. If you are applying for an accounting scholarship, don't restate the information in your application about the coursework you've taken and internships you've held. Write about how you first became interested in the field or about the most valuable experience you had while interning. Or, you may want to write about your analytical ability. Be sure to connect how your analytical skill will contribute to your future as an accountant.

**Convey to interviewers information they can't find in your application.** Share why you plan to enter the field, highlights from your experience and your plans for the future. Recognize that your plans may change, but outline where you see yourself in the career in the next five or 10 years. Describe your goals and how you hope to make inventive contributions.

**Get recommendations from employers if you've had experience in the field.** If you haven't, your employers may still be able to describe skills that you've developed that are necessary for the career. Ask teachers or professors who have taught related subjects.

Remember that your overall objective is to demonstrate your devotion to the career and your ability to excel and make useful contributions to it.

## Awards That Recognize Leadership

When you were a child, being a leader meant you decided which schoolyard game to play during recess. Now, it may mean leading an organization, heralding a cause or influencing the establishment. In the future, it will mean managing and motivating a team of people or making a difference in your community. Scholarship judges recognize the value of supporting students who are promising leaders—in fact this is a quality that almost all scholarships reward. They want to back those who will move and shake their world.

When you apply for scholarships based on leadership (or any award that values leadership), it's not enough to say that you are a leader. You need to prove it to the scholarship judges by sharing your experiences with them. Here are some strategies for applying for leadership-based scholarships:

**To demonstrate your leadership ability, *show* the scholarship judges how you've been a leader.** Describe leadership positions you've held and your responsibilities in each, but don't stop here. Use examples to illustrate how you've successfully led a group, how you've directed or motivated your peers. Give the scholarship judges shining examples of your leadership in action.

**Provide concrete examples of the effects of your leadership.** Did your team meet its goals? Did you lead a new or innovative project? Did you increase membership or participation? Were there changes as a result of your efforts? Results provide solid evidence of the effectiveness of your leadership.

**Recognize that being a leader doesn't just mean being the president of a class or organization.** Leaders are people who are passionate about their cause and who influence other people. Leadership can take many forms, from writing an editorial column to leading a Girl Scout troop. Include both formal and informal leadership roles you've played. This may consist of official positions you've held as well as special projects you've led in which you didn't have an official title. The important thing about leadership is that you have influenced other people and rallied them to take action.

**In applications, highlight your main responsibilities and achievements as a leader.** This will provide a quick overview of your accomplishments. As always select those that best fit the mission of the scholarship.

**In essays, do not just repeat the information that is on your applications.** Provide insight into who you are as a leader. Share an anecdote about one of your experiences as a leader. Describe your philosophy on being a leader. Tell the judges when you first realized the power of leadership and what it meant to you to discover qualities of leadership within yourself. Talk about a leader you admire. Let the scholarship judges know what characteristics a position of leadership brings out in you. It's important that you personalize your leadership experience.

**In interviews, use the same strategies that you have put into action in your essays and applications forms and don't recount information that your interviewers can easily find and read in those documents.** Instead, use the interview time with the judges to provide personal information about your leadership experience or share your personal approach to leadership. Share examples of times you've been a leader. Try to exude confidence in your interview. Since you'll be in the company of other leaders, ask them about their philosophy of leadership, what they did as students and what they find challenging about being a leader in their fields.

**Ask recommenders to describe examples of your leadership ability.** Remind them of projects and events in which you were a leader so they can complete the portrait of you as a strong leader in their letters to the committee.

## Athletic Scholarships

You're the best dribbler, server, runner, pitcher or sprinter at your school. How do you use that talent to pay for college? With an athletic scholarship.

Athletic scholarships are the Holy Grail. At their best, they can cover tuition and fees, room and board and books. That's not bad for doing something you enjoy.

There are two types of athletic scholarships. The first is given by colleges to the best college-bound high school athletes. The second is from organizations that reward high school or college students who participate in athletics but that may or may not base the scholarships on athletic talent.

> ### Grades Count Too
>
> *For athletic scholarships, your scores on the field are important but so are your scores in the classroom. To qualify, you must meet minimum academic requirements.*

## College Athletic Awards

College athletic scholarships are funded by membership revenue from the National Collegiate Athletic Association (NCAA), which encompasses more than 1,200 colleges, conferences and affiliate organizations. The colleges are divided into three divisions, with athletic scholarships awarded for Division I and Division II schools. At Division III schools, student athletes receive scholarships based on financial need but not on athletic talent.

However, don't think that every talented athlete is instantly showered with a full-ride scholarship. It takes more than talent to win and to keep one of these awards. Here are some strategies for winning an NCAA scholarship:

**Remember that academics rule—even in qualifying for athletic scholarships.** You can be the number one player in the country, but if you don't have the grades or tests scores, you won't play competitively in college. The minimum academic requirements for eligibility are that you must do or have the following:

- Graduate from high school.
- Complete a curriculum these 16 core courses:
  **English:** Four years.
  **Mathematics:** Three years of courses at the level of Algebra I or above.
  **Natural or physical science** (including at least one laboratory course, if offered by your high school): Two years.
  **Additional courses:** English, mathematics or natural or physical science: One year.
  **Social science:** Two years.
  **Additional academic courses:** In any of the above subject areas or foreign language, philosophy or comparative religion courses: Four years.
- Have a core-course grade-point average and a combined score on the SAT reading and writing and math sections or a sum score on the ACT based on the NCAA qualifier index scale. In other words, they set minimum scores that you must achieve.

**You don't have to be a football or basketball star to win athletic scholarships.** In fact, you may have better opportunities to win scholarships for less-publicized sports like crew, rugby, volleyball or field hockey. Competition is often less intense for these sports.

**Find schools that match both your athletic and academic goals.** Don't choose a college solely because of its athletic program. The great majority of student athletes don't go professional after graduating. They go to graduate school or find jobs. Select a college that fulfills your academic needs so that you will be prepared for the next step.

**College coaches may not find you, so you must find them.** Unless you are a true superstar, the reality is that coaches don't have the resources to do national searches for student athletes. If you want to be noticed, you are going to need to start the conversation. Do this by writing a letter to coaches at prospective colleges. Build a portfolio as evidence of your athletic ability. Your portfolio should include the following:

- Athletic statistics such as win-loss record, times, averages, etc.
- Records set
- Honors or awards won
- Titles won
- Newspaper clips or website links
- Video links or videos on DVD
- Letters of recommendation from coaches
- Playing schedule

**Keep in touch with the coaches.** Follow up to make sure they received your letter and portfolio. Ask if they need additional information. Get your high school coach to call the college coach on your behalf. Try to keep yourself at the top of their list of whom they want on next year's team.

**If you are fortunate enough to receive an athletic scholarship, realize that you are not guaranteed a free ride for the rest of your academic career.** There are no guaranteed four-year athletic scholarships in Division I, II or III. Athletic scholarships are awarded for a maximum of one academic year and may be renewed each year for a maximum of five years within a six-year period.

**Don't count on that $7 million contract yet.** For a very, very small minority, college segues into professional athletics. According to the NCAA, the odds of a high school football player making it to a professional team are about 6,000 to 1, and the odds for a high school basketball player are 10,000 to 1. Do your best, but keep focused on academics too.

**Get more information.** The more information you have, the better equipped you'll be for facing the stiff competition for athletic scholarships. Speak with your coach and guidance counselors. Also, get more detailed information on eligibility and a directory of schools that have scholarships for each sport from the NCAA website at www.ncaa.org/student-athletes.

## Athletic Organization Awards

There are also scholarships for high school and college athletic competitors and enthusiasts given by aficionado organizations and athletic associations like your school's booster club.

For these scholarships, the level of athletic talent can vary. For some, athletic ability is the key measurement, while others equally weigh additional qualities like leadership, academic achievement or public service. Adapt your application to fit the criteria on which you will be judged. Here are some strategies to help you:

**In your application, concentrate on how you meet the mission of the scholarship.** For example, if you are applying for a scholarship that is based on both athletic and academic achievement, outline your accomplishments on the field and in the classroom.

**Submit a sports portfolio.** Your portfolio brings the judges to the sidelines of your game and enables them to see evidence of your athletic ability. See the previous section for what to include in your portfolio.

**Go beyond your stats.** Describe your motivation for participating in the sport to provide background for your interest. Outline your goals for the future, and let the scholarship judges know where you are headed. While going off to play in the NFL or NBA may be your goal, consider mentioning alternatives to demonstrate that you understand how difficult going professional is and how much you value a solid education.

**Try to make your essays different from what the scholarship committee will expect.** Many athletes write about the time they scored the winning touchdown or hit the winning home run. Take a different approach. Depict the first time you recognized your passion for the sport. Describe an unexpected mentor or role model who influenced and shaped you as an athlete. Explain why the sport is important *besides* scoring points and becoming a professional athlete. Use the essay to share something about yourself, not to just glorify your accomplishments. The scholarship judges will know by your portfolio that you are a talented player. You need to show them that you can be self-analytical about your athletic achievements.

**In interviews, go beyond the information that is in your applications and essays.** Again, don't just recount the winning game or match. Provide insight into your personal motivation and goals. Have anecdotes and examples besides those from game time to illustrate your commitment to the sport. Be ready to discuss your major and classes you'd like to take.

**Encourage your coaches to write about your athletic statistics but also about you as a person in their letters of recommendation.** You may want to ask a teacher or professor who knows you in a different capacity to write a recommendation as well. Request that he or she comment on your integrity and dedication to academics. This will provide a more complete picture of who you are underneath the jersey.

## Scholarships for Public Service

Scholarships offer the opportunity for philanthropy to pay off in cold hard cash. Of course, this should not

---

### Be Honest about Your Commitment

*When applying for scholarships, be honest about how committed you are. If you are not truly devoted to the interest or hobby that you say you are, the judges will see through you.*

be your motivation for volunteering, but it is a nice perk of donating your time and service for a worthy cause. Many organizations provide scholarships to encourage public service among youth. Your challenge becomes how you distinguish your application from those of all the other do-gooders.

**As with other types of scholarships, what's most important for service-based scholarships is fulfilling the mission.** Before you start your application to any one service organization, you must understand what the group is trying to achieve. What is the organization's purpose? Why is it awarding the scholarship? Once you understand this, mold your application to show how you fit the scholarship. Highlight service experience that matches the scholarship's mission.

**When completing the application, include details that define the quality of the contributions that you have made.** List the number of hours you've contributed in service and what you did. Include any responsibilities or leadership positions that you held. Most important, note the effects of your contributions. Give concrete evidence of how your service has produced results. For example, if you volunteered for an adult literacy program, describe how your students improved their scores on a reading test after working with you. If you volunteered for a voter registration drive, recount how many voters you registered. By providing specific results of your work, scholarship judges will see that you not only volunteer but you also make a difference that is measurable and material.

**Personalize your inspiration.** Discuss your motivation for serving and why the causes are important to you. Bring your inspiration to a personal level so that the scholarship committee can understand you better as a person. Be illustrative in your essay, providing lively examples or anecdotes. Don't be afraid to be creative.

**Take a similar approach with interviews.** Go beyond what you have included in your application and essay. Use this time to show interviewers why your volunteer work is important to you personally. Practice sharing experiences and information to illustrate your points. Also take the time to learn about your interviewers' links to public service. Ask members of the scholarship committee how they got involved and what motivates them to continue in areas of service.

Avoid merely stating the facts about your public service in every part of your application. Instead, make your service personal by conveying how it has affected the lives of those you have helped and how it has affected you.

## Awards Based on Ethnic Background

No matter what your ethnic background, there is probably a scholarship for you. Scholarships based on ethnic background are awarded to celebrate the history or culture of an ethnic group, increase the number of minorities in college and encourage minorities to enter certain professions. Regardless of the purpose of the award, here are some points to keep in mind when applying:

**Meet the goal of the scholarship.** It's not enough for you to just be a member of the ethnic group. In other words, if you are applying for an award for Asian Americans, you will not win simply because you are an Asian American. You will win if you fit the mission of the award. If the purpose of the award is to help Asian Americans become leaders in the community, you must not only have the appropriate ethnic background but also demonstrate your leadership skills and show your plans to be involved in the Asian American community in the future.

**Personalize your application.** Instead of making general statements about the culture of your ethnic group or describing its history in your application, write about how your heritage has affected you personally. The scholarship judges are probably already familiar with the culture and history of the group, so describing these will not tell them anything about you. It's important that your application demonstrates the importance of your background to you, how it has shaped who you are, how you identify with it and how you will use it in the future.

**Explain how you will share your knowledge with others.** Remember that scholarship judges want to get the most mileage from the awards they are giving. This means they want to reward students who will make an impact on the future.

---

### "My Hobbies Paid for College"
### Russell Duffy, Scholarship Winner

When I was a freshman in college, my parents asked me to apply for scholarships to help pay my tuition bills. I made a list of all my hobbies and interests. I cross-referenced them with scholarships and found three awards that matched my hobbies: writing, singing and public speaking.

In the spring I applied for all three. For the writing scholarship, I described how I wrote for our school's literary magazine and included clips from pieces I had gotten published. When I applied for the singing scholarship, I included audio and video recordings of performances I'd made in high school and college. For the public speaking scholarship, I had to give a speech as a part of the competition.

It turns out that I won two scholarships for public speaking and singing. I never thought that what I love to do in my free time could help me pay for college, but I won $3,000!

You can show that you will do so by explaining how you have already influenced others.

## Religious Scholarships

When you think of money for education, religion is probably the last thing that pops into mind. However, many religious organizations award scholarships to encourage students to get involved in activities of faith and to promote the growth of that religion. We have a few words of advice for applying for religious-based scholarships.

Most important, only apply for a religious scholarship if you are a true believer in the principles and teachings of that religion. We don't suspect that you would do this, but some students have been known to apply for such scholarships even though the only time they attend church is when their parents drag them out of bed on Christmas and Easter mornings. If you are not truly dedicated to the religion, mission or church, don't pretend to be.

That said, let's discuss what you should do when applying for a scholarship that is supported by a religious organization.

**Emphasize your participation in religious activities in your application.** This may include participating in missionary campaigns, church camps, teaching, volunteering or studying religious traditions. These descriptions will help show the selection committee your dedication to the religion. Also emphasize how religious teaching and faith have helped you in the past and what they mean to your future.

**Go beyond your faith.** Often, religious scholarships are not just about religion. Many recognize students who have done public service, displayed leadership or excelled academically. Include descriptions about your many nonreligious activities in your application and essays as well.

## Awards for Hobbies

You probably didn't know that you can earn money from being an amateur radio operator, a bowler or a Latin speaker, but you can. For almost every hobby there is a scholarship. Organizations composed of enthusiasts want to encourage the growth and popularity of the objects of their affection and thus have established scholarships for students who partake in them.

**Ensure that you fit the mission of the scholarship.** If the scholarship is for true enthusiasts of the hobby, make sure you really are an enthusiast. Don't apply for a philatelic scholarship if the only stamps you've ever touched are those you use to send letters.

**In applications, highlight any honors or awards you have won in the hobby.** If you haven't won any, provide other evidence of your knowledge or skill level. If you are applying for a sewing scholarship and have never won an award in sewing, describe instead how you started a business in which you sold your sewn products. Convey to the scholarship committee your skill level in the hobby whether it's through awards you've won or other personal accomplishments that you've made.

**Use essays as an opportunity to discuss the personal significance of your hobby.** Explain your motivation for becoming involved or discuss role models in the hobby. Make your essay personal with anecdotes, dialogues or active experiences. Don't be afraid to be creative. Convey how the hobby has affected you individually.

**Utilize essays or interviews to demonstrate that you are committed to continuing your hobby.** Discuss your goals so that the selection committee will understand that by awarding the scholarship to you, they will meet their goal of promoting the hobby in the future.

**In interviews, provide insight into how the hobby has affected you.** Then ask interviewers how they got their start in the hobby and about their experiences as well. You know that this is a topic of conversation they will enjoy.

**Get recommendations from those who can vouch for your skill level in the hobby.** If you are applying for a sewing scholarship, get a recommendation from your sewing teacher or from a frequent recipient of some of your projects.

## Scholarships from Your Parents' Employers

One perk that some employers provide is a scholarship fund for the sons and daughters of their employees. Because you must either be an employee or the dependent of an employee, there are a limited number of people who can apply. This does not mean that employer scholarships are easy to win, but it does mean that—unlike scholarships in which every student in the country can apply—the competition for these awards will be significantly less. Here are some strategies to help improve your chances even more:

**Ask your parents to find out who the judges will be.** If the parent(s) who is employed by the provider of the scholarship feels it's appropriate, he or she can informally speak with the judges to get more information on what qualities they are looking for in students who are viable candidates for the award. They might also ask what characteristics were common among students who have won in the past. Warn your parent(s) not to try and lobby for you since this can easily backfire. If your parent(s) is able to gather more information about what the judges are looking for beyond the written guidelines, you will have a better idea of how to shape your application and essay.

**Focus on how you fulfill the mission of the scholarship in the application and essay.** Often the mission will be general, rewarding students for academic achievement and leadership. Review the information in this chapter on applying for scholarships based on academics and leadership.

**Be careful in the interview how you describe your parents.** Be aware that while it's inappropriate and shouldn't happen, what you say could get back to your mom or dad's manager, supervisor or employer. Do not be critical or relate information that could be used against your parents. For example, do not say that your parents dislike their managers or express their beliefs about what changes should be made to the company. Chances are that the judges will not reveal what they learn, but it's better to be cautious.

**Know something about the company.** You may know where your parents work but have no idea what their companies actually do. Sit down with your parents and ask them to describe their jobs and tell you about the company in general. Visit the website to get more information on what the company does and achievements or products that it is most proud of.

## Need-Based Scholarships

Because the purpose of financial aid is to assist those who need help to attend college, it makes sense that financial need is a requirement for many scholarships. To make a case for your need, it's not enough to submit the Free Application for Federal Student Aid (FAFSA) or tax forms. Here is some guidance for applying for need-based scholarships:

**First, try to find out how the organization defines "need" and how much of a role it plays in the selection of scholarship recipients.** Scholarship benefactors and organizations define need differently. You may find that while you are needy according to the guidelines of one scholarship, you may not be according to another. If you are on the borderline of meeting the financial criteria for a specific scholarship but you find out that financial need does not play a large role in selection, you may still have a good chance of winning. However, if you discover that it is the largest factor, you may choose to spend your time applying to a different scholarship that better fits your background and circumstances.

**Don't Assume You Don't Qualify for Need-Based Awards**

*Don't count yourself out of need-based scholarships without first understanding how the judges define financial need. For some, there are specific guidelines, while for others a level of need is preferred but not required.*

**Tell the truth about how much you will really require to attend college.** Most need-based scholarships require documentation of your earnings, taxes paid and projected college expenses so the judges will be able to verify your financial situation.

**Build a case that demonstrates your financial need.** Concisely highlight the main reasons for your need. By showing that your income and assets are X and you anticipate that your college education will cost Y, you can quickly show the difference between the two. Briefly explain special circumstances that affect your need such as the costs of a sibling's education, medical costs or the support of an elderly or ailing relative. This helps the scholarship committee understand your circumstances.

**Money should not be the entire premise of your application.** Include information about your financial background, but spend the rest of the application making a case for why you're qualified to win the award. Your financial situation is just one consideration. Once you've established that you need financial help, prove that you meet the mission of the scholarship. Let the financial forms demonstrate your need. Your application, essay, interview and recommendations should focus on how you fit the scholarship, not on why you need money.

## Recurring Themes

In this chapter, we have outlined strategies that you should use when applying for specific scholarships. Because each is judged by a different group of people and has different qualifications, take an individualized approach to applying to them. However, in your study of these very different types of scholarships, you'll find some recurring themes to take away. In summary, remember to do the following:

- Build a case for why you fit the mission of the scholarship.
- Tell the truth.
- Use essays and interviews to go beyond facts found in your application.
- Share something personal about yourself.

By following these guidelines, you will create the strongest application possible and therefore will have the best chance of coming home with the dough.

## Chapter 12 Summary: Specific Scholarships

**There are scholarships for nearly every talent, hobby or interest imaginable.** Your job is to find those that best match your skills and experience. Then, create an application that builds a case for why you should win the award.

**Scholarships based on major.** Directly or indirectly demonstrate your passion for the field and share your plans to use what you learned in college after graduating.

**Scholarships based on career goals.** Show how much promise you have for contributing to the field in the future and describe your motivation for entering the field as well as your goals for the future.

**Scholarships based on leadership.** Demonstrate how you've been a leader through examples and illustrations, including the results of your work. Remember that you don't have to hold an official position to be a leader.

**College-bound high school athletes.** Keep in mind that your scores on the field are important but so are the scores you get in the classroom. Academic achievement is a must for athletic scholarships. With a few exceptions for nationally recognized athletes, the coaches will not find you. You will need to build a portfolio to showcase your talents and start the communication with them.

**Be realistic about athletic scholarships.** Know that there are many more student athletes than there are scholarships available and that your chances of making it into the professional leagues are about 6,000 to 1 for football and 10,000 to 1 for basketball.

**Scholarships based on service.** Highlight the results of your service work and any responsibilities or leadership positions that you have held. Explain your motivation for participating in service work.

**Scholarships based on ethnic background.** Highlight your contributions to your ethnic community and the role you plan to play in the future.

**Scholarships based on religious belief.** Focus on your contributions to your faith and the community. Share activities and the responsibilities that you have shouldered.

**Scholarships based on a hobby or interest.** Showcase awards or honors you've won for the hobby and evidence of your skill in it.

**Need-based awards.** The definition of financial "need" varies by award, which means that you may qualify for awards even if you think you don't. Build a case that illustrates why you need aid by showing the costs of your education and your family's ability to contribute.

# Guaranteed Scholarships

In this chapter, you'll learn:

- Why guaranteed scholarships do exist

- How to tell if a guaranteed scholarship is actually a scam

- Getting in-state tuition even if you live out of state

# Do Guaranteed Scholarships Really Exist?

Normally, when you hear the words "guaranteed" and "scholarship" used in the same sentence, you should run in the other direction. In previous chapters we warned you about any scholarship that claimed to be "guaranteed." While this is often a sign of a scam, there is one exception. There are scholarships with fixed criteria that are often quantitative. Anyone who meets certain eligibility standards wins one of these scholarships automatically.

This does not mean that anyone <u>can</u> win. You still need to meet the criteria such as getting a specific SAT score. However, because the criteria for winning are quantitative, it takes the uncertainty out of whether or not you will win.

In this chapter we will introduce you to a variety of guaranteed scholarships so that you know how to recognize them. Keep in mind that many of these awards are limited to students who attend particular colleges or are residents of specific states. However, they are numerous enough that you will probably be able to benefit from some of them.

## The Big Picture

The majority of these "guaranteed" awards are sponsored by colleges and state governments. It is important that you carefully research your college, or colleges that you are applying to, as well as your state government to see if they offer any of these awards. Since they are often based on such objective criteria as grades, SAT scores and even state of residency, you don't want to miss any opportunities. Why wouldn't you cash in on a guaranteed scholarship?

## National Merit Scholarships

The PSAT (Preliminary Scholastic Assessment Test) can be one of the most lucrative tests you'll take. The National Merit program, administered by the National Merit Scholarship Corporation, a nonprofit organization, receives the scores for all high school juniors who take the PSAT. Using these scores the National Merit organization selects the highest-scoring students to be named National Merit Semifinalists. About 16,000 students out of the more than 1.6 million students who take the PSAT become Semifinalists.

Being selected a semifinalist is an honor in itself because it means that out of all of the juniors who took the PSAT exam, you are among the top scoring echelon.

Unfortunately you don't automatically win a scholarship with this honor. However, those who are National Merit Semifinalists are invited to compete for a National Merit Scholarship. From the 16,000 Semifinalists, about 7,500 win a National Merit Scholarship that might be one of the following:

- $2,500 from the National Merit Scholarships organization
- Corporate-sponsored Merit Scholarship awards
- College-sponsored Merit Scholarship awards

The key to being honored as a National Merit Semifinalist—and thus being able to compete for some money—is to take the PSAT exam during your junior year.

## GPA and Exam-Based Scholarships

Some colleges want more brains on campus and offer automatic scholarships to academically talented students. These guaranteed awards are based on SAT or ACT scores or GPA. For example, Wilmington College of Ohio offers guaranteed scholarships to all incoming students based on their cumulative grade point average and ACT/SAT composite score:

- $10,500-$13,000 for the Academic Achievement Award
- $5,000-$11,000 for the Recognition Award

Take a look at your school or the schools in which you are interested, and see if they offer similar guaranteed scholarships. You will find that many colleges offer incentives to attract bright students.

## Transfer Student Awards

If you find that your college is not the right fit for you, transferring may be the answer. Unfortunately, your financial aid package does not automatically transfer from one college to another. You will need to reapply. Some colleges make the transition easier.

To encourage students who want to transfer into their college, some schools offer guaranteed awards to incoming transfer students with a minimum GPA in their previous college. For example, Spalding University in Louisville, Kentucky, offers scholarships for transfer students of up to $8,000 for those with a GPA of 3.0 or higher.

> ### The Real Guaranteed Scholarships
>
> *Guaranteed scholarships are usually a scam. But there are a few exceptions to this as you can see from this list of awards that are all but guaranteed if you meet certain requirements.*

| Residency Is Not Always Automatic |
| :--- |
| *Getting residency in a state for the purpose of qualifying for in-state tuition is often different than the rules for being a resident in order to vote or get a driver's license.* |

If you are thinking about transferring, speak with someone in the financial aid office at the colleges you are considering. Ask them what kind of financial aid package you may expect as a transfer student and inquire about automatic scholarships for which you may be eligible.

## State Entitlement Awards

Whether or not you like where you live, there's a benefit to living there. States have financial aid programs for their residents. Some of these programs effectively reward students who perform at a specific academic level in high school. Georgia, for example, has the HOPE program that automatically awards money to high school students who have a B average or higher. Ironically, one of the biggest problems with the program is that many students aren't aware that they are eligible for a HOPE Scholarship and don't claim their money.

Many states offer similar entitlement awards. Some are based on academic merit while others have criteria related to financial need. Awards may be designated for high school seniors, adult students or students in certain fields like nursing, medicine or education. Be aware that some require you to use the money only at a college within your state.

We have a listing of all the state agencies that manage scholarships in the Scholarship Directory section of this book. Contact your agency to make sure you are not leaving any money on the table.

## In-State Tuition for Out-Of-State Students

Getting in-state tuition at a public university can save you thousands of dollars. Take a look at the additional money needed for the University of California at Berkeley if you are from out of state. Those students who are not residents of California will have to pay a non-resident fee of almost $30,000.

If you are an out-of-state student, you will need to pay out-of-state tuition until you can establish in-state residency. This is easier in some states than others. Texas, for example, does not like students to move to their state just to use their fine educational system and then leave. One of the residency requirements is that you live in Texas for 12 months without attending a secondary institution. This makes gaining residency for purposes of reduced tuition at a Texas college far less attractive and almost impossible.

The University of California system, on the other hand, makes it possible but not easy. To become a resident you need to show three things:

**Physical presence.** You must have proof that you remained in the state for more than one year. This means no going home for summer. You actually have to physically be in the state and be able to prove it.

**Intent.** You must establish ties to the state of California that show you intend to make California your home. This requires giving up any previous residence and getting proof of your move such as a California driver's license.

**Financial independence.** If both parents are nonresidents, you must show that you are financially independent from your parents. One way is that you have not been claimed as an income tax deduction by your parents for at least two years.

There is one exception to the problem of establishing residency. Some schools have formed relationships with neighboring states to offer their residents automatic in-state rates from the beginning. The University of Arkansas, for example, offers a Non-Resident Tuition Award for entering freshmen and transfer students from neighboring states that include Illinois, Kansas, Louisiana, Mississippi, Missouri, Oklahoma, Tennessee and Texas. You must meet minimum academic criteria of a 3.0 GPA or higher and have an ACT score of at least 24 or an SAT score of at least 1160. If you meet these academic qualities and are from a neighboring state, you will be awarded a scholarship of up to 90 percent.

## All It Takes to Win Is to Apply

These guaranteed scholarships are wonderful. There is no strategy involved in winning. If you meet the established qualifications, you win. The only challenge is to make sure you are aware that the awards exist. Now that you have an idea of what is out there, it shouldn't be hard to find some in your area. So get out there and stake your claim!

## Chapter 13 Summary: Guaranteed Scholarships

**There really are guaranteed scholarships.** While we have warned you about scholarship scams that guarantee that you will win, there are legitimate awards that are based on quantitative criteria.

**National Merit Scholarships.** You may win scholarships from corporations and colleges based on your performance on the PSAT in your junior year.

**Academic scholarships.** Some colleges automatically award scholarships based on your grades and test scores. These are available for entering freshmen and transfer students.

**State entitlement awards.** You may win scholarships from your state based on your academic performance.

**In-state tuition for out-of-state students.** You can save money by qualifying for residency.

# Unleash the Power of the Internet

. . . . . . . . . . . . . . . . . . . . . . . . . . . . .

In this chapter, you'll learn:

- How to find more scholarships online

- Strategies for applying for scholarships via the Internet

- The importance of researching awarding organizations and past winners

- How to avoid costly scholarship scams on the Internet

. . . . . . . . . . . . . . . . . . . . . . . . . . . . .

## Opening the Scholarship Vault with the Internet

In the pre-Internet days, the only way to find out about scholarships was through books. The only way to research the background of awarding organizations was to write or call. In fact, the only way to apply was with typewriter and paper. The Internet has helped open the possibilities for scholarships by providing more access to awards, an easy method to find out about awarding organizations and the means for applying with your computer. In this chapter, we show you how to take advantage of these high-tech options.

### The Big Picture

Our view of the Internet is that it is a great tool for finding scholarships. But it is not the only tool. The biggest mistake you can make is assuming that once you do a few Internet searches, you are done. While the Internet has made the typewriter and whiteout obsolete, it sometimes makes applying so easy that students get sloppy. Remember, you should treat online applications with just as much care and attention as you would a paper application. Once you hit that submit button it's too late to make any corrections.

## Using the Internet to Find Scholarships

You will find one of the most comprehensive directories of scholarships in the second half of this book. However, no directory has every scholarship available. In fact, new scholarships are formed every day. One of the benefits of using the Internet in your search is that website databases can be updated very quickly. Here are some tips for using the Internet to search for scholarships:

**Look for databases of scholarships that you can search for free.** We have one on our site at **www.supercollege.com**. Our database works like this: You answer questions about your education, academic goals, career goals, activities, parents' activities and employment, religion, talents, ethnicity and additional background information. Our database uses your answers to search thousands of awards and provide matches for scholarships that fit your individual background.

**Searches should always be free.** Never pay for a scholarship search.

**Before beginning your search, prepare a list of your parents' employers and activities as well as your own activities, talents and**

**interests.** This will save time when you are actually using a website to search for scholarships. Having your pertinent information in a concise format will help ensure that you don't forget or miss anything.

**Spend time to complete the questions about your background.** There may be a lot of questions, but the more specific and accurate you can be about your background, the better your results will be.

**Remember that no database is perfect.** Every scholarship database has its shortcomings. The biggest is that none is anywhere near complete. There are millions of scholarships available and online databases only index a few thousand—and often these are the larger national type of awards. Searching the Internet is no substitute for doing your own research. Plus, depending on the quality of the software and your answers to the background questions, you may discover that not all the matches may actually be good fits.

The bottom line is to use the Internet like any good tool. But do realize that it is not perfect and needs to be supplemented with your own detective work.

## Zap! Applying for Scholarships Online

In the old days, you had to lug out the typewriter and whiteout correction fluid every time you wanted to complete an application. It's much easier now. Just connect to the Internet. No correction fluid needed! There are many benefits to applying online. It's easy to correct typos and you don't have to make a trip to the post office. However, for even the most tech-savvy students, applying for scholarships online can be challenging. To help, here are some tips for applying electronically:

**Preview the application.** Before you start completing the application, take a sneak peek at it so that you know what questions are asked and what information you'll need to provide.

**Prepare your materials and answers in advance.** Because you have previewed the questions, you can compose and organize the information in advance. Spend time on your answers. Just because you can apply instantly with the click of a button doesn't mean that you should craft your answers as speedily.

> *Don't Get Careless*
>
> *One unintended consequence of applying to scholarships online is the huge increase in careless mistakes. For some students, filling out an online application is too easy. Without checking spelling and grammar they simply hit the "submit" button. A better idea is to compose your answers to the application separately and then copy and paste them into the online form.*

**Read the directions regarding timing out to see if you need to complete the entire application in a single sitting or if you can save it, return at another time and complete it.** In most cases, you can save your information and complete the application later.

**Compose your essay in a word processing program first, and then upload it.** Don't try to write your essay at the same time you are submitting the application. When submitting your essays online, follow the same strategies that are recommended for submitting them offline. Brainstorm topics, write with passion and get editors to review your work. Don't take shortcuts. Review Chapter 10 for essay-writing strategies.

**Be careful to avoid typos and mistakes.** It's easy to make careless mistakes when you submit your applications online. Take time to review your work.

**Print out what you submit so you have a hard copy.** You can refer to the hard copy when applying to other scholarships, and you will have a spare in case your electronic copy gets lost.

**Read the submission instructions to find any information that you might need to submit offline.** For some scholarships, you complete your application online and then print it out and send it. For others, you submit your application online but send additional information like letters of recommendation or transcripts by regular mail. Follow the directions carefully.

**Get confirmation.** When you submit your application online, most organizations will send you confirmation that they have received your application. If they do not, get confirmation by sending an email.

## Our Favorite Free Scholarship Websites

**SuperCollege**
www.supercollege.com

**MoolahSpot**
www.moolahspot.com

**Sallie Mae**
www.salliemae.com/scholarships

**Adventures in Education**
www.aie.org

**Fastweb**
www.fastweb.com

**Mario Einaudi Center for International Studies**
www.einaudi.cornell.edu/funding

**The College Board**
https://bigfuture.collegeboard.org/scholarship-search

**Chegg**
https://www.chegg.com/scholarships

## How to Be an Internet Private Eye

There's a reason that the Internet was once nicknamed the "Information Super-highway." You can find out the dirt on pretty much anyone, including scholarship organizations. In addition to finding scholarships and applying to them online, use the Internet to research the sponsor organizations and awards. Here are some tips:

**Read the sponsor organization's website to learn more about the mission of the organization and the award that they offer.** This will help you understand what the organization is trying to accomplish by giving the scholarship.

**Request additional information, newsletters or other literature if it's available.** Or, read the literature online. Many organizations have their literature and newsletters accessible on their websites.

**Get information on past winners.** Some organizations list past winners on their websites and include brief biographical information. Again, this will help you understand what kind of student the organization is seeking for its scholarship recipient.

The more you can learn about the organization and the award, the better you can craft your application to fit the scholarship.

> **Use the Internet to Research the Scholarship Organization**
>
> One of the best uses of the Internet is to research the organizations that are giving away the money. Visit their website and see what they are all about before you decide to apply for their scholarship.

## Be Cautious of Scams

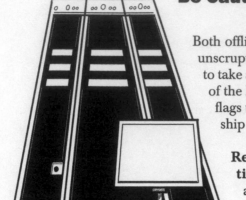

Both offline and online, there always will be that unscrupulous small minority of people who try to take advantage of students' and parents' fears of the high costs of college. Here are some red flags to watch for when you research scholarship possibilities:

**Registration, entry or administrative fee:** Legitimate scholarship and financial aid programs do not require an upfront fee. Never pay to search a scholarship database on the Internet.

**Soliciting your credit card number:** Never give out this kind of financial information to anyone who contacts you.

**No name, address or phone number:** Legitimate online businesses post their contact information on their websites. If no such information exists, the organization—and its scholarship—could be bogus.

**Guarantee:** Remember, there is no such thing as a scholarship you are guaranteed to win. Legitimate scholarships are based on merit or need, not your willingness to pay a registration fee.

Read Chapter 3, *Avoid Scholarship Scams,* for more information on scholarship scams in general. While there is a small group of people who try to take advantage of students, a number of great services can provide scholarship and financial aid guidance—for free. We encourage you to visit SuperCollege.com to learn more.

## Chapter 14 Summary: The Power of the Internet

**The Internet is a great tool for finding scholarships, applying for scholarships and learning more about the sponsoring organizations.** Online scholarship information can be updated very quickly and best of all, it's free! Use it in combination with traditional resources like this book and your high school counselor or financial aid officer.

**Find scholarships online** through websites with free, searchable scholarship databases and through search engines.

**Some scholarships allow you to apply online.** Take advantage of this opportunity to save time and headaches. Be as diligent about the quality of your work when you apply online as when you apply on paper.

**Do online detective work.** Learn more about scholarship sponsors and past winners and use your Internet research skills to improve your application.

**Avoid online scholarship scams.** Be wary of any scholarship services that require a fee, solicit your credit card number, have no contact information or make "guarantees" that sound too good to be true.

**You are welcome to visit our website, SuperCollege.com** (www. supercollege.com). Search our free database of thousands of scholarships, learn more scholarship and financial aid tips and strategies and apply for the SuperCollege.com scholarship.

# Financial Aid Workshop

In this chapter, you'll learn:

- How to get a share of the $241.3 billion in financial aid awarded each year

- What you need to qualify for aid and how to apply

- Eligibility requirements of each financial aid program

- Proven strategies for getting more aid from your college

## Getting the Most Financial Aid You Deserve

How much financial aid do you think is given out each year? $1 billion? $10 billion? How about $50 billion? The answer is more than $241 billion! That is a lot of money. Some families assume that it's very difficult to claim this money. It's not. All you have to do to find out how much financial aid you deserve is simply this: "Ask for it."

The sad reality is that most families do not ask for financial aid. We've heard almost every excuse why families do not apply. The three most common are these:

> *"I don't understand how financial aid works so it must be too complicated."*

> *"My family's income or assets must be too high so I won't even bother applying."*

> *"Deadline? What deadline? Did I miss the deadline to apply?!"*

Banish these excuses—except for the last one which is important—and we'll make sure that you don't miss the deadline. What surprises many families, even those who consider themselves middle or upper-middle class, is that they do qualify for financial aid. Contrary to what you may believe, financial aid is based on more than just income and assets. Other important factors include family size, parents' age and the cost of your college. In fact, the more expensive your college, the more likely you are to get financial aid. You have nothing to lose and everything to gain by applying for financial aid.

## The Big Picture

The term *financial aid* can seem confusing at first since it refers to a cornucopia of money—including grants, loans and even subsidized employment. This money comes from a variety of sources including the federal government, state governments and colleges. These entities have dozens of individual programs (you might have heard of Pell Grants or Direct Subsidized and Unsubsidized Loans) that are under the umbrella term financial aid.

We imagine that right now you are scratching your head and rubbing your temples wondering how you can possibly master the confusing world of financial aid. The good news is that you don't have to. The colleges administer this vast amount of money and decide both the amount and type (i.e., grants or loans) each student receives. Some of these decisions are based on federal guidelines while others are determined by the colleges themselves. But you really don't need to concern yourself with these details. After you apply for financial aid, you will receive an award letter from each college that spells out how much you will get. These award letters will contain everything for which you qualify, including grants, scholarships from the college, student loans and work-study programs. But you won't get this award letter if you don't fill out the applications correctly and submit everything on time.

It is also important to always keep in mind that the financial aid process consists of two phases. The first phase involves mathematical computation. A standard formula calculates how much money your family can contribute to one year of education and therefore how much you qualify for in financial aid. (This number is known as the Expected Family Contribution or the EFC.) But once this number is determined, the second phase of the process involves a real, live human known as a financial aid officer. Financial aid officers have a lot of power and can significantly affect the size and makeup of your financial aid package. They use their professional judgment for special circumstances that are not adequately addressed by the financial aid formulas and provide a critical check to make sure that aid goes to the right students. These financial aid officers are actually some of your strongest allies in receiving financial aid. So while the first phase of financial aid (filling out the forms and calculating your Expected Family Contribution) can seem very inflexible, the second phase of financial aid is all human and in certain instances is very flexible.

## The Financial Aid Cornucopia

The first step to getting your hands on financial aid is to understand what it is. Basically, you may receive any combination of the following types of money. As you read the short description of each, you will see that some forms of aid are better than others.

**Grants/Scholarships:** Money with no strings attached—meaning you don't have to pay it back. This is really the equivalent of hitting the financial aid jackpot. Grants are sometimes called scholarships, and often these terms are used interchangeably. The major grant program from the federal government is the Pell Grant. However, each state and college may also have its own grant programs.

**Loans:** Money you borrow and are required to pay back with interest. In most cases the terms are more generous than other types of loans such as home equity loans. For example, the Direct student loan program does not require that you start to repay your loan until after you graduate. Also, if you qualify for the "subsidized" Direct loan program, the federal government will pay the interest that you owe while you are in college. It's basically an interest-free loan until after you graduate. There are also loans for parents such as the PLUS. Don't discount loans just because they are borrowed money. A low-interest student loan may be just what you need to make up for any shortfall in your ability to pay for tuition.

**Work-Study:** Money you earn the old-fashioned way—by working. But work-study is not your typical part-time job. The government subsidizes your pay so that you earn more and can qualify for choice part-time jobs on campus that students who don't have work-study cannot get. Work-study jobs are often in places like the library or student center and offer good wages along with flexible hours that can accommodate your schedule as a student.

Most financial aid packages are a combination of the above. But as you can see, some forms of financial aid (such as grants) are much more desirable than others (such as loans). When it comes to deciding what your specific package will look like, each college's financial aid officer will make the decision based on rules and guidelines as well as how much money they have to give.

## Five Steps to Getting Financial Aid

We are going to break down the financial aid process into five easy steps. We will also give you a little inside information on how each step of the process works so you can see what factors will affect your outcome. In many ways applying for financial aid is like doing your federal taxes. There are forms to fill out and rules (even loopholes) that can help or hurt your bottom line. Now, we know that no one enjoys filling out a 1040 tax return, but at least in this case there is a good possibility that you will be getting a nice chunk of change back from the government to help you pay for college, so it's certainly worth your time to tackle it.

## Step 1: Fill Out the FAFSA

As with anything from the government, you need to fill out a form. In this case, to be considered for federal financial aid, you will need to complete the Free Application for Federal Student Aid or FAFSA. Most states and many public universities also require this form to be eligible for their aid programs. If you are applying to a private college, you may also have to submit the CSS/PROFILE form, which is similar to the FAFSA. The main difference between the CSS/ PROFILE and FAFSA is not in the data it collects but the formula that is used to determine how much financial aid you deserve. Unfortunately, you don't have a choice in which form the colleges use since they will require either one or both. Also, some colleges have additional forms that you need to fill out.

Since all families should complete the FAFSA (similar to the CSS/PROFILE), let's take a look at it in detail. The FAFSA is a multi-page form that asks for detailed financial information including items from your previous federal income tax return. It's not a difficult form to complete. What is difficult is that you need to collect a lot of information about your income and assets. In fact, the information that you include in your FAFSA should match the numbers on your federal tax return. You may submit the FAFSA to the Department of Education as soon as possible after October 1 of the year before you will be starting or continuing school. If you are a high school student applying to college, this means that after October 1 of your senior year you must submit the FAFSA form. If you are already in college, you must submit the FAFSA each year to continue to receive financial aid.

It's also important that you don't miss the colleges' deadlines—and each school sets its own. Most want you to submit the FAFSA no later than February or March. It is vital that you submit the FAFSA as soon as possible. Financial aid is awarded on a first-come, first-served basis. If you wait until April, it is possible that funds may already be depleted even if you do deserve the help.

There is a big push by the Department of Education, which administers the FAFSA, to get you to fill out the application online. This is not a bad idea since the online form is designed to help prevent errors and give you faster results. You can begin the process by going to the Department of Education's website at www.fafsa.ed.gov. Be sure to download the pre-application worksheets. These will help you collect the information you will need to complete the FAFSA. If you prefer to fill out the FAFSA on paper, get a copy by calling 800-4-FED-AID.

As with all government forms, at first glance the FAFSA may seem intimidating. However, if you spend some time working on it, you'll find that the information is relatively straightforward. To help, here are some tips for completing the form:

> ### The CSS/PROFILE
>
> Many private colleges require the CSS/PROFILE. Think of the CSS/PROFILE as the FAFSA for non-federal financial aid. You will be asked many of the same questions, so get your tax forms out and even your completed FAFSA. Follow the same advice that we have for the FAFSA, and make sure you adhere to the deadlines. The colleges provide the deadlines for the CSS/PROFILE, typically October or November if you have applied to colleges early or February for regular decision. If you are already in college, submit the form as soon as possible, or at the latest, four weeks before the priority filing deadline.

**File the FAFSA as soon as possible after October 1.** This is an important form. Don't procrastinate. Notice how many times we repeat this!

**Follow directions.** The Department of Education reports that delays are caused most often because students or parents don't follow directions when completing the FAFSA. Spend the time to read the directions and follow them completely. If you have questions, don't guess but contact the Federal Student Aid Information Center at 1-800-4-FED-AID.

**Be thorough.** Answer questions completely. Take the time to find the answers to all the information requested.

---

## "I Assumed I Wouldn't Get Aid, but I Was Wrong"
### Jeffrey Newell, College Student

Before my freshman year I spent an entire weekend dutifully completing all the financial aid forms. After spending all that time on the forms, I thought that I would get a sweet financial aid package. My family certainly wasn't at the poverty level, but it wasn't unheard of for students in similar financial situations as mine to get some significant grants.

I was pretty disappointed that after spending all that time gathering financial information and my family's tax return, I only received a medium-size loan. Because my parents were doing okay financially—they own a travel agency—we decided not to take the loan and to squeeze by on what we had.

After my experience in my first year, I decided not to apply for financial aid for my sophomore or junior years. I assumed that I would only be offered a loan anyway, so why waste my time? During those couple of years, business

for my parents went up and down as usual depending on how much people wanted to travel.

Before my senior year, one of my roommates asked how I was doing with my financial aid applications. I said that I don't usually apply. He was shocked and told me I should apply. After some badgering, I obliged and applied just to get him to stop bugging me.

I didn't see a whole lot of difference in my family's financial situation between my senior year in high school and my most recent, but I received an offer for a loan and a grant. A grant? That's money I don't have to repay. After getting the grant, I realized I should have taken the time to apply before. Even though my family's financial situation didn't change dramatically over the years, it changed enough to make the difference between a loan and grant. What I learned: Apply even if you don't think you should.

**Realize that the FAFSA takes time.** Set aside half a day to gather the information and complete the form. Don't think that you can complete it during the commercials of a YouTube video.

**Save time with the Renewal FAFSA.** If you've applied for federal financial aid before, you can usually use the Renewal FAFSA. This form saves you time because many of the blanks are pre-filled with data from the prior year. Ask your school counselor or an employee of the financial aid office for more information.

**If you transfer schools, check with your new school to see what forms you should complete.** Your financial aid package does not automatically transfer with you.

> ### What You Can Afford
>
> *The principle behind financial aid is to determine how much you can afford to pay for college. If you can afford less than the cost, then the difference is need. Financial aid tries to meet this need.*

**Don't think you're on your own.** Use the help provided by your school and by the government. The Department of Education has an entire staff of people to assist you with completing the necessary forms and answering your questions about financial aid. Visit their website at www.fafsa.ed.gov and don't hesitate to contact them by phone or email with your questions.

## Step 2: Review Your Student Aid Report

After you submit the FAFSA, you will need to wait patiently as the Department of Education computers crunch the numbers to determine your Expected Family Contribution. If you submitted the CSS/PROFILE, the computers at the College Board are also furiously working using a slightly different formula. At this stage, the process is completely computational. The same calculations are applied to every student. If you and your friend submitted FAFSAs with identical numbers, the results would be the same for both of you.

The magic number that the computers spit out is your Expected Family Contribution or EFC. This number represents what your family (you and your parents) are expected to contribute toward one year of your education. Whether or not your EFC is accurate is another topic that we will discuss later. But for now let's look at how your EFC is determined:

$$\begin{aligned} &\text{Parent income } \mathbf{X} \text{ up to } 47\% + \\ &\text{Parent assets } \mathbf{X} \text{ up to } 5.65\% + \\ &\text{Student income } \mathbf{X} \text{ } 50\% + \\ &\underline{\text{Student assets } \mathbf{X} \text{ } 20\% =} \\ &\text{Expected Family Contribution} \end{aligned}$$

Now don't have a heart attack. Not all your income or assets are subject to the 47 percent and 5.65 percent assessment rate. There are both income and asset protections that effectively shelter some of your money. Plus, depending on your income, the assessment rate may not be the full 47 percent or 5.65 percent. In fact, the lower your income and assets, the lower your assessment rate.

The best way to get an estimate of what your Expected Family Contribution will be is to use a free online EFC calculator. These calculators let you enter some numbers and quickly get an estimate of your Expected Family Contribution. The College Board's website has a free calculator at http://www.collegeboard.com. You can also adjust the numbers to see how changes in your income and assets affect your EFC.

A few days after you submit the FAFSA, you will receive the Student Aid Report (SAR) from the Department of Education. The SAR includes a summary of the information that you submitted in the FAFSA and shows your Estimated Family Contribution (EFC). Carefully review your SAR. If there are any mistakes, you need to correct them immediately.

## Step 3: Make the College Aware of Special Circumstances, if Necessary

You are not the only one who receives the information in the SAR. Each college that you apply to or the college that you attend will also receive this information along with your Expected Family Contribution. There, the financial aid officer takes this information and uses it to determine your financial need. Determining financial need is fairly easy. All the financial aid officer does is subtract the Cost Of Attendance (COA) from your Expected Family Contribution (EFC).

**Cost Of Attendance –**
**Expected Family Contribution =**
**Financial Need**

The Cost Of Attendance (COA) is the cost of attending your college or university for one year. These costs include the following: tuition and other fees, room and board, transportation between your home and the college, books and other supplies and estimated personal expenses.

Let's take a look at an example:

*You have completed the FAFSA. You have also received your SAR that reports an EFC of $8,000.*

*This means that you and your parents are expected to contribute $8,000 to pay for next year's college expenses. If the college costs $7,000 per year, then you would not receive any financial aid since it's assumed that you can afford it. Remember that your EFC is $8,000 so your family is expected to contribute $8,000, which is more than the cost of attending the college. However, if another college costs $20,000 then you would expect to receive an aid package of $12,000. In other words, at the first college you are not considered to have financial need but at the second college you have a financial need of $12,000.*

> ### No Harm in Asking
>
> There is no guarantee that your school will be able to adjust your financial aid package, but it doesn't hurt to ask. Write a brief letter that contains the most important points about the change in your family's economic situation. Be ready to provide additional information if asked.

It's at this point in the process when the computers stop and the humans take over, that any special circumstances may be considered. Financial aid officers at the colleges have the ability to raise or lower the EFC for a variety of reasons. Therefore, it is crucial that you are open about your family's true financial situation to the financial aid officer. Remember too that all financial aid is based on the prior-prior year's taxes. A lot may have happened this or the previous year that is not reflected by the prior-prior year's tax return. If you want to share additional information, send a letter to the college financial aid office to explain any unusual circumstances that may affect your family's finances. Most colleges include a space on their financial aid forms for you to describe any relevant information such as this. When you are thinking about writing this letter, consider these three points:

**Don't hide the financial dirty laundry.** Many parents feel compelled to hide embarrassing circumstances when filling out financial forms. After all, you are revealing financial strengths and weaknesses to a total stranger. However, if there are special circumstances such as large medical bills, current or impending unemployment, recent or ongoing divorce, siblings attending private elementary or high schools or any additional expenses that may not be reflected in the FAFSA or CSS/PROFILE, tell the financial aid officer. Don't be embarrassed. It could cost you big time.

**Give the college a reason to give more money.** Financial aid officers are numbers people. However, they have wide latitude for interpreting numbers and can apply a variety of standards. They can make exceptions, which can help or hurt your case. To get the most support from these professionals, make a case with numbers. Don't just say that you don't have enough money–show it. Document with numbers why your tax forms don't accurately reflect your true income or expenses.

**Don't ever try to trick the college.** The human being in the financial aid process is also what keeps it safe from trickery. You could, for example, take all the money in your savings account and plunk it down to buy an around-the-world vacation. On paper you'd have no savings. Yet, when the financial aid officer looks at your income, he or she will think it is very odd that someone who earns a decent living and owns a nice house is so cash poor. Not only would the financial aid officer not give you more financial aid, but you would also have depleted your savings.

## Step 4: Compare Award Letters

Every college tries to create a financial aid package that meets your needs using a combination of grants, loans and work-study. However, not every school is able to do this. Some colleges with limited resources may only be able to offer a financial aid package that covers a portion of your entire financial need.

If you are a high school senior, you will typically receive your award letter with your decision letter. The financial aid award letter details how much and what type of financial aid you are being offered. It's not necessary to accept or reject the whole package. You are free to pick and choose. For example, definitely accept any grants or scholarships, but carefully consider loans or work-study.

You should also compare award letters. While one college may cost twice as much as another, you may find that it is also willing to give twice the financial aid. In that case, the actual costs of the two colleges may be the same.

What's most important is what you'll pay out of pocket and how much you'll need to borrow. Compare this among the colleges, not their sticker prices.

### Asking for a Second Opinion

*Asking for a re-evaluation is based on the fact that your current financial situation is not always accurate when looking at only the numbers. There are a lot of other factors that may be important for the college to know.*

## Step 5: If You Need It, Ask for a Re-evaluation

If you feel that the amount of financial aid you are offered by a college is simply not enough, ask for a re-evaluation. To be effective, provide the financial aid office with concrete reasons why their initial assessment was wrong. Start with a letter or call to the financial aid office. Be sure to have all your documents ready, and remember that the squeaky wheel often gets the grease. If you don't say anything about the package, the college will assume that you are happy with it.

If you do ask for a reassessment, don't make the mistake of approaching it like you would buying a car where you haggle with a salesperson over the cost of floor mats and how much below the sticker price you will pay. Financial aid officers are really on your side and they do want to give you every penny that you deserve. However, to make it feasible for them to do so, you need to make a strong (and documented) case for why their initial evaluation was flawed.

Good reasons to ask for a reassessment include the following:

- Unusual medical expenses
- Tuition for a sibling including private secondary or elementary school
- Unemployment of a spouse or parent
- Ongoing divorce or separation
- Care for an aging relative

There is one other situation that may warrant a reassessment. If one college offers you significantly more than your first choice college, it may be possible to use that to get a better package. For example, if you are accepted to College A and College B, but College B offers a more generous financial aid package, you could try to work with College A to raise or match College B's package. First, write a letter to College A, stating that you would like very much to attend the college but that you may not be able to because of the financial aid package offered. Outline in quick bullet points the financial aid package offered by College B. Provide brief reasons why you need a package like that to be offered by College A. Reiterate that you would prefer to attend College A and would like to know if there is anything the financial aid office can do to increase the package. Follow up with a phone call. This does not always work, and some colleges have a strict policy of not matching award offers of other colleges. However, some colleges have the means to be more flexible and just might raise their initial offer.

It's always important to be proactive when it comes to financial aid. If at any point during your time in college your financial circumstances change significantly, contact your school's financial aid office. We recommend first writing a letter that outlines your special circumstances in quick, easy-to-understand bullet points. The financial aid officer will then have all the information he or she needs to reassess your financial situation. Follow up with a telephone call to check on any additional information and on the status of your inquiry.

## A Re-evaluation Success Story

If you find it hard to believe that a single letter can result in a larger financial aid package, here is the proof. The following is a letter one student wrote to the Harvard financial aid office while she was a student there. Before writing the letter, she had received only a small loan from Harvard despite the fact that her father had been laid off for over a year. The student composed this letter to explain her family's extenuating circumstances, describing their actual income and expenses. Her letter paid off—she got a $8,500 grant for each semester that she had left in school!

## Reassessment Letter to Harvard

Dear Sir or Madam:

I am writing to request that my financial aid package for the fall semester be reconsidered. My family and I were disappointed with the amount we were offered because in addition to my father having been unemployed for over a year, my older sister will be a sophomore in college, and my mother, a part-time teacher, has received no income since June because of summer break.

We understand that nearly every family must undergo an amount of hardship to send its members to college. However, because my parents wish to continue financing my sister's and my education, they are worried about how they will pay for their own expenses. They have been using my mother's income to basically cover their mortgage payments and their savings to pay for everything else. In February, my parents had $38,000 in savings. In the last six months, their savings has decreased by about $20,000. They now have $18,000 to contribute to my sister's and my college expenses as well as to spend on their and my younger brother's food and basic necessities. They don't know how long their savings will last without a change in the amount of aid I will receive.

At the end of this month, my sister will begin her sophomore year at USC. The cost will be $77,459, and she has received $53,901 in financial aid. This makes my parents' contribution amount to $23,558, of which they will borrow half. One of the things you might be able to address is why my sister's financial aid package was dramatically higher than mine.

Since July of last year my father has been unemployed. His severance pay ended in October, and his unemployment benefits have been depleted since February. Although he has applied for over a dozen positions, his prospects for finding a job in his specialty are slim.

My parents and I have discussed the possibility of having me take a year off so that I may work to help pay for tuition, but we'd much rather that I finish school now and work after I have received my degree.

Please contact my parents or me with any further questions you may have. Thank you very much for your time and consideration. I hope that this information is helpful in your review of my application.

Sincerely Yours,

There's no guarantee that a letter like this will work, but if your family's situation changes, get in touch with your financial aid office immediately.

## Exchanging One Kind of Money for Another

In an ideal world, you would receive a financial aid package from the school, and any external scholarships you won would be a bonus on top of the package. Unfortunately, most colleges deduct the amount of scholarships that you win from the financial aid package. We believe that this is a huge disservice to students, diminishing the appeal of scholarships.

Fortunately, this trend is not universal and is showing signs of changing. By taking a proactive stance, you can help accelerate this change. If you find yourself in this situation, contact the financial aid office first. Explain that you applied for the scholarships because you needed money in addition to your financial aid package. If they haven't already, ask if they will reduce your student contribution or loans instead of reducing the amount of your grants.

Another course of action is to contact the organization that awarded the scholarship. If they are aware of this problem, some organizations won't award scholarships to students whose colleges reduce their aid package. If you can get the organization to write a letter of support or to provide a copy of its policy, you have a good chance of getting your college to reassess the reduction of your financial aid.

If this does happen and the college will not help you, at the very least let the college know that you are disappointed with their policy and hope that it will change. Also, it is better for you to receive financial aid in the form of scholarships, which you do not need to repay, than nearly any other form of financial aid. Plus, since financial aid budgets and demand vary each year, you may not receive the same amount in financial aid next year. If you have a renewable scholarship, at least you can count on it for all four years.

## Declaring Independence

Some students mistakenly believe that if they declare independence from their parents, they will get more

> ### Acronym Review
>
> *In case the acronyms are a bit confusing, here's a quick review. You submit the Free Application for Federal Student Aid (FAFSA) to the government. In return, you get the Student Aid Report (SAR), which determines your Estimated Family Contribution (EFC). The EFC is used by your school to develop a financial aid package.*

financial aid. Unfortunately, declaring independence for the purposes of financial aid is based on strict guidelines. In most cases, you are considered dependent on your parents, and their income and assets are considered in financial aid. You're considered to be independent if one of the following is true:

- You will be 24 or older by December 31 of the award year.
- You're married.
- You're enrolled in a graduate or professional degree program.
- You have legal dependents other than a spouse.
- You're an orphan or ward of the court.
- You were determined to be homeless.
- You are currently serving on active duty in the U.S. armed forces for purposes other than training.
- You're a veteran of the U.S. Armed Forces.

If you are independent, only you and your spouse's (if you have one) income and assets will be considered. Some parents don't support their children or provide funds toward their college expenses, even though according to the above guidelines they are still considered dependent. If this is your situation, it is vitally important that you include a detailed letter explaining this to the financial aid office.

## Strategies That Can Help You Get More Financial Aid

Just like with tax planning, good financial aid planning can help you qualify for more financial aid. Just remember that financial aid is always based on the prior, prior year's taxes, which means that any actions you take must be done two years in advance.

The following are generalized strategies that may not be appropriate for your individual situation. These are not hard and fast rules since what might be good for one family may be unworkable for another. Before taking any action, speak with an accountant. Note that these suggestions are directed to both you and your parents.

**Limit your child's assets.** Looking at the calculation that determines the Expected Family Contribution, you can see that if you put money into a child's name, it will be assessed by 20 percent. But if you keep the money in your name it will only be assessed by up to 5.65 percent. For every $100 in the student's name, you will be expected to spend $20 to pay for college. However, for every $100 in your name, you will be expected to spend only $5.65. That's a big difference. Any money that is in your child's bank account is considered your child's asset. If a relative would like to give a gift of cash or stock to your child, ask if he or she is willing to either give it to you or wait until your child graduates from college. Or your generous relative could make the gift directly to your child's 529 Savings Plan.

Putting money in your child's name is generally a bad idea when it comes to financial aid. Of course, there may be some good tax reasons for doing this, especially if you know that you won't qualify for financial aid. Balance the desire to save on taxes with the effect that putting money into a child's name will have on financial aid. It's important to speak with an accountant about the benefits of this strategy so that your specific situation is considered.

> ### No Credit, No Problem
>
> *One advantage of federal student loans is that they are guaranteed by the federal government. This means even if you have no credit history you can still qualify for a student loan.*

**Spend UGMA funds two years before your child graduates.** Let's say that you have put some money into a custodial account for your child. Why not spend this money while your child is still in high school instead of leaving it to be counted against your financial need? Now if you go crazy and spend it on luxuries, then this won't help. However, let's say that when your child turns 16 and gets his or her driver's license, you plan to buy a used car. Instead of using your own money, let your child use his or her custodial account. As long as you don't spend more than you normally would and buy a BMW instead of a Corolla, then you'll put your child in a better position to receive more financial aid. If you plan to do this, make sure to withdraw whatever amount of money that you plan to spend before January 1 of your student's sophomore year. Always keep in mind that financial aid is based on the prior, prior year's tax returns, which for the typical student who enters college in the fall will cover January 1 of the sophomore year through December 31 of the junior year.

**Consider deferring bonuses and raises.** Imagine this scenario. It's November 2020 and your child is graduating from high school and starting college in the fall of 2021. Your boss tells you that you will get a bonus or significant raise. If you take the bonus now, then that money will be used when determining your child's financial aid package for the 2022-2023 school year. Remember that financial aid is always based on the prior, prior tax year. If you delay taking the bonus for two months until January 2021, then that money will not be used in your child's student financial aid calculations until he or she applies for financial aid for the third year of college. But since you will have spent some (maybe even a significant amount) to pay for the first year, you will have fewer assets that will be counted toward the third year of college. This also buys time to save since you know that the bonus or increase in salary will reduce your financial aid in the third year.

Before you utilize this strategy, be sure that you are going to get financial aid in the first place. Run your numbers through one of the free EFC calculators. Also consider other factors. Will your boss still be in the mood to give you a bonus next year? Sometimes it's better to just take the money. This tactic would be much more lucrative if your child were entering his or her senior year in college in 2022. Deferring your raise or bonus in this situation would mean that it would not be counted at all during your child's education.

**Consider alternative forms of bonuses.** If you have the flexibility, it may make sense to take your bonus or even a pay raise in some other form than cash. For example, instead of taking a raise, you might swap one day a week of working from home which would lower childcare costs. Or you might convert your bonus from a cash payment to training or classes that you were planning to pay for yourself. A bonus or raise that does not show up as income will not be subjected to financial aid consideration. However, carefully weigh the costs of forgoing a cash bonus or raise. If you can use the money to pay down credit card debt (with its high interest rate), for example, you are probably much better off doing that.

**Time stock sales.** When you sell a stock can have an impact on financial aid. Let's say you have a stock that has appreciated by $10,000. If you sell the stock after January 1 of your child's sophomore year in high school, the earnings are considered income for the first year of college and will be assessed at up to 47 percent. From the $10,000 gain, as much as $4,700 can be counted by the financial aid formula as going to pay for college. But let's say that instead you sell the stock before January 1 of your child's sophomore year. The proceeds will not be counted as income but instead show up as an asset. As a parental asset, this money can only be assessed at a rate up to 5.65 percent, which means only $565 is considered as available to pay for college.

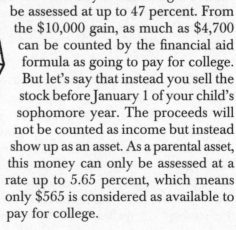

**Build your 401K or IRA accounts.** Under both the federal and institutional methodologies, your retirement accounts are not considered assets that can be used to pay for college. Plus, under current tax laws you can withdraw money from these accounts and use them to pay for college without paying a penalty. So don't neglect your retirement as you save for your child's college needs.

**Use 529 Savings Plans and Coverdell Educational Savings Accounts to build a college nest egg tax free.** Both 529 Savings Plans and Coverdell ESAs allow you to invest money without paying taxes on the gain as long as it is used for educational expenses. As a bonus, both of these accounts are considered assets of the parent(s), which means that they have minimal impact on financial aid. Don't neglect these two savings vehicles for building tax-free college savings.

## A Quick Word about Saving for College

While this chapter focuses on financial aid, we cannot stress enough how important it is for you to have a strong savings plan. Your personal savings is your best ally when it comes to paying for college. Scholarships will always be competitions with no guarantees that you'll win. Financial aid changes each year, depending on the budgets of the government and college. There is no guarantee—even if you deserve it—that you will receive all the financial aid that you need to pay for school. Plus, since your savings are your money, you have total freedom to use it at whichever college you want. Nothing is as flexible as your own money.

If you want to learn more about saving for college, we recommend *1001 Ways to Pay for College,* which has a whole chapter on how to create a smart savings plan.

## The Federal Financial Aid Programs in Detail

The reward for tackling tax forms and financial aid applications is a package that may consist of federal and state aid. To help you understand what you are offered, here are some descriptions of the possibilities.

We begin with the grants. These are like scholarships in that they represent free cash that does not have to be repaid. Just remember that these are only for a year, and you must reapply each year to continue to receive them.

## Federal Pell Grants

Details: For undergraduate study, with the exception of post-baccalaureate teacher certification programs. You can be enrolled less than half-time. Provides every eligible student with funds.

Based on: Financial need as determined by your Estimated Family Contribution and Cost Of Attendance, full-time or part-time status and length of enrollment.

Amount: Varies based on funding. The maximum amount for the 2019-20 school year is $6,195.

How you get the money: Grant that can be credited to your school account, pay you directly or do a combination of both.

## Federal Supplemental Educational Opportunity Grants (FSEOGs)

Details: Grants for undergraduates with the most financial need, i.e., the lowest Expected Family Contributions. FSEOGs do not need to be repaid. The government provides limited funds for individual schools to administer through this program. This means there is no guarantee that every eligible student will receive an FSEOG.

Based on: Financial need, when you apply and the availability of funds at your school. Priority is given to those who receive Federal Pell Grants.

Amount: $100-$4,000 per year.

How you get the money: The school will credit your account, pay you directly or both.

## Iraq and Afghanistan Service Grant

Details: Grants for students whose parent or guardian died while serving in the U.S. Armed Forces. Students must meet all the qualifications for Federal Pell Grants except for the financial need requirement.

Based on: Full-time or part-time status and length of enrollment.

Amount: $6,195 not to exceed the cost of attendance.

How you get the money: Grant that can be credited to your school account, pay you directly or do a combination of both.

## TEACH Grant Program

Details: Grants for undergraduate, postbaccalaureate or graduate students who plan to become elementary or secondary teachers.

Based on: Applicants must complete the FAFSA, although financial need is not required. Students must also be taking or planning to take teaching courses, score above the 75th percentile on a college admissions test or have a minimum 3.25 GPA and agree to work at a low-income school in a high-need field.

Amount: Up to $4,000 per year.

How you get the money: Grant that can be credited to your school account, pay you directly or do a combination of both.

After the grants, which are really the best types of free cash for college, comes the work-study program.

## Federal Work-Study

Details: Provides jobs for undergraduate and graduate students with financial need, allowing them to earn money while attending school. The focus is on providing work experience in your area of study. Generally, you will work for your school on campus or for a nonprofit organization or public agency if you work off campus. You will have a limit on the hours you can work in this program. The government provides limited funds for individual schools to administer this program.

Based on: Financial need, when you apply and the availability of funds at your school.

Amount: Federal minimum wage or higher.

How you get the money: Paid by the hour if you're an undergraduate. Paid by the hour or a salary if you're a graduate school student.

## Student Loans

The last type of aid is a loan. Did we just hear you groan? Before you think that loans are for the birds, you should know that most students who go to college borrow money to pay for tuition. In addition, the terms for most student loans are extremely favorable and better than almost any other type of consumer loan.

There are two types of loans: Subsidized loans are based on financial need. They are subsidized because the government subsidizes the interest payments so that you are not charged interest until repayment, usually after you graduate. Unsubsidized loans are not based on financial need. You are charged interest from the time the loan is disbursed until it is paid off. However, the interest rates are still usually lower than other types of loans. In one school year, you may have both subsidized and unsubsidized loans.

## Direct Loans

Details: These are low-interest Direct Loans from the federal government to help pay for an education at a four-year college or university, community college or trade, career or technical school. Direct Loans are no longer given by sources other than the government such as banks or credit unions.

Amount: For dependent undergraduate students, you can borrow a maximum of $5,500 (up to $3,500 subsidized) if you're a first-year student in a full academic year program. You may borrow $6,500 (up to $4,500 subsidized) if you have completed your first year of study and are enrolled in a full academic year program or $7,500 (up to $5,500 subsidized) a year if you've completed two years of study and are enrolled in a full academic year program. For independent undergraduate students or dependent students whose parents are not able to get a PLUS loan, you can borrow a maximum of $9,500 if you're a first-year student in a full academic year program ($3,500 of this amount can be subsidized). You may borrow $10,500 if you've completed your first year of study and are enrolled in a full academic year program ($4,500 of this amount can be subsidized) or $12,500 a year if you've completed two years of study and are enrolled in a full academic year program ($5,500 of this amount can be subsidized).

Interest and fees: The interest rate is currently fixed at 5.05 percent for unsubsidized loans and at 5.05 percent for subsidized loans. There is also a fee of 1.059 percent of the loan.

How you get the money: The money will be disbursed to your school by the Department of Education. The money must first be used for tuition, fees and room and board. After these expenses are paid, you will receive the remaining amount by check or cash.

How you repay the money: You will begin to repay your loan after you graduate, leave school or drop below half-time enrollment. You can pay using one of seven methods: the Standard Repayment Plan of a fixed amount per month for up to 10 years; the Extended Repayment Plan, which extends the repayment period to generally between 12 and 25 years; the Graduated Repayment Plan, in which your payments start lower and increase generally every two years; the Revised Pay As You Earn Repayment Plan (REPAYE), in which payments are 10 percent of discretionary income; the Pay As You Earn Repayment Plan (PAYE), in which the maximum monthly payment is 10 percent of discretionary income; the Income Based Repayment Plan, in which monthly payments are 10 or 15 percent of discretionary income; or the Income Contingent Repayment Plan (ICR), in which monthly payments are the lesser of 20 percent of discretionary income or the amount you would pay with a fixed payment over 12 years. For more details and a repayment estimator to compare plans, visit https://studentaid.gov/manage-loans/repayment/plans.

> ### *Investment in You*
> ---
> *Don't discount a loan right away. Remember that your education is an investment in your future. It's perfectly normal to borrow some money, and why not do so at the lowest interest rate possible?*

In certain situations, you can receive a deferment to temporarily postpone payments on your loan. For subsidized loans, you do not pay interest during the deferment period. For unsubsidized loans, you do. Under certain circumstances you can receive forbearance, a limited and temporary postponement or reduction of your payments, if you are unable to meet your repayment schedule and are not eligible for a deferment. These circumstances may include poor health, serving in a medical or dental internship or residency or if the payments exceed 20 percent of your monthly gross income. For both subsidized and unsubsidized loans, you pay interest during the forbearance period. Deferments and forbearance must be approved by the Direct Loan Servicing Center. More information is available at https://studentaid.ed.gov/sa/.

## PLUS Loans for Graduate and Professional Degrees

<u>Details</u>: Loans for graduate and professional degree students that are not based on financial need.

<u>Amount</u>: The maximum is the Cost of Attendance minus other financial aid in the Direct Loan program.

<u>Other details</u>: The interest and fees and how you get the money is the same as the PLUS Loans below.

## PLUS Loans

<u>Details</u>: Loans for parents with good credit histories to pay for their dependent undergraduate students' educations. Available through the Direct PLUS Loan. This program is available for parents of undergraduate students who are enrolled at least half time. FFEL PLUS Loans available through banks and private lenders are no longer available.

<u>Based on</u>: These loans are not based on financial need.

<u>Amount</u>: The maximum is the Cost of Attendance minus any other financial aid you receive. For example, if your Cost of Attendance is $10,000 and you receive $6,000 in financial aid, the maximum amount your parents can borrow is $4,000.

<u>Interest and fees</u>: The interest rate is fixed at 7.08 percent. There is also a fee of 4.236 percent of the loan.

<u>How you get the money</u>: The money will be disbursed to your school by the Department of Education. The money must first be used for tuition, fees and room and board. After these expenses are paid, your parents will receive the remaining amount by check or cash.

<u>How you repay the money</u>: Repayment begins within 60 days after the first loan disbursement, and interest starts to accumulate from the first disbursement.

You can pay using one of three methods: the Standard Repayment Plan of a fixed amount per month; the Extended Repayment Plan, which extends the repayment period; or the Graduated Repayment Plan, in which your payments start lower and increase every two years.

In specific situations, you can receive a deferment to temporarily postpone payments on your loan or forbearance, a limited and temporary postponement or reduction of your payments if you are unable to meet your repayment schedule and are not eligible for a deferment.

## Consolidation Loans

<u>Details</u>: Allows students and parents to consolidate a number of federal financial aid loans into a single loan to simplify repayment. This allows the borrowers to make one payment per month and in

some cases obtain a lower interest rate. All the federal loans described in this chapter can be consolidated. Contact the Loan Origination Center's Consolidation Department at 800-557-7394 or visit https://studentaid. gov/app/launchConsolidation.action.

Direct Consolidation Loans are provided by the U.S. Department of Education. They can be one of three types: Direct Subsidized Consolidation Loans, Direct Unsubsidized Consolidation Loans or Direct PLUS Consolidation Loans.

Eligibility: You can get a Consolidated Loan once you've started repayment or during deferment or forbearance. If you are in school, you can apply for a Direct Consolidation Loan if you are attending at least half time and have at least one Direct Loan or FFEL Loan in an in-school period. You may be eligible for a Consolidated Loan if you are in default on a Direct Loan.

Interest and fees: The interest rate is fixed throughout the repayment period and is the weighted average of the loans being consolidated.

## Getting More Help

In this chapter, we have given you a basic understanding of how the financial aid process works and what you need to do to apply. For information on state programs, contact your state's higher education agency, which is listed in the directory. Also, consider our book, *1001 Ways to Pay for College,* since it includes additional material on financial aid, tax advantages and long-term college savings programs. You can also get help with applying for federal financial aid by contacting the Federal Student Aid Information Center at the following address:

Federal Student Aid Information Center
P.O. Box 84
Washington, DC 20044-0084
800-4-FED-AID

## Chapter 15 Summary: Financial Aid Workshop

**Each year more than $241.3 billion in financial aid is awarded.** Your mission is to make sure some of that money comes to you. Unlike scholarships in which you need to compete for the funds, in most cases, if you qualify for federal financial aid, you will receive it. Your responsibility is to learn about the different options open to you and to apply.

**There are three types of financial aid:** Grants, which do not need to be repaid; loans, which allow you to borrow money and must be repaid; and work-study, which allows you to work at a part-time job while attending school.

**Qualifying for federal financial aid.** You need to have financial need, which is determined by the cost of attending your college (Cost of Attendance) and the amount that the government determines your family can contribute toward your education (Estimated Family Contribution). There are additional requirements including: graduating from high school, working toward an eligible degree program and being a U.S. citizen, U.S. national or U.S. permanent resident.

**To apply, you must complete the Free Application for Federal Student Aid (FAFSA) and/or the** CSS/PROFILE. Do this online or with old-fashioned paper.

**After the FAFSA.** You will receive a Student Aid Report (SAR) from the government which determines your Estimated Family Contribution (EFC), or the amount that your family is expected to contribute. Your school's financial aid office will develop a financial aid package using this information that may be a combination of scholarships, loans, grants or work-study.

**The scholarship dollars you win may affect your financial aid package.** They reduce your Cost of Attendance. Realize that this may not be bad if your package is composed of more scholarship dollars, which do not need to be repaid, and less loan dollars, which, of course, need to be repaid.

**There may be flexibility.** Once you've received the financial aid package from your college, especially if there are extenuating circumstances such as medical or dental expenses, tuition for a sibling or a change in your parents' employment situation, things can still change. In some cases, there is also flexibility when you are deciding between two colleges with differences in their financial aid packages.

# Free Cash for Graduate School

In this chapter, you'll learn:

- **How to adjust your strategy to win graduate financial aid**

- **Why not all graduate aid is equal**

- **Step-by-step strategies for completing fellowshlp and grant proposals**

- **Tips for acing the interviews**

- **How to keep the money you've won**

# The Long and Expensive Path of Graduate School

Typically spanning two to eight years, graduate school can be a long and arduous path. With the stresses of dissertations, oral exams, board exams, research and the quest to publish, the less you need to worry about paying for your education the better. While grad student life is hardly equated with luxury, there are a lot of financial aid resources available from graduate schools, the government and private organizations. The challenge is to find these resources, and because they are limited, make your work in your particular field stand out so that you get some of this aid.

Your approach to graduate financial aid will be different than it was to undergraduate financial aid. While undergraduate scholarships are often based on involvement in activities, leadership or special skills, the majority of graduate scholarships and fellowships are based primarily on academics and research. Crafting your applications for graduate school aid requires its own set of unique strategies.

Another difference is that the community of applicants and judges is often smaller in graduate studies. Graduate students who apply will have more similar backgrounds than undergraduate students. This means that you will need to be particularly strategic about how to set your application apart from those of other students. Because you know that the selection committee will probably be professors or other specialists in your field of study, you need to craft your application materials to impress this very demanding crowd.

The strategies in this chapter are specifically designed for graduate school scholarships and fellowships. Hopefully we can help ease the stress of at least one aspect of graduate school life. As for the dissertation, we're sorry—you're on your own.

## The Big Picture

As you go from undergraduate to graduate school, the intensity of academics increases. The same holds true for financial aid. For graduate school, financial aid is not based on leadership or extracurricular activities. Research and academics count most.

Our approach to graduate financial aid is to focus on demonstrating your long-term commitment to academics and research. Judges are no longer casual members of clubs or volunteers. They are the small circle of leaders in your future career field—professors, deans and academic institutional heads. To win you must show them the intensity of your passion for your field and your ability to contribute to its advancement. You must demonstrate your ability to think critically and innovatively.

# Understanding Graduate Financial Aid

The first step to getting graduate school financial aid is to learn about all the options that are available to you. There are several forms of financial aid, each with its own requirements and benefits. Here is a brief overview:

**Scholarships:** Often given by private organizations, scholarships are typically awarded in general fields of study. They are usually open to both undergraduate and graduate students. Scholarships are based on merit, with some based on financial need as well. They do not need to be repaid.

> ### New Approach
>
> *Your approach to graduate financial aid should be different than it was to undergraduate financial aid. The majority of graduate scholarships and fellowships are based primarily on academics and research.*

**Grants:** Unfortunately, only undergraduate students are eligible for Pell Grants or Federal Supplemental Educational Opportunity Grants (FSEOG) from the government under most circumstances. However, there are special federal grants for students entering the health and medical fields from the National Health Services Corps and the Armed Forces.

In addition, there are various types of research grants for graduate students. Provided by the federal and state governments, graduate schools or private organizations, this form of aid does not need to be repaid. For graduate students, grants often fund a specific project, research study or dissertation. These grants can pay for the costs of materials and sometimes even travel to research centers. They can also provide you with the right to use facilities and libraries to which you might not normally have access.

**Fellowships:** Provided by graduate school departments, private organizations and states, fellowships support graduate and post-graduate studies, research or work placement. They typically fund research or study in a particular area at a specific university. Only open to graduate students, fellowships are based on academic merit, with a minority based on financial need as well. They do not need to be repaid and can fund tuition and/or research expenses, with many providing stipends for living expenses. However, don't expect to start living a life of luxury—the stipends are still not enough to raise you above the poverty line. Some require recipients to work as Teaching or Research Assistants.

**Federal aid:** Funded by the government, federal financial aid includes loans and grants. These are based entirely on financial need. For more information, see Chapter 15, *Financial Aid Workshop*.

**Employment:** Many graduate schools supplement students' education with employment opportunities to research or teach. For some schools, such employment is a requirement to graduate or a part of the financial aid package.

**Loan repayment programs:** Some cities and states offer loan repayment programs. Under these programs graduate students can have their loans repaid by the city or state if they agree to work in specific occupations. Upon graduation from medical school, a state may agree to repay your student loan if you work in an area of the state that needs more doctors. Some cities are encouraging students to become teachers by agreeing to repay their graduate student loans if they work in certain school districts.

## More Than Money

In addition to providing financial relief, scholarships, grants, fellowships and teaching assistantships can assist you in your career and add prestige to your curriculum vitae. As you apply for these programs, you may need to complete an application or make an in-person case to the committee that grants research appointments. In doing this, you gain experience presenting your research proposal and you hone your skills of persuasion, both necessary skills in academia. These financial aid programs also help you build the foundation of your academic reputation and introduce your work to others in your field. You have the prospect of networking with professors and other academics who will be your supporters in the future. Keep these additional opportunities in mind as you apply for graduate financial aid programs.

## It's All about Academics

An emphasis on academics is a chief factor that differentiates graduate school grants, scholarships and fellowships from undergraduate awards. Undergraduate

awards may be based on criteria like leadership, activities, hobbies, talents or athletic ability. Graduate awards, however, are almost entirely based on academics, achievement in a particular field of study and your potential contribution to the future of that field.

Remember this focus on academics when applying for graduate awards. Throughout applications, proposals, essays and interviews, emphasize your contribution to and passion for the academic field spotlighted by the award. Other factors such as leadership and interpersonal skills are important in how they equip you to succeed in the field, but the main emphasis should be on your ability to contribute to the collective knowledge in a specific area.

When applying to graduate programs, check websites and catalogues to find out who the professors are in the department you wish to join. Familiarize yourself with their books and articles and explain how your plans fit with their academic interests. If you are not able to visit a campus, call individual professors to discuss their program and your plans. They will appreciate your attempts to introduce yourself, your knowledge of their work and your efforts to find out more about the department's program.

Concentrate on the mission of financial aid awards. The mission may be simple: to advance a field by supporting those who study it. Or the mission may be more complex, furthering a specific agenda or encouraging study of specific areas. The government, for example, funds the study of certain languages that are considered to be strategically important. Even if you are studying economics in 17th century Russia, you could qualify for a FLAS award since part of your coursework would include the study of the Russian language.

Learn more about an award's mission by reading the literature published by the organization, viewing its website or speaking with the award administrator. A great way to see the group's mission in action is to find out information about previous winners. Ask the organization for a list of these students. If you are already in graduate school, there are probably some winners in your department who are a few years ahead of you. Contact them to find out details about their background, their approach to applying and any helpful hints they can provide about the award's selection.

By understanding the mission of the award and the awarding organization, you will know how well you fit with what it is trying to achieve. You will also be able to shape the application, proposal, essay and interview to reflect the mission of the award, making you a stronger candidate in the eyes of the selection committee.

## Applications: Your Stats Sheet

Applications are like baseball cards. Flip over a baseball card and you'll find the most important statistics about the player such as his batting averages and home runs. Similarly, applications are the place for the most important statistics about your achievements. Selection committees use them as a quick way to learn the key facts about you. Because you are vying to be noticed and working with both the limited space provided and the limited attention span of selection committees, follow these strategies to make the most of your applications:

**Make application triplets.** Before starting, if you only have one copy of the application, make at least three copies of it. Use one for practice to make sure the most important information you need to convey fits in the space given. Keep the others in case you make an egregious error and need to start over, something that will most likely happen at 3 a.m. the day the application is due. Of course if

> **Applications Are Building Blocks**
>
> *Use applications as building blocks to construct a case for why you should win the award. Present information that demonstrates your academic commitment and achievements.*

you printed the application off of the Internet or will complete the application online, this is not an issue.

**Build a case for how you fit the mission of the award.** Always keep the mission of the award at the forefront of your thinking so that you can provide evidence and examples of how you fulfill it. If the award's objective is to support students who show promise in your academic field, highlight your classes, awards and accomplishments in that area.

**Know your audience.** Try to find out as much information as you can about the selection committee. You will complete an application differently if the selection committee is composed of professors in your department than if it is made up of employers at a biomedical company trying to build relationships for future recruitment. For a selection committee of professors, focus on research, teaching and publishing. On the other hand, for employers at a biomedical company, highlight how your research has commercial applications as well as related work experience. By knowing your audience, you can shape your application accordingly.

**Focus on your key achievements.** With the limited space applications provide, concentrate on only the most important information. Prioritize information that shows direct contributions or achievements in your field, including classes, awards, lectures given, teaching experience, published works, abstracts, current unpublished projects and related work experience. Give secondary priority to information that demonstrates skills that are not direct achievements but that are still important to the field.

**Neatness counts.** Remember that a sloppy application conveys that you don't take the award seriously. Committee members may also think that if you are careless in completing your application, you may be equally careless in your studies. Neither of these are impressions that you want to make. If the error is noticeable enough, use the extra copy you made of your application and start over. It will take extra time, but it's worth it.

**Make copies after completion.** Take a photo or save an electronic copy of your application for your records. The next time you are completing an application, you can use the copy as a cheat sheet which will save you valuable hours in reassembling your information since you've already prioritized and written descriptions of your accomplishments.

**Check to make sure you have everything gathered together.** Before submitting or mailing your applications, ensure that you have included everything. You can be disqualified for missing a single piece.

For more information on applications, refer to Chapter 7, *Create Stunning Scholarship Applications.*

## Recommendations: Getting Professorial Praise

Throughout your applications you have the opportunity to praise yourself and your accomplishments in glowing words of admiration. Recommendations offer professors and others the opportunity to do the same and to confirm that you are as great as you say you are. To get the most powerful recommendations possible, follow these strategies for selecting and preparing your recommenders:

**Be strategic about whom you ask.** The most important principle for selecting recommenders is how well they know you. You may have received the highest grade in class, but if your professor couldn't pick you out from a crowd, he or she is not the best person to ask. Select those with whom you've worked closely and who can speak meaningfully about your abilities. An equally important measure is the ability of the recommender to vouch for your talent and achievements in the academic field. Choose professors and others who can describe first-hand how competent you are in your studies. If you are new to graduate work, don't hesitate to ask your former undergraduate professors to write a recommendation. This is perfectly acceptable.

**Do the grunt work for your recommenders.** To make writing recommendations easier, provide all the background information and forms they need for the task:

> **Cover letter:** A brief letter describing the awards you are applying for, their deadlines and helpful reminders of information they may want to include in the recommendations.

> **Curriculum vitae:** A concise overview of your academic honors, coursework and achievements.

> **Recommendation paperwork:** Any forms that your recommenders need to complete with blanks for your personal information pre-filled by you.

Give this information to your recommenders so that they have everything they need to get started.

**Finally, write a thank you note for their help.** Even though writing recommendations is a part of the job for professors, recognize that they have taken time from their busy schedules to help you.

For more recommendation strategies, see Chapter 9, *Get the Right Recommendations.*

## Essays: Getting Personal

### Focus on the Essay

*Selection committees use essays to learn more about you on a personal and professional level beyond the straight facts of your application. Use the essay to explain your motivations and goals and how you view your field of study. Essays are your best opportunity to set your application apart from the others.*

If the application is your formal introduction to the selection committee, then the essay is the part of the conversation in which you get more personal. You can use the essay to describe in more detail your academic interests, goals and contributions. Because essays allow you to share more of yourself beyond the application form, they offer your best opportunity to set your application apart from those of other applicants. The following strategies will help you create an essay with impact:

**Focus on the progress you have made in your field.** The best essay is one that gets the selection committee excited about your work and makes them want to fund your education so that you can complete it. Tempt them with what you have done, reveal some early results even if they are only preliminary or describe the plans for your future research. Give the selection committee a tantalizing view into what you are learning. Take advantage of knowing who is on the committee and what their interests are.

**Give them something they can't get anywhere else.** Don't just restate what is written in your application or curriculum vitae. If you do this, you will simply waste space. Essays should provide information and insight about you that is not included in the applications.

**Get personal.** Reveal something about yourself. What motivated you to choose this area of study? What do you feel is the most exciting thing about your field? Who has been a mentor for you? What do you hope to accomplish after you get your degree? Answering a question like one of these will give the selection committee insight into your thoughts and help to distinguish you beyond your achievements.

**Know and understand your audience.** Adjust your message and level of formality based on who will read your work. Your essay should be more formal and academic in nature if the intended audience is composed of professors than if it is made up of community leaders. As you write, think about who will read your essay.

**Get editors.** Don't rely on yourself for the entire direction of your essays. Professors, colleagues and family members make great editors. They can offer suggestions for improvement, expand on ideas you have and make sure you don't have any mistakes. They may even remember something great that you forgot to mention in your essay. The more help you can get from others, the better your essays will be.

**Be creative.** When it comes to describing your coursework and achievements in the application, there isn't much room for creativity. Not so for essays. Be as ingenious as you can, as long as it is appropriate. Use anecdotes, dialogue and action to make your essay come alive. If appropriate, discuss your unique approach or how you got started in the field. Use illustrations to show that you have the skills needed or to reflect your dedication to your studies. After reading many essays that are alike, the selection committee will appreciate one that takes chances with a little creativity. If you are worried about being too imaginative, ask a professor for feedback.

**Address intellectual issues.** Graduate school is a world unto itself. The setting is different from undergraduate school in that specialists devote themselves to technical and intellectual issues in a chosen field. Demonstrate your knowledge of these issues and your ability to discuss the latest developments. You don't need to be long-winded about this—be brief, concise and to the point, just like research—but remember that it is important to let your readers know that you understand the field in which you, too, will become a specialist.

**Be yourself.** Most important, make sure that your essay echoes who you really are. Only write what is comfortable for you. In trying to make your essay different from the others, don't do so by adopting an alter ego. Be yourself and use your accomplishments in the field to make you stand out.

Refer to Chapter 10, *Secrets to Writing Winning Essays*, for more help with essays.

## Research Grant Proposals: Application Heavies

If scholarship essays are the featherweights of graduate financial aid, grant proposals are the heavyweights. Unlike normal scholarship essays, research grant proposals require outlining specific academic objectives and implementation plans. Provided by the government, graduate schools and private organizations, most graduate grants award aid for a specific project, study or dissertation. Because the awarding organizations have limited funds, their objective is to get the most academic mileage out of the least amount of money. When applying for grants, follow the strategies for essays above, but keep these additional points in mind:

**How will your research benefit the field?** Awarding grants is not a selfless task. The committee wants the bragging rights for backing research that advances the field. To fulfill this need, explain the potential signifi-

> *Be Detailed in Your Proposal*
>
> *Research grant proposals require more details than regular essays. Impress the selection committee by showing them that you've thought through all the steps and potential obstacles to successfully complete the project.*

cance of your research on the field. Show why your research is meaningful. Include specific applications of your research if they are not immediately apparent.

**What is your plan of action?** It's important to convey that you have goals for your research, but it's equally important to explain how you're going to get there. An essential component of a grant proposal is an outline of your plan of action. Include measurable objectives, a timeline and budget. Make it clear that you have an organized plan for accomplishing your objectives. Everyone knows that research takes more time than you think and costs more than you budget. Show the committee an aggressive but realistic plan and they will be impressed. It is also important to indicate the limits of your project—what you will not address as well as what you propose to accomplish.

**How does the grant fit with the future you?** The selection committee realizes that few people do research for philanthropic reasons. They want to know what's in it for you, your reasons for being interested in the research and how it fits with your future career plans. Explain how you hope to use what you learn in the future and what your future plans are.

**What specifics can you offer?** Be as specific as possible to show the seriousness of your efforts. Don't just offer your hypothesis. Describe the line of reasoning that you have taken to reach it. Offer an excerpt of the sources you plan to use. Explain who your advisors will be and their roles. You must show the committee how committed you are to the project. Giving them a taste of what you have found so far is a great way to demonstrate your seriousness.

## Interviews: Interaction with a Purpose

For some awards, the interaction gets even more personal than can be conveyed via essays or proposals. Some require interviews with one or more members of the selection committee who will use an interview as a way to get to know you beyond your application. This face-to-face time will also serve as an opportunity for the committee to delve deeper into your academic interests. The most important rule is never go to an interview without having done your homework. Here are your assignments:

**Know the purpose.** Understand the purpose of the award and the awarding organization. Research both by speaking with members of the organization, reading the group's literature and speaking with past recipients of the award.

**Practice.** Practice doing mock interviews before the real thing. Ask a friend or family member to ask you questions and practice answering them. To get even more out of mock interviews, record them for review afterward.

**Have an interactive conversation.** Don't just speak about yourself and your accomplishments. Your interviewers have probably worked in the field for a number of years. Use this time to find out more about how they got to where they are and to discuss their thoughts on the future of the field. Try to engage them in your project. Ask their opinions on what they think the results might be. Be sure to prepare questions in advance so that you have an arsenal of thoughtful and provocative questions.

> ### Maximize Your Resources
>
> *The best way to get money for graduate school is to find out as much information as you can. Look around you—there are resources in your department, on the Internet and on campus. Use them!*

**Be ready for anything.** Most interviews are straight-forward, with interviewers asking questions you can generally anticipate. However—especially for graduate awards—interviewers have been known to throw in a curveball or two. Some professors treat interviews as a time to bolster their egos and ask esoteric questions about their fields. If you are surprised with one of these questions, take a second to think and do your best. You can always say that you don't know the answer now but would be happy to get back to the professor. After the interview, find the answer and email it that day. Chances are, if you were stumped, so were the other applicants and it could impress the scholarship judges that you took the time to research the question and find an answer. There really is no fool-proof way to prepare for this kind of question, except to ask your mock interviewer to toss in a few outlandish questions to get you thinking on your feet.

**Remind yourself to overlook the prestige of your interviewers.** Professors can be intimidating. Remember that they are real people. Treat them with deserved respect but don't be intimidated by them. If you don't have experience speaking with professors or if you find yourself extremely nervous around them, set up some office hours with professors on your campus to talk about the field and to ask about the award. Get used to talking one-on-one with professors before you walk into your first interview.

**Know what members of the committee have published.** If you know who your interviewers will be, read their work and be conversant about it. The opinions presented in their published work will be useful in predicting how they may react to your work and opinions.

You can find more interview strategies in Chapter 11, *Ace the Interviews.*

## Renew Your Award

*Get to know
your award, its
requirements and
restrictions so that
you can keep what
you've earned
and use it to its
fullest potential.
Pay attention to the
small print when you
receive an award.*

# Get Paid to Step into a Classroom or Lab

After you've exhausted the resources for winning money for your education, you can always resort to the traditional method: Working for it. Many schools offer opportunities to earn money through on-campus employment. In fact, for some schools and fellowships, it's a requirement.

Typical employment opportunities are teaching or researching. Grad students offer schools an additional pool of young and enthusiastic instructors for undergraduate courses. Grad students also assist professors with conducting research. In the sciences, lab work is a staple of the graduate school education.

To find out about opportunities for employment at your school, go to your department or your school's career services office. Be prepared with a curriculum vitae that outlines your desired type of work and qualifications. If that doesn't work, approach individual professors and ask about opportunities directly. You may even be able to create a position for yourself.

## Keep Your Aid Flowing

Despite your wishes, once you win a research grant, fellowship or scholarship, you can't take the money and run. You don't need to pay the money back, but you still have some responsibilities for maintaining your award. Here are some tips for carrying out the responsibilities of your award:

**Get to know your grant, fellowship or scholarship administrators.** Along with assisting with the administrative paperwork, administrators associated with your award will be able to answer your questions about the details of your award as well as offer advice on how to maximize the benefits of it.

**Be aware of your award's term and requirements.** Take time to understand the particulars of your award. How long does the award last? What happens if you take a leave of absence, study part time or quit your studies? Is the award renewable? If it is, what do you need to do to renew it?

**Learn about restrictions for spending the dough.** Some awards are limited to tuition only. Others can be used for books, travel or even living expenses. Some provide the money directly to your school while others provide a check made out to you. Make sure that you understand what you can spend the award money on and what sort of records you need to keep.

**Know what happens once you're finished with your studies.** Understand who owns the equipment that you purchase and if the awarding organization has any kind of ownership of your work. Keep records of your expenditures including receipts.

**Learn the tax implications of your award.** Speak with the award administrator or the IRS (www.irs.gov or 800-829-1040).

**Keep the awarding organization up to date on your progress.** Provide the organization with a summary report or copy of the finished product after you have finished your work. If your work is published, be sure to credit the various groups that have given you awards. This is not only good manners, but it will also help ensure that the award is around in the future.

## Getting More Help

Now that you are armed with strategies for winning scholarships and fellowships, don't stop here. Investigate these additional resources to lighten the burden of being a poor grad student. Here are some sources:

**Your department.** Inquire about awards and employment opportunities. Read newsletters distributed by your department and check the department bulletin board.

**Your peers.** There's probably a small circle of people who also study your field. Ask fellow students about awards they know of or that they have won themselves.

**Award administrators.** Speak with award administrators to see if they know of other awards that may be applicable to you.

**Professors.** Communicate your goals for the future so that if your professors come across an appropriate program or award, they will think of you. Share ideas for research and employment. Your professors may be able to help you develop proposals to fund your ideas.

**Financial aid office.** Make sure you have the most up-to-date information on programs offered by your school's financial aid office. Meet at least twice a year with a financial aid advisor to review your situation.

**Career services office.** Use this office to investigate potential employment opportunities.

**Internet.** Search websites that offer information and scholarship databases for graduate students. Our site, SuperCollege.com (www.supercollege.com), has a free searchable database of thousands of scholarships.

**Associations.** Professional and academic associations are a great source of awards for advanced studies. For some of them, you don't even need to be a member to apply.

**Your surroundings.** On-campus organizations, employers and community groups often award scholarships and fellowships. Wherever you are, keep an eye out for opportunities.

# Chapter 16 Summary: Free Cash For Graduate School

**Priorities change.** While undergraduate awards are often based on a combination of academics, leadership and activities, graduate awards are almost always based solely on academics and research. You will need to adjust your strategy to highlight your commitment to your field.

**Different types of money.** Graduate financial aid comes in several formats: Federal loans need to be repaid, while scholarships, grants and fellowships do not. Some graduate programs require teaching or research as a part of their financial aid packages.

**Prestige and money.** Graduate financial aid not only provides financial reward but enhances your curriculum vitae as well.

**Applications: Your time to shine.** Applications offer you the opportunity to build a case for how you fit the mission of the award. Know who your audience will most likely be and present the information that will show them that you are the best fit for the award.

**Help your recommenders help you.** When asking others to write your recommendation letters, provide everything they need, including a cover letter, curriculum vitae and accompanying paperwork. Make their job as easy as possible.

**Show your academic might in essays.** Address academic issues and demonstrate how, through your research or projects, you fit the requirements for the award.

**Research grant proposals are the application heavies.** You must provide detailed information about the project you propose, your plan of action and the potential benefits you can make to your field of study.

**Practice for interviews.** Learn as much as you can about the awarding organization and the interviewers themselves. Then practice with mock interviewers.

**Responsibly maintain what you've won.** Each award has its own requirements and restrictions. Get to know them so you hold onto your winnings and use the award to its fullest extent.

**Don't be afraid to ask for help.** If you look around your campus, there are many resources for you to use from professors to the financial aid office to fellow students. Take advantage of them all when finding money for grad school.

# How to Keep the Money You Win

• • • • • • • • • • • • • • • • • • • • • • • • •

# CHAPTER 17

In this chapter, you'll learn:

- **How to ensure you keep the financial aid and scholarship dollars you win**

- **Our advice for approaching and winning scholarships**

- **A special request from Gen and Kelly**

• • • • • • • • • • • • • • • • • • • • • • • • •

# You're There!

When you learn to skydive, your first lesson does not start with jumping out of an airplane. First you go through training in which you learn techniques and safety measures—on the ground. Only after practicing on the ground can you take to the sky.

In your scholarship education, you have just completed the ground training and are ready to take the plunge. As you move from the strategies for applying for scholarships to actually applying for them, we have a few words of advice on how to keep the dollars you earn and how to stay motivated.

# Keeping the Dollars That Are Yours

Let's jump ahead to after you win a cache of scholarship dollars. It would be nice once the scholarship checks were written if you could run off for that well-deserved trip to the Bahamas. Alas, there are restrictions on how you can spend the cash and how you must maintain your scholarship. (Besides, everyone knows that Hawaii is the place to go.) Here are some tips to keep in mind:

> ## Lessons into Action
>
> *You've just learned step-by-step strategies for every piece of the scholarship process from finding scholarships to writing winning applications to using the Internet to expand your search. Now it's time to search our comprehensive Scholarship Directory and put these lessons into action.*

**Get to know your scholarship and financial aid administrators.** These people will be able to answer questions about your award and make sure you are spending it the way you should.

**Give the scholarship committee members proof if they want it.** Some awards require that you provide proof of enrollment or transcripts. Send it to them.

**Be aware of your award's requirements and what happens if something changes.** How long does the award last? What happens if you take a leave of absence, study part time, study abroad, transfer schools or quit your studies? College is full of possibilities! Do you have to maintain a minimum grade point average or take courses in a certain field?

**Know if there are special requirements for athletic scholarships.** If you've won an athletic scholarship, you are most likely required to play the sport. (You didn't get that full ride scholarship for nothing!) Understand the implications of what would happen if you were not able to play because of circumstances such as an injury or not meeting academic requirements.

**Find out if the award is a cash cow (renewable).** If an award is renewable, you are eligible to get it every year you are in school. If so, find out what you need to do and when you need to do it to renew. Some awards just require a copy of your transcript, while others require you to submit an entirely new application.

**Understand restrictions for spending the dough.** Some awards are limited to tuition. Others can be used for books, travel or even living expenses. Some provide the money directly to your school; others provide a check made out to you. Understand what you can spend it on and what sort of records you need to keep.

**Learn the tax implications of your award.** Speak with the award administrator or your pals at the IRS (www.irs.gov or 800-829-1040).

> ### Neither Easy Nor Quick
>
> *Applying for scholarships is not easy. It requires time, patience and perseverance. The competition is tough. As you are applying, remind yourself that the reward is even greater. And when you receive your college diploma, you will feel deep satisfaction from knowing that you played a significant role in paying for this education.*

**Be aware of requirements after you graduate.** Some awards such as ROTC scholarships require employment after graduation. Because these arrangements can drastically affect your future, learn about the requirements now.

**Keep the awarding organization up to date on your progress.** Write the organization a thank you note, and keep them updated on your progress at the end of the year. This is not only good manners, but it will also help ensure that the award is around in the future.

## Parting Words

I (Gen) remember when I won the Sterling Scholarship, one of the highest honors for students in Hawaii. The awards ceremony was televised live throughout the state. For weeks before submitting my application, I prepared for the competition, compiling a 50-page application book, practicing for the eight hours of interviews and enlisting the help of no less than three teachers from my high school. Even though the scholarship was only $1,000, my parents still keep the trophy on display and share with unwitting visitors the videotape of my triumph. I realize now that I was able to put in such extensive effort because of my outlook on the award. I knew whether I won or lost, I would gain the experience of building a portfolio,

becoming a skilled interviewee, working closely with my teachers and meeting some incredible students.

While scholarships are primarily a source of funding for your education, approach them in the same way you do your favorite sport or hobby. I also played for my school's tennis team—and lost just about every match. Yet, I continued because I enjoyed the sport and found the skills a challenge. If you approach your scholarships in this manner, you'll probably win more of them and have fun in the process. Treat them like a chore, and you'll hate every minute, neglecting to put in the effort required to win.

The bottom line is that if you are going to take the time to apply, you should take the time to win. The secrets, tips and strategies in this book will put you within striking distance. Follow them and you'll win more and more often.

This book is unique in that it really is two books in one. Now that you know how to win, it's time to begin finding scholarships to put these strategies to use. The second half of this book is a complete listing of scholarships and awards and is indexed by various criteria so you can quickly find those that match your interests and qualifications. And, because we know you just can't get enough of us, we also encourage you to visit our website, SuperCollege.com, for the most up-to-date information on scholarships and financial aid.

We both wish you the best of luck.

## A Special Request

As you jump headlong into the wonderful world of scholarships, we have a special request. We would love to hear about your experiences with scholarships and how this book has helped you. Please send us a note after you've finished raking in your free cash for college.

Gen and Kelly Tanabe
c/o SuperCollege
2713 Newlands Avenue
Belmont, CA 94002

## Onward!

Let's fly! Flip the page and start finding scholarships. It's time to put all the strategies and tips you've just learned to work for you!

# Winning Scholarship Essays and Applications

APPENDIX

# Winning Scholarship Essays

It's one thing to study the theory behind the pheromones of love, but it is entirely a different thing to experience the euphoria, quickened heartbeat and walking on clouds of love. In a similar way, you have seen the theory behind writing a powerful scholarship essay. It is now time to see this theory in action.

The following essays were written by students who won scholarships. In each essay you will see how winning principles are put to use. The results are essays that inspire, provoke and most important, win money.

*As with any example essay, please remember that this is not necessarily the way your essay should be written. Use these example essays as an illustration of how a good essay might look. Your essay will naturally be different and unique to your own style and personality.*

## Winning Essay #1: Bet You Can't

The next essay was written in response to the question, "What book has had a significant influence on your life?" The scholarship was sponsored by—you guessed it—a local library. The writer, who wishes to remain anonymous here, knew that to stand out she had to write about something original. Forget Twain, Hawthorne or Emerson—she knew every other essay would be about icons like them. She also knew that while she had to write about a unique book she also needed to show how it had affected her life, and she wanted to show the scholarship committee a part of her personality that would demonstrate her future potential. Although the library scholarship committee was not interested in supporting future librarians, it did want to give money to young people who will improve the community in the future. Since she knew that the readers would be librarians volunteering their time after work, she was determined to keep the essay within the 500-word limit. No overworked librarian would be able to get through a 10-page tome. Here is her essay. You can see for yourself how memorable it is.

### Bet You Can't

The book offered a simple challenge: "Bet you can't evenly fold a paper more than eight times." So I tried. But, even after constructing a large piece of paper out of four newspaper sheets taped together, I still could make no more than eight even folds. Although this might seem like proof that indeed a paper cannot be folded more than eight times, I still believe that it can be done. In fact I believe that every impossible task listed in the book titled appropriately *Bet You Can't* is possible.

I bought *Bet You Can't,* a short paperback printed on cheap newsprint paper, when I was in elementary school. Yet, it still sits on my bookshelf between *Shakespeare's Greatest Works* and *The History of the American Revolution.* I could never get myself to pack it away with my other childhood books because I could never accept the fact that there were things that could not be done. After all, if we could discover how to split an atom with a laser and perfect a way to bake cheese inside pizza crust, surely we could find a way to fold a paper more than eight times.

I am a firm believer that there are no limits to what men and women can achieve. I truly feel that the only barriers are those that we impose upon ourselves. And this is precisely why I find *Bet You Can't* so frustrating and why I refuse to accept what it claims is impossible.

Some might say that I am ignoring reality, that I am naive to believe that human beings are capable of everything. I imagine that these same people take great pleasure in reading a book like *Bet You Can't* because it emphasizes the limits, reveals man's weakness and validates their pessimistic view of the world. They must love taunting someone like me with such a book. Be that as it may, I refuse to accept their outlook and refuse to let a book like *Bet You Can't* exist uncontested.

Where would we be today if we had listened to those who make words like "impossible," "undoable" and "utterly futile" their mantra? How much poorer would we be if people like Newton, Roosevelt or King had heeded the advice of their contemporaries and abandoned what they were told could not be done?

I know that it may be mathematically true that you cannot fold a paper evenly more than eight times, but that does not keep me from trying. And I know that one day I will achieve that elusive ninth fold.

## Why This Essay Won

This essay has three key strengths: First, the writer makes her essay stand out from the rest by selecting a book that most likely no other student selected. (Other students probably chose books they read in school.) When you are writing your essay, remember to write about a unique topic or approach the topic in a creative way.

Second, the writer passionately presents her conviction that there is nothing that people can't accomplish. This optimism and belief in the strength of humanity are traits that scholarship committees like. It is always a good idea to write your essay in a way that highlights your positive characteristics. Plus, taking a stand and being resolute in your ideas will make your essay stand above the many others that stick to vague generalizations and lack conviction.

Third, even though the topic of this essay is a book, the writer keeps her work focused on herself. She spotlights how her life has been affected by the book and does not waste any space with a book report or summary. Remember: You can't answer why you deserve to win if you don't write about yourself.

## Winning Essay #2: Public Service

Brian Babcock-Lumish won both the Marshall and Truman Scholarships, highly prestigious awards that draw applicants from across the country. He wrote the following essay for the Truman Scholarship, which awards $30,000 to each of the 80 winners. The Truman places a heavy emphasis on leadership and public service, which is clear from the several essays that each applicant needs to write. In this essay Brian was asked, "Describe your most satisfying public service activity." A graduate of the U.S. Military Academy at West Point, he focuses on the idea that service is embodied in the Army and now is inextricable from his own life. From Bowie, Maryland, he is studying Russian and East European Studies at Oxford as a part of the Marshall Scholarship.

### Public Service

*Brian's contributions reflect his own opinions, not those of the U.S. military.*

My most satisfying public service has been my time as an enlisted soldier in the US Army. Even as a young private, I knew that I was a part of something greater than myself. The nature of the US-Russian relationship has changed in the last decade, yet I was still playing a vital role as a Russian linguist. The military depends on area experts versed in the language, culture and politics of a region. It was my duty to be that expert.

I must admit that my service in the military was not originally motivated by the greater good. I joined as a way to pay for college and pick up a useful skill. West Point and a military career were the last things on my mind. During my year and a half as an enlisted soldier, I grew to appreciate our country's need for those who are willing to make the sacrifices that the military requires. My view began to change from one of self-interest to one of selfless service.

Selfless service is now an explicit part of the Army's core values. As my role in public service has changed from enlisted soldier to future officer, my commitment to public service has only grown. At one time, my life was entrusted to the officers over me. In a short time, I will be that officer. The service that the military renders to society - namely, national security - is one that I am proud to be a part of.

As an officer, I will have a more direct way to impact the bigger picture, whether it be as a tactical commander or strategic adviser. Regardless, the military's ability to fulfill its mission depends on young soldiers — soldiers like the one I once was and the ones I will soon be commanding.

Having been a soldier who understood the Army life and its difficulties, I will be in a better position to lead my own soldiers. My service as a private in the Army in which I will soon be a lieutenant has taught me valuable lessons about my beliefs and myself. That initial period of service gives me greater confidence in my ability to continue my service as an Army officer.

## Why This Essay Won

The power of this essay comes from the fact that Brian convinces us that public service is the foundation of both his present career and life. Brian allows us to trace his beginning as a lowly private who had very little appreciation for the concept of service and joined the Army to simply gain skills and pay for college who then grows to understand the value of service to both his country and fellow soldiers. Brian shows us how his commitment to service on various levels has become ingrained in his life and affects almost everything that he does. It is clear that he has a passion for his service in the military.

The essay also shows how Brian's commitment to service will continue to play a significant role in his future as a leader. Although the essay asks about a past experience, Brian successfully lays out a vision of how his own concept of service will be transmitted to the soldiers he will lead. When you finish this essay you not only understand Brain's most significant public service activity but you are also sure that this experience will continue to have an impact on him throughout his future.

## Winning Essay #3: Cultural Heritage

When asked to write about her ethnic and cultural heritage, Elisa Tatiana Juárez could have detailed countless influences from her Hispanic background. She chose instead to recount a single event: a trip to Mexico. As you read her essay, you will notice how focusing on this trip allows Elisa to illustrate how her cultural heritage has influenced her and how she weaves in some of her accomplishments. With this essay, she won a scholarship from the Presbyterian Church, USA.

A graduate of Coral Reef Senior High School in Miami, Elisa is a student at Brown University. In addition to this award, she won the National Hispanic Heritage Youth Award for Science and Technology and the Science Silver Knight Award.

## Cultural Heritage

The hour hand of the clock is rapidly approaching two in the morning. I look at my clothes thrown about my room. I can't take my shorts so I pull them out of the suitcase. Papi says it's not safe. I tuck a conservative looking blouse in between a box of Equal and a large bag of Jolly Ranchers. We have been buying gifts and treats for my family in Mexico for almost a month, and we still aren't packed. I look at myself in the mirror. Long blonde hair, light skin and clear eyes. Where did I come from?

You look at me and there is no way that I can convince you that my native language is Spanish and that I learned English by watching "Sesame Street" with my Papito. If I tell you that I am Mexican, you would look at me and ask if I was joking. If you ate at my house the chances of eating meat and potatoes are slim to none. Instead, you would find quesadillas con frijoles y salsa ranchera served on our blue and white Mexican dishes.

In just under five hours I will be on a plane to Mexico to see my family. When I get off the airplane the smell of Mexico will make me feel at home. The overcrowding of the streets, the crazy Mexican drivers and the cries of the street vendors all remind me of how lucky I am. Arriving at my abuelita's house I know she will be there to give me un abrazo y un beso. She will then take me by the hand and lead me to the table where we will all sit around and talk about the flight while eating the ever-popular bolillos and pan dulce from the bakery down the street. When I visit I feel like I am the only guera in the whole city. But this never makes me feel singled out or uncomfortable.

I smile at the adventures that await me. Every time I go to Mexico I learn so many new and different things about my past. I do not only focus on events such as the Mexican War of Independence, but I also learn about the people who carry Mexico in their veins. My family is from Mexico, DF (Mexico City), and my maternal great grandfather was one of the first Presbyterian pastors in the country. He helped start a seminary in the north. During the revolution, when he had to leave the country, he started a Presbyterian church in a small town in Arizona that is still there.

During my last visit to Mexico I became even more aware of the extreme poverty conditions in my country. Around that time I had won several awards internationally for my scientific research. Where's the connection? For a long while now I have been considering becoming a doctor as my career. In Mexico I noticed the enormous demand for doctors, but the poverty level among the citizens was incredible. This sparked my interest in possibly becoming a medical missionary. I realized that my potential for becoming a doctor could be used for helping other people less fortunate than I am. I do not think that I would have been able to realize my full potential to help others had I not been from a different culture.

Being Mexican has made me realize the importance of growing up in a multi-cultural home. I am very lucky to be able to share my experiences with other people to assist them in understanding other cultures. I feel like I can be a voice to those who cannot speak. At a recent Montreat Conference I learned that barely 5 percent of the Presbyterian Church (USA) is considered multi-ethnic. In a country where the Anglo population in many cities, like Miami, is a minority, this seems to me to be a critical issue. Because of my background I feel very strongly about this and have been motivated to make a difference. I am on the Montreat Youth Planning Committee and encouraged the team to select a black pastor from South Africa as the pastor for two weeks. I plan on using this experience as a vehicle to share with other students the importance of knowing other cultures. I want to share with them the meaning of my trip to Mexico.

## Why This Essay Won

Typically when students write about their ethnic or cultural heritage, they write about predictable topics such as the value of education, a history lesson or the importance of working hard. There is little creativity in these types of essays. Elisa, on the other hand, creates a vivid and memorable story. Reading her essay gives us a mental picture of who she is and the influence of her visit to Mexico. She gives us a slice of her life instead of a long (and unoriginal) description of her entire upbringing.

Notice also how Elisa incorporates some of her achievements within the essay. When describing her reaction to the poverty of Mexico she explains her desire to enter the medical field and alludes to her past achievements in the sciences. She does not have to go into detail about these achievements since they are explained in her application, which the judges would have already read.

The same is true for her description of the importance of growing up in a multi-cultural home. Not only does Elisa cite a national statistic that surprises us, but she also describes how she is working to change that fact through her involvement with the Montreat Youth Planning Committee, a national conference of the Presbyterian Church. Clearly these are issues that are important to the judges (who are affiliated with the Presbyterian Church) and underscore Elisa's leadership within the youth group.

## Winning Essay #4: Only Two Hands

The sky was the limit for this national essay competition. Applicants may write a 500- to 1,000-word essay on the topic of their choice. Katy Hoyer, a student at Castle View High School in Castle Rock, Colorado, chose to write about her dedication to helping her neighbor Belle who is afflicted with epilepsy. Her essay earned her a $5,000 scholarship and a free online PSAT study program. She admits that even though she won an essay competition, she sometimes experiences writer's block but gives advice for applicants who face the same problem. "If you are having trouble finding a topic for an essay, I would recommend talking to teachers, parents, and friends to see if they can help trigger a good idea. It also helps to read the essays of other students and learn why they wrote on that particular topic," she said.

### Only Two Hands

"Race you to the kitchen!" Belle shouted as she dashed away, her hands full of plates. Laughing, I grabbed a stack of dessert bowls and charged after her. Belle and her husband Roger had been sharing meals at least once a week with my family for the eight years we had been neighbors. Belle and I, although separated in age by fifteen years, had become close friends as we became dish-washing partners after every shared meal. I really admired Belle because even though she was suffering from a debilitating illness, she always maintained a cheerful attitude.

Belle laughed as she threw some soap suds at me. I turned towards her, ready to retaliate. Suddenly, Belle's face blanched and became a mask of fear. She slumped to the floor as if the life had drained from her body. Belle's body arched backwards as though she had been hit with 10,000 volts, stiffened, and began to strain so hard that I could hear all her joints popping as if some savage beast was inside her, trying to get out. Belle was epileptic and I knew she was having a grand mal seizure. The macabre scene lasted for only a few minutes, but even so, Belle had bit and mangled her tongue, causing thick, bloody foam to dribble down her chin. Belle's body relaxed and she began to quake all over in a palsied finale to this frightening dance of pain. When her seizure was over, I gently wiped the blood off her face and Roger carefully helped her to their bedroom. She was confused and crying. As I quietly left, I lamented the fact that after years of pills, doctors, and hospitals, she still did not have complete control for her seizures. Belle suffered from these break through seizures every few months. It sickened me to think of the fear and pain that she lived with daily.

As I plodded home, I began thinking about how much I wanted to help Belle. Back in my room, I turned to the Internet to see if I could find anything which might help to prevent grand mal seizures. What I found was a mix of superstition, witchcraft, and space-age technology. Some people swore that swimming with dolphins would cure epilepsy. Others stuck silver needles in their brains, hoping to stop seizures. I did find some "real" discoveries in medical science, but nothing that I could do myself. I was just about to give up when I came across something that made my face brighten. The "Sonata for Two Pianos" by Mozart had been shown in studies to help stop seizures from progressing into the grand mal stage. I play piano. Maybe I could learn the song and help Belle. My search for this seemingly magic song was rewarded a few days later when I found an arrangement at the music store.

As soon as I could, I started practicing the song, spending hours at a time trying to perfect it. It took me several months to learn it, and some parts really taxed my abilities to the limit. Sometimes I got so frustrated and wanted to cry; the piece was written to be played by four hands at two pianos, and unless I grew two more hands, I wasn't sure it would work. Was I wasting my time? I really wanted to help Belle, though, so I kept at it, trying to figure out a way to play the mystical melody with only two hands.

While learning the song, I continued researching epilepsy and learned that seizures usually start with what is called an aura. It's a funny feeling that can warn the epileptic that a grand mal is coming. I needed to be able to play this song well and right away when Belle's aura began. I wanted to be ready to play the song if she ever had a seizure when we were near a piano.

The evening arrived when Roger and Belle were going to eat at our house. I wanted so badly to help her if she should have a grand mal while visiting. The evening started out cheerfully. We were all laughing and teasing each other; the last thing on any of our minds was Belle's epilepsy. But, after she finished her apple pie a la mode, her face turned ashen. She looked terrified and gasped out, "Oh, no, no." I couldn't believe this was happening; things had seemed so normal. I rushed to the piano and began Mozart's song, half thinking myself silly for believing it would work. I was sweating and gritting my teeth, willing myself to play this piece and play it well. As Roger sat next to Belle on the floor, holding her hand, Belle's strained face—like a flower opening in the sunshine—slowly changed from white to rosy pink. The look of fear vanished from her eyes as she realized she wasn't going into a grand mal. Slowly she lifted her face and looked at me.

"Katy, what happened? What did you play? Where did you find it?" She paused and wiped tears from her face. "Thank you so much," she murmured. I left the piano bench and walked over to her where she sat on the floor, still amazed at what had been avoided. I sat down beside her and told her, "I wanted so much to help you, Belle. I can't believe it worked!"

Although the music had helped that evening, it didn't always work. Belle eventually had brain surgery, which the doctors hoped would reduce the frequency of her seizures. But even so, when she awakened from the anesthesia, Roger and I were waiting at her bedside with a recording of Mozart's "Sonata for Two Pianos", just in case.

### Why This Essay Won

The essay has a catchy opening, which is a definite advantage. Since the competition recently received 9,000 entries, it helps to have a start that draws the judges into it.

From there, Katy takes the reader on an emotional journey, beginning with the touching friendship she has developed with Belle, climaxing with Belle's violent seizure and concluding with Katy's dedication to helping her friend. Katy's description is very vivid, especially of Belle's seizure and as the reader it is easy to envision what Katy saw.

What's most effective about this essay is Katy's genuineness. The way that she analyzes the situation and explains her quest to help, you can tell that these are her true thoughts and feelings, not embellished ones meant to merely evoke sympathy. She takes the reader into her mind, shares her unrestrained thoughts and, in doing so, allows us to get to know her.

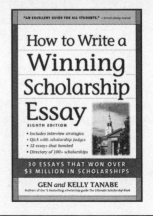

## Winning Essay #5: The Gift

Writing about an influential person can be a challenge. Some applicants think they need to write about someone famous. Some write about their mom or dad but don't offer anything original about their parents. And some write only about the influential person but don't share anything about themselves. Michael accepted the challenge and chose to write about his sister, and he did so taking an unexpected angle along the way. With this essay for Ohio Wesleyan University, Michael won one of the university's Legacy grants for the children and grandchildren of alumni worth $10,000 a year.

### The Gift

"Well, Michael, at least I get better grades than you do!" For some, these words from a sibling could provoke a fight, but when I hear them from my younger sister, Kate, I smile and realize how lucky I am that she is able to taunt me at all. Though it has taken years to unwrap, I am beginning to appreciate fully the gift that I received seventeen years ago.

Kate's birth forever changed the lives of my family members and many of our friends. She was born severely brain damaged due to a placental abruption, and she struggled to survive during her first weeks of life. She depended on a ventilator to breathe and suffered unrelenting seizures. The doctors told my parents that if Kate survived, she would never walk, talk, smile, or even recognize her family.

Kate defied the doctors' predictions and has done miraculously well. Not only can she walk, talk, and smile, but she also runs, sings, and laughs with her many friends. She is passionate about music, movies, basketball, and boys. She is now seventeen years of age, has a great social life, and, yes, gets excellent grades at her school for children with learning differences.

Kate's success is partly the result of years of hard work. The early years of my sister's life were filled with special doctors and therapists, anti-seizure medications, a special diet, surgeries, special equipment, and special schools—all for my special sister. Sometimes Kate did not seem so special to me. She talked, looked, and acted differently than "normal" children. Because of her brain injury, Kate lacks the discretion filter between her thoughts and her verbal expressions. My great-aunt jokes that Kate says what everybody else is thinking. As a child, I was often embarrassed by this behavior. My friends acted uneasy around Kate and tried to ignore her. Part of my maturation process involved understanding that Kate cannot magically correct some of her behavioral issues. As the years went by, I wanted to understand better Kate's life outside of our home.

One of my most rewarding experiences involved volunteering for Kate's Special Olympics basketball program. Kate loves basketball, and I saw this as an opportunity to spend time with her. I operated the scoreboard, worked as a referee, and served as the team's assistant coach. Kate was the star player on her team. She sank three-pointers with the one-hand shot that she perfected in our backyard (she cannot use her right hand due to her hemiplegia). Her teammates loved Kate, and they revered me because I was her older brother. At first, I was uncomfortable with the attention from all of these "special" athletes, but I quickly found myself becoming enthralled by their unbridled joy, kindness toward each other, and sportsmanship. These children taught me more about life than I could ever teach them about basketball. And I will never forget how proud I was of my sister during those games.

I know many people whose decisions regarding their careers have been affected by Kate. My cousin graduated from college with a degree in finance. She was inspired by Kate's tenacity in overcoming her challenges and decided to leave her banking career to obtain a master's degree in special education. She now teaches autistic children. Our childhood babysitter likewise became a middle school education teacher and continues to be one of Kate's best friends. I think that my path will be in the field of public service. This past summer, I interned for the President of the Boston City Council, the Honorable Michael Flaherty. The job put me in direct contact with many indigent, homeless, and mentally ill citizens. I can thank my sister for the fact that I treated these people with the dignity and respect that they deserved.

I grew up helping Kate struggle to learn to walk, control her seizures with burdensome diets, recover from surgeries performed to address the physical effects of cerebral palsy, and to learn basic skills like reading and arithmetic. I now appreciate that this experience taught me to be compassionate, to not be judgmental, and about the importance of service to others. I choose to treat Kate's boasting about her school grades as a lesson to work harder to reach my own potential. Thank you, Kate.

## Why This Essay Won

One of the biggest mistakes that students make when writing about an influential person is that they write only about the influential person and not about themselves. Michael did not make this mistake. He has a nice balance between describing his sister and himself. With such limited space for the essay, this can be a challenge.

Throughout his essay, Michael is not afraid to express his true feelings, which makes him very relatable. He doesn't paint a rosy portrait of his loving relationship with his sister from her birth but instead explains how it has taken time and maturity for him to accept and form a relationship with his sister. By expressing his doubts about and frustration with the needs of his sister, he demonstrates that he is human. This makes his eventual coming to terms with his sister's experiences even more rewarding.

## Winning Essay #6: Career Plans

One of the biggest pitfalls in writing an essay about your career plans is writing only about the career and not about yourself. A student at Farrington High School in Honolulu, Hawaii, Karen Galario Gabbuat knew this and made a point of connecting her career choice to her experiences. She said, "I realized that the best way to answer is to write about the experiences that I had and relate them to the question." By providing concrete examples of how she has already demonstrated traits needed as a pediatric nurse, she made it clear that she is serious about the career and is well suited for it.

Karen also realized that she needed to make her essay stand out. She said, "I knew that there was a lot of competition, and I realized that I needed to express myself and show who I am in the essays that I wrote. I had to show to the scholarship committee that I am different from the other applicants." Her essay won her a scholarship as a high school junior through the GEAR UP Hawai'i/SuperCollege Scholarship.

### Career Plans

The little boy's eyes were shut tight and his hands held onto the wheelchair as if it were a roller coaster ride. Once we reached the radiology department, I stood in front of him and told him that everything would be fine. I said, "Once the 'photographer' is done taking pictures of your hip, I'll be waiting outside, ready to bring you safely to your mother." From then on, it became an inspiration for me to pursue a career as a pediatric nurse. This career may not have a high ranking position, but pediatric nurses achieve great things.

First, through this career, I would like to improve my communication and interaction skills with adolescents and children. For example, before tutoring Margaret, a 4th grade student, I introduced myself with a smile and spoke to her in a jovial voice. I would try to make her feel comfortable by telling her some of my favorites. Then she would respond back by telling her own favorites; then it led to a conversation and it would be easy for me to feel comfortable around her. Pediatric nurses deal with children from infants to adolescents, and communication is important because they see these children every day when they are being checked for any improvements in their conditions.

Interacting and communicating with children is important, and these two things led to a friendship with Margaret over a short period of time. For example, I would show my concern by asking how her day went because I knew her attitude would affect the results of her tutoring. As I kept on tutoring her, our friendship grew and it was easy for us to talk about the many reading skills she needed to work on. As a pediatric nurse, you check up on your patients to see if they made any progress within your shift and you make conversation by asking how they are feeling about their day. Being polite and amiable to the patients will let them know that you are not only there to do your job but be a friend to them while they are trying to recover.

Lastly, what I hope to achieve in this career is being able to make a difference in a child's life even during the smallest treatments. For example, volunteering at Kapi`olani Women and Children Medical Center gave me an idea of what these children are going through such as during chemotherapy or recovery from an accident. The comfort and support the pediatric nurses give to their patients encourages them to fight their battles so that they are not left forlorn.

Pediatric nurses may not have a high ranking position, but they can achieve a lot. Communication, interaction, understanding, friendship, and making a difference are the many things a pediatric nurse can accomplish. I feel that becoming a pediatric nurse will give me the opportunity to attain this as well.

## Why This Essay Won

Karen made solid connections between her interest in becoming a pediatric nurse and the skills that she has learned while volunteering. Instead of just stating that she wants to become a pediatric nurse, she shows her ability to develop a quick rapport with children and her admiration of the pediatric nurses at work. These specifics help us as the readers to envision her in this profession.

## Winning Essay #7: No Child Left Behind: Well-Intentioned but Flawed

While many scholarship competitions ask students to write about a personal experience, the Resolve to Evolve Scholarship requires students to tackle a serious national topic. Jeffrey Lee rose to the challenge with this essay. The essay topic was, "Has the No Child Left Behind Act been successful in fulfilling its purpose? Why or why not?" Jeffrey is a student at the Wharton School at the University of Pennsylvania.

## No Child Left Behind: Well-Intentioned but Flawed

Flawed. Well-intentioned but flawed. That is how the No Child Left Behind (NCLB) Act is likely to be remembered after it is finally repealed, having caused great harm to the American education system. At the time of its passing, it was yet another attempt by the politicians to deal with an underperforming system through "returning to the basics," specifically the areas of math and language arts, commonly known as "reading, writing, and arithmetic." But instead of promoting achievement, it has resulted in a system where low-performing schools are awarded for minor improvements, high-performing schools punished with less funding for gifted students, and schools that fit neither of those criteria left in the lurch.

As George W. Bush said upon signing NCLB into law: "there's no greater challenge than to make sure that …every single child, regardless of where they live, how they're raised, the income level of their family…receive[s] a first-class education in America." Unfortunately, No Child Left Behind has not lived up to its name. Initially, NCLB was intended to improve the performance of U.S. primary and secondary schools by increasing standards of accountability for states, school districts, and schools, providing parents more flexibility in choosing which schools their children could attend, and mandating that all teachers be "highly qualified" in their subjects of instruction. While good in principle, issues in implementation have in fact hindered progress and proven a deterrent to educational excellence, with problems such as underfunding and ill-thought regulations and penalties in regard to "improvement" leading to a mindset that promotes a gaming of the system rather than true student learning.

One of the most problematic provisions of NCLB calls for schools to exhibit constant academic improvement in order to continue to receive federal funding, with annual standardized multiple choice exams becoming the default measure of student performance (provisions allegedly having been made for English language learners). Aside from the inherent unfairness of such exams due to socioeconomic concerns, and the failure of states to provide accommodations to English language learners, this leads to two major issues: the lowering of standards to show greater "improvement" and teaching solely what is on the exam, instead of going on to more relevant applications. This is in light of recent studies calling into question the practice of determining educational quality by testing students, suggesting Problem-Based Learning as an alternative, which would require more funding and an individuated approach to education. Once again, the NCLB act points to the American tendency toward standardization, a principle that has become outmoded as colleges seek students passionate about a single field, not well-rounded individuals.

Besides testing, the various financial incentives for both underperforming and high performing schools also contribute to the devaluation of educational achievement. With more money devoted to low achieving schools that show improvement, and less to high achievers that have little room to improve, academic achievement is paralyzed and penalized at a certain level, encouraging slow progress in order to allow for greater potential improvement in future years. Furthermore, the distribution of already limited education funds under NCLB is questionable; in California, schools are given extra funding for not passing the California High School Exit Exam (CAHSEE), essentially punishing successful schools. This allocation of resources not only affects the schools in general, but also the teachers, who must spend their own money to obtain essential teaching supplies. According to a study conducted by Quality Education Data (QED), an education market research and database company, high school teachers spent an average of $427 of their own money on teaching supplies. And those going beyond the requirements suffered even more, with teachers at my school spending up to $12,000 of their own money a year for materials to enhance students' learning experiences.

This points to the most alarming issue of all, that even these mandates to improve education are underfunded, because educational funding is simply too limited, encompassing only a minute portion of the national budget. If improving education is so important to lawmakers, then why is education only 2% of the budget, as opposed to say, military spending, which takes up a much larger 16%? With the way in which NCLB is structured, paralyzing academic achievement, encouraging lower standards of learning, and distributing the name, home phone number, and address of every student enrolled to military recruiters, this seems to indicate that it may simply be another tool to funnel underperformers into the personnel-starved military, using the promise of a better life and skills not learned in school to do so.

While NCLB was well-intentioned at the outset, it has proven detrimental to the state of the American education system, and as such, alternatives to the tired "back to the basics" approach must be considered. In the last decade, Problem-Based Learning has emerged as a viable instructional strategy that centers on the student as an individual, with the role of the teacher moving away from instructor to facilitator of learning. This bottom-up approach to responsibility in learning has been shown to enhance content knowledge and foster the development of communication, problem-solving, and self-directed learning—valuable skills not traditionally taught in the classroom. That, as well as the establishment of individual school and community based Passionate Pursuits programs, where schools would aid students to bring their interests to fruition, would shift accountability from an institution-centered approach to an individual-centered approach—and those with a modicum of control of their environment, who feel that their education is relevant, have generally performed better on any measure of success, testing or otherwise. Of course, none of this improvement, or even maintenance of the status quo, is possible without more funding, as the number and needs of students continue to increase with each passing year, and until education is once again a priority in fact rather than in name, there will not come the day when in reality, no child is left behind.

## Why This Essay Won

The simple reason why this essay won is that Jeffrey takes a strong stand about the No Child Left Behind Act and then supports his position with research and reasoning. There is no doubt about Jeffrey's position. From the beginning he states clearly that he believes the program has not succeeded. Then, he gives solid reasons that support his point of view by explaining why it's unfair to require schools to show constant academic improvement through testing and by describing how the financial incentives don't make sense. He presents quotes, facts and statistics to back up his position. At the conclusion, he does not merely make his case, but he provides direction for solving the problem. He outlines the need for increased educational spending and a different approach to teaching such as Problem-Based Learning. Jeffrey's essay demonstrates that it's important to not just make statements but to support any statements with examples. Examples help the reader understand the issue and prevent the essay from being filled with general statements. His essay also shows that even a serious topic can presented in a way that's easy for those not as familiar with the issue to understand.

## Winning Submission #8: Shawn Smith

Works are judged based on their originality, technical skill and emergence of a personal vision or voice in The Scholastic Art & Writing Awards. According to Bryan Doerries, associate executive director, programs, "Shawn Smith's work blurs the boundaries between jewelry and sculpture."

## Winning Submission #9: Wilmer Wilson

Wilmer Wilson's photographs boldly explore the politics of racial identity, utilizing the medium to its fullest potential by experimenting with gray scale, light, text and even contact sheets to convey his personal perspective.

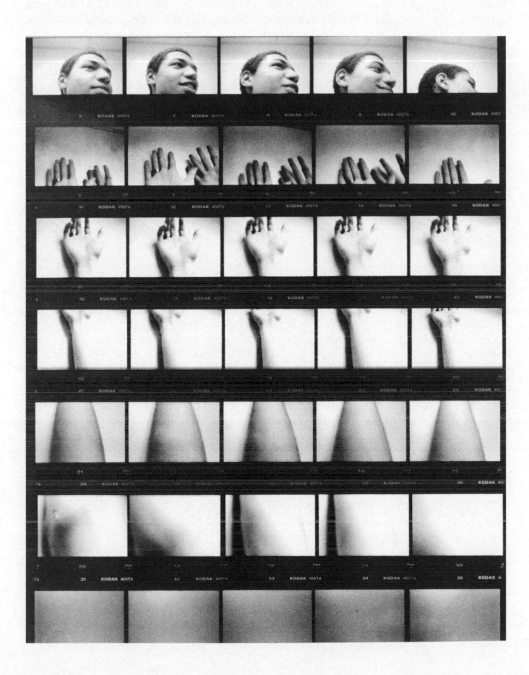

## Be Inspired

We hope the essays and applications in this appendix have inspired you to write your own winning scholarship essay. It's interesting to note that these essays are not masterpieces in terms of pure writing skill. But what all the essays do very well is convey to the scholarship judges why the student deserves to win. The writers have clearly done their homework on the mission of the scholarships and have used that information as a guide on which part of their lives and activities to highlight. You don't need to be a great writer to write a winning scholarship essay, but you do need to spend the time and effort to write an essay that is original, shares a slice of your life, and, most important, gives the scholarship judges a reason to give you their money.

# 175 Scholarships (Almost) Anyone Can Win

DIRECTORY

## $1,000 JumpStart Scholarship

College JumpStart Scholarship Fund
4546 B10 El Camino Real
No. 325
Los Altos, CA 94022
http://www.jumpstart-scholarship.net
**Purpose:** To recognize students who are committed to using education to better their life and that of their family and/or community.
**Eligibility:** Applicants must be 10th, 11th or 12th grade high school, college or adult students. Applicants may study any major and attend any college in the U.S. Applicants must be legal residents of the U.S. and complete the online application form including the required personal statement. The award may be used for tuition, room and board, books or any related educational expense.
**Amount:** $1,000.
**Number of Awards:** 3.
**Deadline:** April 15.
**How to Apply:** Applications are available online.

## $1,000 Moolahspot Scholarship

MoolahSPOT
2713 Newlands Avenue
Belmont, CA 94002
http://www.moolahspot.com/index.cfm?scholarship=1
**Purpose:** To help students pay for college or graduate school.
**Eligibility:** Students must be at least 16 years or older and plan to attend or currently attend college or graduate school. Applicants may study any major or plan to enter any career field at any accredited college or graduate school. A short personal statement is required.
**Amount:** $1,000.
**Number of Awards:** Varies.
**Deadline:** December 31.
**How to Apply:** Applications are only available online.

## $1,000 Plan for College Sweepstakes

Sallie Mae
300 Continental Drive
Newark, DE 19713
https://salliemae.com/scholarshipsearch
**Purpose:** To help students pay for college, Sallie Mae is awarding this $1,000 Plan for College Sweepstakes.
**Eligibility:** Enter to win $1,000 when you register for Sallie Mae's free college planning tools, resources and calculators. It's fast, easy, free and no essay required.
**Amount:** $1,000.
**Number of Awards:** 1 per month.
**Deadline:** December 31.
**How to Apply:** Applications are available online.

## $1,000 Scholarship Detective Launch Scholarship

Scholarship Detective
http://www.scholarshipdetective.com/scholarship/
**Purpose:** To help college and adult students pay for college or graduate school.
**Eligibility:** Applicants must be high school, college or graduate students (including adult students) who are U.S. citizens or permanent residents. Students may study any major. The funds may be used to attend an accredited U.S. institution for undergraduate or graduate education.
**Amount:** $1,000.
**Number of Awards:** 2.
**Deadline:** December 31.
**How to Apply:** Applications are available online.

## 1 for 2 Education Foundation Scholarship

1 For 2 Education Foundation
4337 E. Grand River
Suite 198
Howell, MI 48843
Email: info@1for2edu.org
https://www.1for2edu.com/#section-41
**Purpose:** To support highly motivated students who agree to "pay it forward."
**Eligibility:** Applicants must be enrolling as full-time students at an accredited four-year college or university and maintain a 3.0 GPA. Recipients agree to provide scholarships in the future.
**Amount:** Varies.
**Number of Awards:** Up to 10.
**Deadline:** February 15.
**How to Apply:** Applications are available online.

## A Voice for Animals Essay Contest

Humane Education Network
P.O. Box 7434
Menlo Park, CA 94026
Phone: (650) 854-8921

http://www.hennet.org/contest.php
**Purpose:** To support students who wish to have a voice for animals.
**Eligibility:** Applicants must be high school students who plan to study any major. Applicants must write an essay as part of their application.
**Amount:** Varies.
**Number of Awards:** Varies.
**Deadline:** April 30.
**How to Apply:** Applications are available online.

## ACT Student Champions

ACT
Phone: 319-337-1270
http://www.act.org/content/act/en/public-affairs/college-and-career-readiness-champions.html
**Purpose:** To reward students who have made exemplary college and career readiness efforts.
**Eligibility:** Applicants must be graduating high school seniors who have taken the ACT. Students must have a composite ACT score of 22 or have earned a minimum 3.0 grade point average. Applicants must demonstrate that they have overcome challenges and are tenacious in their pursuit of goals.
**Amount:** $500.
**Number of Awards:** 50.
**Deadline:** October 31.
**How to Apply:** Applications are available online.

## Adult Skills Education Award

Imagine America Foundation
12001 Sunrise Valley Drive
Suite 203
Reston, VA 20191
Phone: 571-267-3010
Email: Leed@imagine-america.org
https://www.imagine-america.org/students/scholarships-education/
**Purpose:** To support adult learners with tuition assistance and college scholarships to career colleges.
**Eligibility:** Applicants must be U.S. citizens or permanent residents enrolling in a participating career college. Applicants must also either have a high school diploma, GED or pass an Ability to Benefit test. The minimum age requirement for application is 19. Applicants must also complete the NCCT Educational Success Potential Assessment. Selection is based on the overall strength of the application.

**Amount:** $1,000.
**Number of Awards:** Varies.
**Deadline:** June 30.
**How to Apply:** Applications are available online.

## Adult Students in Scholastic Transition (ASIST)

Executive Women International (EWI)
3860 South 2300 East
Suite 211
Salt Lake City, UT 84109
Phone: 801-355-2800
Email: ewi@ewiconnect.com
http://ewiconnect.com/scholarships/
**Purpose:** To assist adult students who face major life transitions.
**Eligibility:** Applicants may be single parents, individuals just entering the workforce or displaced workers.
**Amount:** $2,000-$10,000.
**Number of Awards:** 13.
**Deadline:** Varies by chapter.
**How to Apply:** Contact your local EWI chapter.

## AFSA National Essay Contest

American Foreign Service Association (AFSA)
2101 East Street NW
Washington, DC 20037
Phone: 202-944-5504
Email: dec@afsa.org
http://www.afsa.org
**Purpose:** To support students interested in writing an essay on foreign service.
**Eligibility:** Applicants must be U.S. Citizens, high school students and have parents who are not members of the Foreign Service. Students must attend a public, private, parochial school, home school or participate in a high school correspondence program in any of the 50 states, the District of Columbia or U.S. territories or must be U.S. citizens attending schools overseas. The current award is $2,500 to the student and an all expenses paid trip to Washington, DC, for the winner and parents.
**Amount:** $2,500.
**Number of Awards:** 1.
**Deadline:** April 6.
**How to Apply:** The registration form is available online. Applicants must write a 750- to 1,000-word essay on the topic provided.

## Ag Day Essay Contest

Agriculture Council of America
11020 King Street, Suite 205
Overland Park, KS 66210
Phone: 913-491-1895
Email: jenam@nama.org
https://www.agday.org/essay-contest
**Purpose:** To support agricultural awareness while encouraging students to pursue higher education.
**Eligibility:** Applicants must be in 9th to 12th grade during the current school year and be a U.S. citizen. The contest requires an essay or video response to the given prompt on the website.
**Amount:** $1,000.
**Number of Awards:** 2.
**Deadline:** January 31.
**How to Apply:** Applications are available online.

## Akash Kuruvilla Memorial Scholarship

Akash Kuruvilla Memorial Scholarship Fund Inc.
P.O. Box 140900
Gainesville, FL 32614
Email: akmsfinfo@gmail.com
https://www.facebook.com/AKMSF/
**Purpose:** To continue the legacy of Akash Jacob Kuruvilla.
**Eligibility:** Applicants must be entering or current full-time college students at an accredited U.S. four-year college or university. They must demonstrate academic achievement, leadership, integrity and excellence in diversity. Selection is based on character, financial need and the applicant's potential to impact his or her community.
**Amount:** $1,000.
**Number of Awards:** 2.
**Deadline:** June 28.
**How to Apply:** Applications are available online. An application form, essay, personal statement, one recommendation letter and resume are required.

## Alpha Kappa Alpha Financial Need Scholars

Alpha Kappa Alpha Educational Advancement Foundation Inc.
5656 S. Stony Island Avenue
Chicago, IL 60637
Phone: 800-653-6528
Email: akaeaf@akaeaf.net
https://akaeaf.org/scholarships
**Purpose:** To assist undergraduate and graduate students who have overcome hardship to achieve educational goals.
**Eligibility:** Applicants must be studying full-time at the sophomore level or higher at an accredited institution and have a GPA of 2.5 or higher. Students must also demonstrate leadership, volunteer, civic or academic service. The program is open to students without regard to sex, race, creed, color, ethnicity, religion, sexual orientation or disability. Students do NOT need to be members of Alpha Kappa Alpha. Deadline is April 15 for undergraduate students and August 15 for graduate students.
**Amount:** Varies.
**Number of Awards:** Varies.
**Deadline:** April 15 and August 15.
**How to Apply:** Applications are available online. An application form, personal statement and three letters of recommendation are required.

## American Bar Association Law Day Art Contest

American Bar Association (ABA)
321 North Clark Street
Chicago, IL 60654
Phone: 312-988-5000
http://www.americanbar.org
**Purpose:** To encourage students to learn about the legal system.
**Eligibility:** Applicants must be high school students in grades 9-12 or the equivalent within the United States. Students must create an art piece representing the theme for Law Day.
**Amount:** $750.
**Number of Awards:** 2.
**Deadline:** March 31.
**How to Apply:** Applications are available online.

## American Fire Sprinkler Association High School Senior Scholarship Contest

American Fire Sprinkler Association
12750 Merit Drive
Suite 350
Dallas, TX 75251
Phone: 214-349-5965
Email: scholarship@firesprinkler.org
https://www.afsascholarship.org/high-school-contest/
**Purpose:** To provide financial aid to high school seniors and introduce them to the fire sprinkler industry.

**Eligibility:** Applicants must be high school seniors who plan to attend a U.S. college, university or certified trade school. Students must read the "Fire Sprinkler Essay" available online and then take an online quiz. Applicants receive one entry in the scholarship drawing for each question answered correctly.
**Amount:** $2,000.
**Number of Awards:** 10.
Scholarship may be renewable.
**Deadline:** April 1.
**How to Apply:** Applications are available online.

## Americanism Essay Contest

Fleet Reserve Association (FRA)
FRA Scholarship Administrator
125 N. West Street
Alexandria, VA 22314
Phone: 800-372-1924
Email: news-fra@fra.org
http://www.fra.org
**Purpose:** To recognize outstanding student essayists.
**Eligibility:** Applicants must be in grades 7 through 12 and must be sponsored by a Fleet Reserve Association (FRA) branch or Ladies Auxiliary unit. They must submit an essay on a sponsor-determined topic. Selection is based on the overall strength of the essay.
**Amount:** $2,500-$5,000.
**Number of Awards:** Varies.
**Deadline:** December 1.
**How to Apply:** Entry instructions are available online - look under "events and programs" link. An essay and cover sheet are required.

## Americorps National Civilian Community Corps

AmeriCorps
1201 New York Avenue NW
Washington, DC 20525
Phone: 202-606-5000
Email: questions@americorps.org
https://www.nationalservice.gov/programs/americorps
**Purpose:** To strengthen communities and develop leaders through community service.
**Eligibility:** Applicants must be U.S. citizens who are between 18 and 24 years of age. Recipients must live on one of five AmeriCorps campuses in Denver, Colorado; Sacramento, California; Baltimore, Maryland; Vinton, Iowa or Vicksburg, Mississippi. Applicants must

commit to 10 months of service on projects in areas such as education, public safety, the environment and other unmet needs. The projects are located within the region of one of the four campuses.
**Amount:** $5,775.
**Number of Awards:** Varies.
**Deadline:** Varies.
**How to Apply:** Applications are available online.

## Americorps Vista

AmeriCorps
1201 New York Avenue NW
Washington, DC 20525
Phone: 202-606-5000
Email: questions@americorps.org
https://www.nationalservice.gov/programs/americorps
**Purpose:** To provide education assistance in exchange for community service.
**Eligibility:** Applicants must be United States citizens who are at least 17 years of age. They must be available to serve full-time for one year at a nonprofit organization or local government agency with an objective that may include to fight illiteracy, improve health services, create businesses or strengthen community groups.
**Amount:** Varies.
**Number of Awards:** Varies.
**Deadline:** Varies.
**How to Apply:** Applications are available online.

## Annual Community Volunteer Scholarship

Dealhack
140 Broadview Avenue
Suite 31
Toronto, ON Canada M4M
https://dealhack.com/scholarship
**Purpose:** To assist students with exceptional volunteer involvement.
**Eligibility:** Applicants must be enrolled as full-time students at a college or university in the U.S. or Canada. Students must demonstrate outstanding community volunteer involvement.
**Amount:** $1,500.
**Number of Awards:** 1.
**Deadline:** June 30.
**How to Apply:** Applications are available online.

## Anthem Essay Contest

Ayn Rand Institute
P.O. Box 57044
Irvine, CA 92619
Phone: 949-222-6550
Email: essays@aynrand.org
https://www.aynrand.org/contests
**Purpose:** To honor high school students who distinguish themselves in their understanding of Ayn Rand's novel "Anthem".
**Eligibility:** Applicants must be eighth to twelfth grade students who submit a 600-1,200-word essay that will be judged on both style and content, with an emphasis on writing that is clear, articulate and logically organized. Winning essays must demonstrate an outstanding grasp of the philosophical meaning of "Anthem".
**Amount:** $25-$2,000.
**Number of Awards:** 59.
**Deadline:** April 30.
**How to Apply:** Essay is required for the contest. There is no application.

## Applying for the College Success Scholarship

Study.com
100 View Street #202
Mountain View, CA 94041
https://study.com/pages/Academic_Awards_Home.html
**Purpose:** To support students who are pursuing a higher education.
**Eligibility:** Applicants must be citizens of the United States who are either graduating high school seniors or students currently enrolled at an accredited college or university. Students must have a minimum of 30 semester hours or 40 quarter hours remaining in their program until graduation.
**Amount:** $1,000.
**Number of Awards:** 1.
**Deadline:** April 1.
**How to Apply:** Applications are available online.

## Art Awards

Scholastic Art and Writing Awards
557 Broadway
New York, NY 10012
Phone: 212-343-6100
Email: info@artandwriting.org
http://www.artandwriting.org/scholarships/
**Purpose:** To reward America's best student artists.

**Eligibility:** Applicants must be in grades 7 through 12 in American or Canadian schools and must submit artwork in one of the following categories: art portfolio, animation, ceramics and glass, computer art, design, digital imagery, drawing, mixed media, painting, photography, photography portfolio, printmaking, sculpture or video and film. There are regional and national levels.
**Amount:** Varies.
**Number of Awards:** Varies.
**Deadline:** Varies.
**How to Apply:** Applications are available online. The deadlines vary by state but start in December. There is an online form to find out the deadline for your state.

## Atlas Shrugged Essay Contest

Ayn Rand Institute
P.O. Box 57044
Irvine, CA 92619
Phone: 949-222-6550
Email: essays@aynrand.org
https://www.aynrand.org/students/essay-contests
**Purpose:** To honor students who distinguish themselves in their understanding of Ayn Rand's novel "Atlas Shrugged".
**Eligibility:** Applicants must be high school seniors, college undergraduates or graduate students who submit an 800-1,600-word essay which will be judged on both style and content with an emphasis on writing that is clear, articulate and logically organized. Winning essays must demonstrate an outstanding grasp of the philosophical meaning of "Atlas Shrugged".
**Amount:** $100-$25,000.
**Number of Awards:** 59.
**Deadline:** September 19.
**How to Apply:** Essay is required for the contest. There is no application.

## AU Student Essay Contest

Americans United for Separation of Church and State
Attn.: Essay Contest Submission
1901 L Street NW
Suite 400
Washington, DC 20036
Phone: 202-466-3234 x427
Email: campus@au.org
http://www.austudents.org/essaycontest/
**Purpose:** To emphasize the importance of the separation of church and state.
**Eligibility:** Applicants must be current high

school juniors or seniors in the U.S. Students must submit an essay discussing potential violations of church-state separations as found in the topics listed on the website.
**Amount:** $1,500.
**Number of Awards:** 3.
**Deadline:** May 1.
**How to Apply:** Applications are available online.

## AXA Achievement Scholarships

AXA Achievement Scholarship
c/o Scholarship America
One Scholarship Way
St. Peter, MN 56082
Phone: 800-537-4180
Email: axaachievement@scholarshipamerica.org
https://us.axa.com/axa-foundation/about.html
**Purpose:** To provide financial assistance to ambitious students.
**Eligibility:** Applicants must be U.S. citizens or legal residents who are current high school seniors and are planning to enroll full-time in an accredited college or university in the fall following their graduation. They must show ambition and drive evidenced by outstanding achievement in school, community or workplace activities. A recommendation from an unrelated adult who can vouch for the student's achievement is required.
**Amount:** $2,500.
**Number of Awards:** Up to 12.
**Deadline:** December 15.
**How to Apply:** Applications are available online.

## BankMobile Financial Literacy Scholarship

BankMobile
401 Park Avenue South
New York, NY 10016
Phone: 917-543-3254
Email: scholarship@bankmobile.com
https://www.bankmobile.com/scholarship
**Purpose:** To support student financial literacy.
**Eligibility:** Applicants must be undergraduate or graduate level students, U.S. citizens and have a minimum 3.0 GPA. Students must submit an essay explaining the importance of financial literacy in both their lives and their career. Special consideration is given to applicants who are actively promoting financial literacy within their community.
**Amount:** $1,500.

**Number of Awards:** 1.
**Deadline:** July 17.
**How to Apply:** Applications are available online and must include an official transcript (high school or college) and the essay.

## Barbizon's College Tuition Scholarship

Barbizon Modeling & Acting Centers
4950 W. Kennedy Boulevard
Suite 200
Tampa, FL 33609
Phone: 888-999-9404
http://www.barbizonmodeling.com/scholarships/
**Purpose:** To support students who wish to continue their education.
**Eligibility:** Applicants must be legal U.S. residents who are planning to attend an accredited college or university. Students must fill out an entry form for the sweepstakes and must be accepted at an accredited college or university within three years of graduation.
**Amount:** $100,000.
**Number of Awards:** 1.
**Deadline:** December 31.
**How to Apply:** Applications are available online.

## Be the Boss Scholarship

GoSkills
555 Bryant Street
#901
Palo Alto, CA 94301
Phone: 650-822-7732
Email: support@goskills.com
https://www.goskills.com/Scholarship
**Purpose:** To encourage women to start their own online business.
**Eligibility:** Applicants must be female high school or college students interested in starting their own online business. Students must submit their business plan to apply.
**Amount:** $2,000.
**Number of Awards:** 2.
**Deadline:** September 15, March 15.
**How to Apply:** Applications are available online.

## Bellhops' Moving Forward Scholarship

Bellhops Inc.
1100 Market Street
Suite 502

Chattanooga, TN 37402
Phone: 888-836-3939
Email: scholarship@getbellhops.com
https://www.getbellhops.com/scholarship/
**Purpose:** To help students pursue higher education.
**Eligibility:** Applicants must be graduating high school seniors or current college students. Students must complete an application and essay as well as provide academic transcripts and a photo. Applicants must have a grade point average of 3.0 or higher.
**Amount:** $3,000.
**Number of Awards:** 1.
**Deadline:** September 15.
**How to Apply:** Applications are available online.

## Beyond the Boroughs Scholarship

Beyond The Boroughs
282 Katonah Avenue
Suite 122
Katonah, NY 10536
Phone: 914-458-2926
http://www.beyondtheboroughs.org
**Purpose:** To support students with financial need in pursuing a bachelor's degree.
**Eligibility:** Applicants must be accepted to an accredited four-year college. A minimum GPA of 2.5 is required. Selection is primarily based on demonstration of financial need, academic achievement, work history and extracurricular involvement.
**Amount:** $20,000.
**Number of Awards:** Varies. Scholarship may be renewable.
**Deadline:** March 15.
**How to Apply:** Applications are available online.

## Bob Bennett Memorial Scholarship

Unity One Credit Union
6701 Burlington Boulevard
Fort Worth, TX 76131
Phone: 817-306- 3100
http://www.unityone.org
**Purpose:** To support students pursuing a higher education.
**Eligibility:** Applicants must be either graduating high school seniors or current college students. Students must write an essay as part of their application.
**Amount:** $250-$1,000.
**Number of Awards:** 3.
**Deadline:** April 26.

**How to Apply:** Applications are available online.

## Bonner Scholars Program

Bonner Foundation
10 Mercer Street
Princeton, NJ 08540
Phone: 609-924-6663
Email: info@bonner.org
http://www.bonner.org/apply
**Purpose:** To award four-year community service scholarships to students planning to attend one of 75 participating colleges.
**Eligibility:** Students must complete annual service requirements as stipulated by the organization. Awards are geared toward students demonstrating significant financial need. Scholarship recipients are named Bonner Scholars.
**Amount:** Varies.
**Number of Awards:** Varies.
**Deadline:** Varies.
**How to Apply:** Contact the admission office at each participating school to request an application.

## Bright!Tax Global Scholar Initiative

Bright!Tax
244 Fifth Avenue
New York, NY 10001
Phone: 212-465-2528
Email: inquiries@brighttax.com
http://www.brighttax.com/scholarships.html
**Purpose:** To support students wishing to study abroad.
**Eligibility:** Applicants must be U.S. citizens who want to study abroad for at least one full semester at an accredited institution. Selection is based on academic and extracurricular achievement, community involvement, future ambitions and financial need.
**Amount:** $1,000.
**Number of Awards:** Minimum of 2.
**Deadline:** June 1, November 1.
**How to Apply:** Applications are available online.

## Bruce Lee Scholarship

U.S. Pan Asian American Chamber of Commerce
1329 18th Street NW
Washington, DC 20036
Phone: 800-696-7818
Email: info@uspaacc.com
http://uspaacc.com/

**Purpose:** To support the higher education goals of students of all ethnic backgrounds.

**Eligibility:** Applicants must be U.S. citizens or permanent residents and be high school seniors who will pursue post-secondary educations at an accredited institution in the U.S. Students do not need to be Asian Americans. Selection is based on character, the ability to persevere over adversity, academic excellence with at least a 3.3 GPA, community service involvement and financial need. Applicants must be able to attend the Excellence Awards and Scholarships Dinner during the CelebrAsian Annual Conference (in May).

**Amount:** Varies.

**Number of Awards:** Varies.

**Deadline:** March 27.

**How to Apply:** Applications are available online.

## Burger King Scholars Program

Burger King Scholars Program
5505 Blue Lagoon Drive
Miami, FL 33126
Phone: 305-378-3000
Email: bdorado@whopper.com
http://www.bkmclamorefoundation.org

**Purpose:** To provide financial assistance for high school seniors who have part-time jobs.

**Eligibility:** Applicants may apply from public, private, vocational, technical, parochial and alternative high schools in the United States, Canada and Puerto Rico and must be U.S. or Canadian residents. Students must also have a minimum 2.5 GPA, work part-time an average of 15 hours per week unless there are extenuating circumstances, participate in community service or other activities, demonstrate financial need and plan to enroll in an accredited two- or four-year college, university or vocational/technical school by the fall term of the graduating year. Applicants do NOT need to work at Burger King, but Burger King employees are eligible.

**Amount:** $1,000-$50,000.

**Number of Awards:** Varies.

**Deadline:** December 15.

**How to Apply:** Applications are available online and may only be completed online.

## C.I.P. Scholarship

College Is Power
1025 Alameda de las Pulgas
No. 215
Belmont, CA 94002

http://www.collegeispower.com/scholarship.cfm

**Purpose:** To assist adult students age 18 and over with college expenses.

**Eligibility:** Applicants must be adult students currently attending or planning to attend a two-year or four-year college or university within the next 12 months. Students must be 18 years or older and U.S. citizens or permanent residents. The award may be used for full- or part-time study at either on-campus or online schools.

**Amount:** $1,000.

**Number of Awards:** Varies.

**Deadline:** December 31.

**How to Apply:** Applications are available online.

## Carson Scholars

Carson Scholars Fund
305 W Chesapeake Avenue
Suite 310
Towson, MD 21204
Phone: 877-773-7236
Email: katie@carsonscholars.org
http://carsonscholars.org/scholarships/

**Purpose:** To recognize students who demonstrate academic excellence and commitment to the community.

**Eligibility:** Applicants must be nominated by their school. They must be in grades 4 through 11 and have a GPA of 3.75 or higher in English, reading, language arts, math, science, social studies and foreign language. They must have participated in some form of voluntary community service beyond what is required by their school. Scholarship recipients must attend a four-year college or university upon graduation to receive funds.

**Amount:** $1,000.

**Number of Awards:** Varies.

**Deadline:** January 10.

**How to Apply:** Applications are available from the schools of those nominated. Only one student per school may be nominated.

## Chinese American Citizens Alliance Foundation Essay Contest

Chinese American Citizens Alliance
1044 Stockton Street
San Francisco, CA 94108
Phone: 415-829-9332
Email: info@cacanational.org
http://www.cacanational.org

**Purpose:** To provide a forum for expression

for future leaders of the United States.

**Eligibility:** Applicants must be high school students in grades 9 through 12. Students do NOT need to be Chinese Americans. They must write a 500-word essay on a topic chosen by the Chinese American Citizens Alliance. The essay must be written on a given date at the student's local lodge or other designated location.

**Amount:** Up to $1,000.

**Number of Awards:** 13.

**Deadline:** February 26.

**How to Apply:** Applications are available online. An application form and essay are required.

## Christophers Video Contest for College Students

Christophers
5 Hanover Square
22nd Floor
New York, NY 10004
Phone: 212-759-4050
Email: youth@christophers.org
https://www.christophers.org/video-contest-for-college-students

**Purpose:** To support college students who believe in The Christophers' mission that any one person can make a difference.

**Eligibility:** Applicants must be current undergraduate or graduate level college students and U.S. citizens. Selection is based on the video submitted and how well it depicts the theme of "One Person Can Make a Difference."

**Amount:** $500-$2,000.

**Number of Awards:** 3.

**Deadline:** December 17.

**How to Apply:** Applications are available online. Students must also submit a video of five minutes or less communicating the theme.

## CIA Undergraduate Scholarship Program

Central Intelligence Agency
Office of Public Affairs
Washington, DC 20505
Phone: 703-482-0623
https://www.cia.gov/careers/student-opportunities

**Purpose:** To encourage students to pursue careers with the CIA.

**Eligibility:** Applicants must be high school seniors or college freshmen or sophomores. High school students must have an SAT score

of 1500 or higher or an ACT score of 21 or higher, while all applicants must have a GPA of at least 3.0. Applicants must demonstrate financial need, defined as a household income of less than $70,000 for a family of four or $80,000 for a family of five or more. They must meet all criteria for regular CIA employees, including security checks and medical examinations. Applicants must commit to a work experience each summer during college and agree to CIA employment for 1.5 times the length of their CIA-sponsored scholarship.

**Amount:** Varies.

**Number of Awards:** Varies. Scholarship may be renewable.

**Deadline:** June 15.

**How to Apply:** Applications are available online. A resume, SAT/ACT scores, family income information, copy of the FAFSA or Student Aid Report, transcript and two letters of recommendation are required.

## Clean Water Scholarship Competition

Waterlogic
Phone: 866-917-7873
Email: info@waterlogicusa.com
https://www.waterlogic.com/en-us/scholarship-competition/

**Purpose:** To support students pursuing a higher education who have demonstrated a sincere interest in increasing global access to clean water.

**Eligibility:** Applicants must be U.S. citizens entering college for the upcoming fall semester or be currently enrolled as undergraduate students with a 3.0 GPA. Students must write an essay as part of their application.

**Amount:** $1,500.

**Number of Awards:** 1.

**Deadline:** May 31.

**How to Apply:** Applications are available online.

## Clubs of America Scholarship Award for Career Success

Clubs of America
484 Wegner Road
Lakemoor, IL 60051
Phone: 800-258-2872
https://www.greatclubs.com/scholarship/

**Purpose:** To support undergraduate students in funding their education.

**Eligibility:** Applicants must be enrolled at an accredited U.S. educational institution. A

minimum GPA of 3.0 is required. Students must submit an essay explaining their career goals. Selection is based on the overall strength of the submission.
**Amount:** $1,000.
**Number of Awards:** 1.
**Deadline:** August 31.
**How to Apply:** Applications are available online.

## Coca-Cola All-State Community College Academic Team

Coca-Cola Scholars Foundation
P.O. Box 442
Atlanta, GA 30301
Phone: 800-306-2653
Email: Scholars@coca-cola.com
http://www.coca-colascholarsfoundation.org/apply/
**Purpose:** To assist community college students with college expenses.
**Eligibility:** Applicants must be enrolled in community college, have a minimum GPA of 3.5 on a four-point scale and be on track to earn an associate's or bachelor's degree. Students attending community college in the U.S. do NOT need to be members of Phi Theta Kappa. Fifty students will win a $1,500 scholarship, fifty students will win a $1,250 scholarship and fifty students will win a $1,000 scholarship.
**Amount:** $1,000-$1,500.
**Number of Awards:** 150.
**Deadline:** October 25.
**How to Apply:** Applications are available online. Nomination from the designated nominator at your school is required. A list of nominators is available at http://www.ptk.org.

## Coca-Cola Scholars Program

Coca-Cola Scholars Foundation
P.O. Box 442
Atlanta, GA 30301
Phone: 800-306-2653
Email: Scholars@coca-cola.com
http://www.coca-colascholarsfoundation.org/apply/
**Purpose:** Begun in 1986 to celebrate the Coca-Cola Centennial, the program is designed to contribute to the nation's future and to assist a wide range of students.
**Eligibility:** Applicants must be high school seniors in the U.S., be U.S. citizens, nationals or permanent residents and must use the awards at an accredited U.S. college or university. Selection is based on the transcript, school profile, school and non-school related clubs and organizations, honors and awards and volunteer service. Application period typically reopens on August 1st of each year.
**Amount:** $20,000.
**Number of Awards:** 150.
Scholarship may be renewable.
**Deadline:** October 31.
**How to Apply:** Applications are available online.

## College Prep Scholarship for High School Juniors

QuestBridge
120 Hawthorne Avenue
Suite 103
Palo Alto, CA 94301
Phone: 888-275-2054
Email: questions@questbridge.org
http://www.questbridge.org
**Purpose:** To equip outstanding low-income high school juniors with the knowledge necessary to compete for admission to leading colleges.
**Eligibility:** Applicants must be high school juniors who have a strong academic record and an annual household income of less than $60,000. Many past award recipients have also been part of the first generation in their family to attend college. Scholarships are open to all qualified students, regardless of race or ethnicity.
**Amount:** Varies.
**Number of Awards:** Varies.
**Deadline:** March 20.
**How to Apply:** Applications are available on the QuestBridge website in February. An application form, transcript and one teacher recommendation are required.

## CollegeNET Scholarships

CollegeNET Scholarship Review Committee
805 SW Broadway
Suite 1600
Portland, OR 97205
Phone: 503-973-5200
Email: scholarship@collegenet.com
http://www.collegenet.com
**Purpose:** To assist college applicants.
**Eligibility:** Applicants must sign up at the website and visit and participate in forums. Recipients are determined by votes on the website.

**Amount:** Varies.
**Number of Awards:** Varies.
**Deadline:** Weekly.
**How to Apply:** Applications are available online.

## Coolidge Scholarship

Calvin Coolidge Memorial Foundation Inc.
P.O. Box 97
Plymouth, VT 05056
Phone: 802-672-3389
Email: coolidgescholars@coolidgefoundation.org
https://coolidgescholars.org/
**Purpose:** To reward high school juniors who have achieved academic excellence and have an interest in public policy.
**Eligibility:** Applicants must be U.S. citizens planning on enrolling full-time in an accredited U.S. college or university. Students must apply during their junior year in high school. Selection is based on academic excellence, interest in public policy and appreciation for Coolidge values and demonstrated humility and leadership.
**Amount:** Full tuition.
**Number of Awards:** 2.
**Deadline:** January 16.
**How to Apply:** Applications are available online through the website and include an essay, a transcript, a resume and two letters of recommendation.

## Cottage & Bungalow Scholarship

Cottage & Bungalow
P.O. Box 384
Tullahoma, TN 37388
Phone: 844-677-6604
Email: scholarships@cottageandbungalow.com
https://www.cottageandbungalow.com/scholarship.html
**Purpose:** To support creativity in education.
**Eligibility:** Applicants must be legal U.S. students or hold a valid student visa and be at least 18 years of age by December 31 of the current year. Students must be currently enrolled or enrolling in an accredited U.S. institution as a full-time undergraduate or graduate student. Applicants must submit an essay on the given topic on the website.
**Amount:** $500.
**Number of Awards:** 1.
**Deadline:** February 1.
**How to Apply:** Applications are available online.

## Cottage Inn Scholarship

Cottage Inn
4390 Concourse Drive
Ann Arbor, MI 48108
Phone: 734-663-2470
Email: info@cottageinn.com
http://www.cottageinn.com/cottage-inn-scholarship/
**Purpose:** To reward those who embrace education.
**Eligibility:** Applicants must be U.S. residents and be enrolled in or accepted into an accredited college or university in the U.S. Students will need to submit an essay. Minimum 3.0 GPA required.
**Amount:** $500-$2,500.
**Number of Awards:** 3.
**Deadline:** May 31.
**How to Apply:** Applications are available online and must include an official transcript and an acceptance letter to the college or university you will be attending.

## Countdown to College Scholarship

Potential Magazine
61 Market Place
Montgomery, AL 36117
Phone: 334-518-7810
http://potentialmagazine.com
**Purpose:** To support high school students in pursuing post-secondary education.
**Eligibility:** Applicants must be subscribed to the Countdown to College eNewsletter.
**Amount:** $500.
**Number of Awards:** 1.
**Deadline:** May 4.
**How to Apply:** Applications are available online.

## Courageous Persuaders Video Contest

Courageous Persuaders
Email: sherp@dada.org
http://courageouspersuaders.com/official-rules/
**Purpose:** To reward students who understand the dangers of underage drinking and texting while driving.
**Eligibility:** Applicants may enter as an individual or as a team. Students must be a high school student, in grades 9-12 (ages 19 and under) and a United States or Canadian citizen attending a United States (or U.S. territories) or Canadian high school. Students must submit a 30-second commercial about the dangers of

underage drinking or the dangers of texting while driving.
**Amount:** $3,000.
**Number of Awards:** 18.
**Deadline:** January 31.
**How to Apply:** Applications are available online.

## Create Real Impact Contest

Impact Teen Drivers
Attn.: Create Real Impact Contest
P.O. Box 161209
Sacramento, CA 95816
Phone: 916-733-7432
Email: info@impactteendrivers.org
http://www.createrealimpact.com
**Purpose:** To raise awareness of the dangers of distracted driving and poor decision making.
**Eligibility:** Applicants must be legal U.S. residents who are between the ages of 14 and 22. They must be enrolled full-time at an accredited secondary or post-secondary school. They must submit an original, videotaped creative project that offers a solution to the problem of distracted driving. Selection is based on project concept, message effectiveness and creativity.
**Amount:** $500 and $1,500.
**Number of Awards:** 13.
**Deadline:** March 19.
**How to Apply:** Contest entry instructions are available online. A videotaped creative project is required.

## Create-a-Greeting-Card Scholarship

Gallery Collection
Prudent Publishing
65 Challenger Road
P.O. Box 150
Ridgefield Park, NJ 07660
Phone: 800-950-7064
Email: service@gallerycollection.com
https://www.gallerycollection.com/greeting-cards-scholarship.htm
**Purpose:** To reward high school, college students and members of the United States armed forces who enter a contest to create a Christmas card, holiday card, birthday card or all-occasion greeting card.
**Eligibility:** Applicants must be U.S. citizens or legal residents who are at least 14 years old. The submission must include original artwork or photographs. Those members of the United States armed forces must not be older than 34.

Selection is based on the overall quality of the submission including creativity, uniqueness and suitability.
**Amount:** $1,000-$10,000.
**Number of Awards:** 2.
**Deadline:** March 2.
**How to Apply:** Applications and submissions may be made online or mailed directly to the scholarship administrator at the Gallery Collection. Entry form and greeting card submission are required. Online submissions are preferred.

## Davidson Fellows Scholarships

Davidson Institute for Talent Development
9665 Gateway Drive
Suite B
Reno, NV 89521
Phone: 775-852-3483
Email: DavidsonFellows@davidsongifted.org
http://www.davidsongifted.org/
**Purpose:** To reward young people for their works in mathematics, science, technology, music, literature, philosophy or "outside the box."
**Eligibility:** Applicants must be under the age of 18 and be able to attend the awards reception in Washington, DC. In addition to the monetary award, the institute will pay for travel and lodging expenses. Three nominator forms, three copies of a 15-minute DVD and additional materials are required.
**Amount:** $10,000-$50,000.
**Number of Awards:** Varies.
**Deadline:** February 12.
**How to Apply:** Applications are available online.

## Davis-Putter Scholarship Fund

Davis-Putter Scholarship Fund
P.O. Box 7307
New York, NY 10116
Email: information@davisputter.org
http://www.davisputter.org
**Purpose:** To assist students who are both academically capable and who aid the progressive movement for peace and justice both on campus and in their communities.
**Eligibility:** Applicants must be undergraduate or graduate students who participate in the progressive movement, acting in the interests of issues such as expansion of civil rights and international solidarity, among others. Applicants must also have demonstrated

financial need as well as a solid academic record.
**Amount:** Up to $10,000.
**Number of Awards:** Varies.
**Deadline:** April 1.
**How to Apply:** Applications are available online.

## Delete Cyberbullying Scholarship Award

Delete Cyberbullying
2261 Market Street #291
San Francisco, CA 94114
Email: help@deletecyberbullying.org
http://www.deletecyberbullying.org
**Purpose:** To get students committed to the cause of deleting cyberbullying.
**Eligibility:** Applicants must be a U.S. citizen or permanent resident and attending or planning to attend an accredited U.S. college or university for undergraduate or graduate studies. Applicants must also be a high school, college or graduate student or a student planning to enter college.
**Amount:** $1,000.
**Number of Awards:** 1.
**Deadline:** June 30.
**How to Apply:** Applications are available online. An application form and an essay are required.

## Dell Scholars Program

Michael and Susan Dell Foundation
P.O. Box 163867
Austin, TX 78716
Phone: 512-329-0799
Email: apply@dellscholars.org
http://www.dellscholars.org
**Purpose:** To support underprivileged high school seniors.
**Eligibility:** Students must be participants in an approved college readiness program, and they must have at least a 2.4 GPA. Applicants must be pursuing a bachelor's degree in the fall directly after graduation. Students must also be U.S. citizens or permanent residents and demonstrate financial need. Selection is based on "individual determination to succeed," future goals, hardships that have been overcome, self motivation and financial need.
**Amount:** Varies.
**Number of Awards:** Varies.
Scholarship may be renewable.
**Deadline:** December 1.

**How to Apply:** Applications are available online. An online application is required.

## Delta Theta Chi Sorority National Memorial Scholarship

Delta Theta Chi Sorority
Attn: Cindi Cook
2614 S. Lulu
Wichita, KS 67216
http://www.deltathetachi.org/Scholarships.html
**Purpose:** To support the pursuit of higher education.
**Eligibility:** Applicants must provide transcripts for the past four years. Students graduating high school or current undergraduate freshmen must provide official documentation of grade point average, SAT and/or ACT scores. Applicants must complete the application in full, including the essay, and provide at least one letter of reference.
**Amount:** $2,600.
**Number of Awards:** 2.
**Deadline:** February 1.
**How to Apply:** Applications are available online.

## Dietspotlight.com Scholarship

DietSpotlight.com
75 Valencia Avenue
Suite 1000
Coral Gables, FL 33134
https://www.dietspotlight.com/scholarship/essay/
**Purpose:** To encourage students who are pursuing a health-related degree to create an obesity conscious community.
**Eligibility:** Applicants must be enrolled in a health-related degree program and submit a personal essay using between 900-1,500 words. Students must provide their name and address along with the essay in a Word or PDF format to be considered.
**Amount:** $3,000.
**Number of Awards:** 4.
**Deadline:** December 31.
**How to Apply:** Applications are available online.

## Digital Privacy Scholarship

Digital Responsibility
3561 Homestead Road #113
Santa Clara, CA 95051-5161
Email: scholarship@digitalresponsibility.org

http://www.digitalresponsibility.org

**Purpose:** To help students understand why it's important to be cautious about what they post on the Internet.

**Eligibility:** Applicants must be a high school freshman, sophomore, junior or senior or a current or entering college or graduate school student of any level. Home schooled students are also eligible. There is no age limit. Students must also be a U.S. citizen or legal resident.

**Amount:** $1,000.

**Number of Awards:** 1.

**Deadline:** June 30.

**How to Apply:** Applications are available online.

## DirectTextbook.com Scholarship Essay Contest

DirectTextbook.com
1525 Chemeketa Street NE
Salem, OR 97301
Phone: 503-930-4568
Email: service@directtextbook.com
https://www.directtextbook.com

**Purpose:** To support students who write an essay.

**Eligibility:** Applicants must be U.S. citizens enrolled in a two- or four-year institution in the fall semester. Students must have a grade point average of 2.5 or higher. Applicants must provide a completed application and an essay.

**Amount:** $1,000-$3,000.

**Number of Awards:** 3.

**Deadline:** July 25.

**How to Apply:** Applications are available online.

## Distinguished Young Women Scholarship Program

Distinguished Young Women
751 Government Street
Mobile, AL 36602
Phone: 251-438-3621
Email: lynne@ajm.org
http://distinguishedyw.org/scholarships/

**Purpose:** To provide scholarship opportunities and encourage personal development for high school girls through a competitive pageant stressing academics and talent as well as self-expression and fitness.

**Eligibility:** Teen girls are selected from state competitions to participate in a national pageant. Contestants are judged on a combination of scholastics, personal interview, talent, fitness and self-expression. Applicants should be a high school student at least in their sophomore year. Students must be U.S. citizens, have never been married and have never been pregnant.

**Amount:** Varies.

**Number of Awards:** Varies.

**Deadline:** Varies.

**How to Apply:** Applications are available online.

## Don't Text and Drive Scholarship

Digital Responsibility
3561 Homestead Road #113
Santa Clara, CA 95051-5161
Email: scholarship@digitalresponsibility.org
http://www.digitalresponsibility.org

**Purpose:** To help students understand the risks of texting while driving.

**Eligibility:** Applicants must be a high school freshman, sophomore, junior or senior or a current or entering college or graduate school student of any level. Home schooled students are also eligible. There is no age limit. Students must also be a U.S. citizen or legal resident.

**Amount:** $1,000.

**Number of Awards:** 1.

**Deadline:** September 30.

**How to Apply:** Applications are available online.

## DoSomething.org Monthly Scholarships

Do Something (Scholarships)
19 West 21st Street, Floor 8
New York, NY 10010
Phone: 212-254-2390
Email: scholarships@dosomething.org
https://www.dosomething.org/us/about/easy-scholarships

**Purpose:** To assist students who participate in a social issue campaign.

**Eligibility:** Applicants must be age 25 or younger and be U.S. or Canadian citizens. There is a new scholarship each month. Selection is based on a random drawing of all students who participate in the campaign.

**Amount:** Varies.

**Number of Awards:** Varies.

**Deadline:** Varies.

**How to Apply:** Applications are available online.

## Dr. Alma S. Adams Scholarship

Truth Initiative
900 G Street, NW
Fourth Floor
Washington, DC 20001
Phone: 202-454-5555
Email: adamsscholarship@truthinititative.org
http://truthinitiative.org/Adams-Scholarship
**Purpose:** To support students who have a passion to help reduce the use of tobacco products in priority underserved populations.
**Eligibility:** Applicants must be U.S. citizens or legal residents. Students should be pursuing a degree in public health, communications, social work, education, liberal arts or a related field and have a minimum GPA of 2.0. Applicants must provide proof of community service activities such as (but not limited to) activism, outreach or peer counseling in tobacco prevention or control. Financial need is considered.
**Amount:** $5,000.
**Number of Awards:** 2.
**Deadline:** April 30.
**How to Apply:** Applications are available online and must include a SAR report.

## E-waste Scholarship

Digital Responsibility
3561 Homestead Road #113
Santa Clara, CA 95051-5161
Email: scholarship@digitalresponsibility.org
http://www.digitalresponsibility.org
**Purpose:** To help students understand the impact of e-waste and what can be done to reduce e-waste.
**Eligibility:** Applicants must be high school, college, graduate or home schooled students. There is no age limit. Students must also be U.S. citizens or legal residents. A 140-character message about e-waste is required to apply. The top 10 applications will be selected as finalists; finalists will be asked to write a full length 500- to 1,000-word essay about e-waste. Only online applications are accepted.
**Amount:** $1,000.
**Number of Awards:** 1.
**Deadline:** April 30.
**How to Apply:** Applications are available online.

## eCampus Tours Scholarship Giveaway

Edsouth
eCampusTours
P.O. Box 36014
Knoxville, TN 37930
Phone: 865-342-0670
Email: info@ecampustours.com
http://www.ecampustours.com
**Purpose:** To assist students in paying for college.
**Eligibility:** Eligible students include U.S. citizens, U.S. nationals and permanent residents or students enrolled in a U.S. institution of higher education. Winners must be enrolled in an eligible institution of higher education, as stipulated in the eligibility requirements, within one year of winning the award. Scholarship awards will be paid directly to the college.
**Amount:** $1,000.
**Number of Awards:** 2.
**Deadline:** March 31.
**How to Apply:** Applications are available online or by mail. Registration with eCampusTours is required.

## Educational Advancement Foundation Merit Scholarship

Alpha Kappa Alpha Educational Advancement Foundation Inc.
5656 S. Stony Island Avenue
Chicago, IL 60637
Phone: 800-653-6528
Email: akaeaf@akaeaf.net
https://akaeaf.org/scholarships
**Purpose:** To support academically talented students.
**Eligibility:** Applicants must be full-time college students at the sophomore level or higher, including graduate students, at an accredited school. They must have a GPA of at least 3.0 and demonstrate community involvement and service. The program is open to students without regard to sex, race, creed, color, ethnicity, religion, sexual orientation or disability. Students do NOT need to be members of Alpha Kappa Alpha. The application deadline is April 15 for undergraduates and August 15 for graduates.
**Amount:** Varies.
**Number of Awards:** Varies.
**Deadline:** April 15 (undergraduates) and August 15 (graduates).
**How to Apply:** Applications are available online. An application form, personal statement and three letters of recommendation are required.

## Explore the World Scholarship

Hostelling International USA
8401 Colesville Road
Suite 600
Silver Spring, MD 20910
http://www.hiusa.org/travel-scholarships
**Purpose:** To support students who wish to study abroad or participate in service abroad.
**Eligibility:** Applicants must be between 18 and 30 years of age and a U.S. citizen or permanent resident. Students should be able to prove financial need, live in one of the metropolitan areas listed on the website and plan to travel abroad on an education, volunteer or service learning trip.
**Amount:** $2,000.
**Number of Awards:** 104.
**Deadline:** March 2.
**How to Apply:** Applications are available online.

## Family Travel Forum Teen Travel Writing Scholarship

Family Travel Forum
135 West 20th Street
5th Floor
New York, NY 10011
Phone: 212-595-6074
Email: editorial@travelbigo.com
https://myfamilytravels.com/Teen_travel_writing
**Purpose:** To aid college-bound students who have written the best travel essays.
**Eligibility:** Applicants must be members of the MyFamilyTravels.com online community and be between the ages of 13 and 18. They must be in grades 8 through 12 and must be attending a U.S. or Canadian high school, U.S. or Canadian junior high school, U.S. home school or an American school located outside of the U.S. They must submit an essay about a significant travel experience that occurred within the past five years and that happened when the applicant was between the ages of 12 and 18. Selection is based on originality, quality of storytelling and grammar.
**Amount:** $1,000.
**Number of Awards:** 3.
**Deadline:** July 12.
**How to Apply:** Application instructions are available online. An essay submission form and essay are required.

## FMAA Scholarship Program

Flag Manufacturers Association of America
994 Old Eagle School Road
Suite 1019
Wayne, PA 19087
Phone: 610-971-4850
https://fmaa-usa.com/Scholarship.php
**Purpose:** To support graduating high school seniors who create a video on the United States flag.
**Eligibility:** Applicants must create a video essay discussing what the United States flag means to them as a young American in today's world. Students must post their one and a half to two minute video online.
**Amount:** Up to $3,000.
**Number of Awards:** 5.
**Deadline:** May 30.
**How to Apply:** Applications are available online.

## Foreclosure.com Scholarship Program

Foreclosure.com
1095 Broken Sound Parkway, NW
Suite 200
Boca Raton, FL 33487
Phone: 561-988-9669 x 7387
Email: scholarship@foreclosure.com
http://www.foreclosure.com/scholarship/
**Purpose:** To support current undergraduate college students who are interested in addressing critical issues facing the nation, namely issues involving real estate/housing.
**Eligibility:** Applicants must be U.S. citizens 13 years of age or older who are currently enrolled as undergraduate college students. They must write an essay between 800 and 2,000 words providing creative solutions to a given topic involving critical issues facing the nation centered around real estate/housing. Selection is based upon the overall strength of the essay and application.
**Amount:** $1,000-$5,000.
**Number of Awards:** 5.
**Deadline:** December 15.
**How to Apply:** Applications are available online. An application form and essay are required.

## Frame My Future Scholarship Contest

Church Hill Classics
594 Pepper Street

Monroe, CT 06468
Phone: 800-477-9005
Email: info@diplomaframe.com
http://www.diplomaframe.com
**Purpose:** To help success-driven students attain their higher education goals.
**Eligibility:** Applicants must be high school seniors or current college students who plan to enroll full-time for the following academic year. Students must be residents of the United States, including APO/FPO addresses but excluding Puerto Rico. Employees of Church Hill Classics and affiliated companies, their family members and individuals living in the same household are not eligible.
**Amount:** $500-$5,000.
**Number of Awards:** 3.
**Deadline:** April 1.
**How to Apply:** Applications must be submitted online. An entry form and original piece of artwork are required.

## Free Speech Essay Contest

Foundation for Individual Rights in Education
510 Walnut Street
Philadelphia, PA 19106
Phone: 215-717-3473
Email: rahul.truter@thefire.org
https://www.thefire.org/resources/high-school-network/essay-contest/
**Purpose:** To encourage students to promote the freedom of speech.
**Eligibility:** Applicants must be juniors or seniors in U.S. high schools including home-schools or U.S. citizens attending overseas schools. Students must submit an essay pertaining to the topic of free speech and censorship.
**Amount:** Up to $10,000.
**Number of Awards:** 7.
**Deadline:** December 31.
**How to Apply:** Applications are available online.

## Fulbright Grants

U.S. Department of State
Office of Academic Exchange Programs, Bureau of Educational and Cultural Affairs
U.S. Department of State, SA-44
301 4th Street SW, Room 234
Washington, DC 20547
Phone: 202-632-3238
Email: fulbright@state.gov
https://us.fulbrightonline.org/

**Purpose:** To increase the understanding between the people of the United States and the people of other countries.
**Eligibility:** Applicants must be graduating college seniors, graduate students, young professionals and artists. Funds are generally used to support students in university teaching, advanced research, graduate study or teaching in elementary and secondary schools.
**Amount:** Varies.
**Number of Awards:** Varies.
**Deadline:** October 8.
**How to Apply:** Applications are available online.

## G2 Crowd Entrepreneurial Scholarship

G2 Crowd
20 N. Upper Wacker
Chicago, IL 60606
Phone: 847-748-7559
https://learn.g2crowd.com/scholarship
**Purpose:** To support entrepreneurial-minded students.
**Eligibility:** Applicants must be enrolling in or currently enrolled as a full-time student at an accredited U.S. university and hold a minimum GPA of 2.5. Students must write an essay pertaining to entrepreneurialism.
**Amount:** $5,000.
**Number of Awards:** 4.
**Deadline:** February 29, May 31, August 31, November 30.
**How to Apply:** Applications are available online.

## GE-Reagan Foundation Scholarship Program

Ronald Reagan Presidential Foundation
40 Presidential Drive, Suite 200
Simi Valley, CA 93065
Phone: 844-402-0354
Email: ge-reagan@scholarshipamerica.org
https://www.scholarsapply.org/ge-reagan/
**Purpose:** To reward students who demonstrate leadership, drive, integrity and citizenship.
**Eligibility:** Applicants must be high school seniors and pursue a bachelor's degree at an accredited U.S. college or university the following fall. Students must demonstrate strong academic performance (3.0 or greater GPA or equivalent), demonstrate financial need and be a U.S. citizen. Funds may be used for student tuition and room and board.
**Amount:** $10,000.

**Number of Awards:** Varies.
Scholarship may be renewable.
**Deadline:** January 3.
**How to Apply:** Applications are available online. The competition will close earlier than the deadline once 25,000 applications are received.

## Gen and Kelly Tanabe Student Scholarship

Gen and Kelly Tanabe Scholarship Program
2713 Newlands Avenue
Belmont, CA 94002
Phone: 650-618-2221
Email: scholarships@gkscholarship.com
http://www.genkellyscholarship.com
**Purpose:** To assist high school, college and graduate school students with educational expenses.
**Eligibility:** Applicants must be 9th-12th grade high school students, college students or graduate school students who are legal U.S. residents. Students may study any major and attend any college in the U.S.
**Amount:** $1,000.
**Deadline:** December 31.
**How to Apply:** Applications are available online.

## George Montgomery/NRA Youth Wildlife Art Contest

National Rifle Association
11250 Waples Mill Road
Fairfax, VA 22030
Phone: 800-672-3888
Email: grantprogram@nrahq.org
https://awards.nra.org/awards/
**Purpose:** To support young artists and encourage awareness of local game birds and animals.
**Eligibility:** Applicants must be in grades 1 through 12 and submit an original artwork depicting any North American game bird or animal that may be legally hunted or trapped. NRA membership is not required. Art is divided into categories based on grade level and is judged on effort, creativity, anatomical accuracy and composition.
**Amount:** Up to $1,000.
**Number of Awards:** Varies.
**Deadline:** November 3.
**How to Apply:** Application information is available online. A statement of authenticity signed by a parent, guardian or teacher must be submitted along with the artwork.

## George S. and Stella M. Knight Essay Contest

National Society, Sons of the American Revolution
1000 South Fourth Street
Louisville, KY 40203
Phone: 502-589-1776
Email: sdelong1@san.rr.com
http://www.sar.org
**Purpose:** To reward students who have written outstanding essays on the American Revolution, the U.S. Constitution or the Declaration of Independence.
**Eligibility:** Applicants must be U.S. citizens or legal residents. Students must be high school sophomores, juniors or seniors. Applicants must submit an 800- to 1,200-word essay on some topic that is related to the Declaration of Independence, the American Revolution or the U.S. Constitution. Selection is based on the overall strength of the essay.
**Amount:** $1,000-$5,000.
**Number of Awards:** 3.
**Deadline:** December 31.
**How to Apply:** Applications are available online.

## Global Citizen Scholarship

EF Educational Tours
EF Center Boston
Two Education Circle
Cambridge, MA 02141
Phone: 800-665-5364
Email: EF.Global.Citizen@ef.com
https://www.eftours.com/global-citizen
**Purpose:** To help students reflect on their place in the world through writing and then have a chance to experience it first-hand.
**Eligibility:** Applicants must be college-bound high school students in the U.S. or Canada nominated by their schools and must write an essay or create a video or digital media project on a topic related to global citizenship. The award involves a paid educational trip to Europe.
**Amount:** Educational tour expenses.
**Number of Awards:** Varies.
**Deadline:** December 31.
**How to Apply:** Applications are available online on the EF Tours Facebook page.

## Gloria Barron Prize for Young Heroes

Barron Prize
P.O. Box 1470
Boulder, CO 80306
http://www.barronprize.org
**Purpose:** To reward young people who have organized and led extraordinary service projects.
**Eligibility:** Applicants must be residents of the U.S. or Canada between the ages of 8 and 18. Students must be currently working on a service project or have completed a service project within the past year. Selection is primarily based on demonstration of generosity, tenacity and positive impact on the world.
**Amount:** $5,000.
**Number of Awards:** 15.
**Deadline:** April 15.
**How to Apply:** Applications are available online.

## Go! Overseas Study Abroad Scholarship

Go! Overseas Study Abroad Scholarship
2040 Bancroft Way
Suite 200
Berkeley, CA 94704
Phone: 415-796-6456
Email: scholarship@gooverseas.com
http://www.gooverseas.com/study-abroad/
**Purpose:** To aid students who have been accepted into a study abroad program.
**Eligibility:** Applicants must be current college or graduate students who have been accepted into a study abroad program for the coming academic year. Selection is based on application creativity and display of analytical thinking.
**Amount:** $500.
**Number of Awards:** 2.
**Deadline:** May 6, December 2.
**How to Apply:** Applications are available online. An application form and essay are required.

## GoBankingRates

GOBankingRates
1700 E. Walnut
Lost Angeles, CA 90245
Email: info@gobankingrates.com
https://www.gobankingrates.com/scholarships/
**Purpose:** To assist with the expense of post-secondary education.
**Eligibility:** Applicants must be legal U.S. residents at least 18 years of age and a graduating high school senior or currently enrolled freshman, sophomore or junior at an accredited U.S. college or university. Students must submit an essay along with their application.
**Amount:** $2,500.
**Number of Awards:** 1.
**Deadline:** June 15.
**How to Apply:** Applications are available online.

## Goedeker's Appliances Annual College Book Scholarship

Goedeker's
13850 Manchester Road
Ballwin, MO 63011
Email: scholarship@goedekers.com
http://www.goedekers.com/college-scholarship
**Purpose:** To offset the cost of higher education.
**Eligibility:** Applicants must be currently enrolled or enrolling in an undergraduate or graduate college and have a minimum grade point average of 3.0.
**Amount:** $500.
**Number of Awards:** 3.
**Deadline:** July 7.
**How to Apply:** Applications are available online.

## Goodshop Scholarship

Goodshop
550 Montgomery Street
9th floor
San Francisco, CA 94111
Email: information@goodshop.com
https://www.goodsearch.com/scholarship/
**Purpose:** To support students who write about causes they support.
**Eligibility:** Applicants must write an essay on the topic provided.
**Amount:** $500-$1,000.
**Number of Awards:** 2.
**Deadline:** December 31.
**How to Apply:** Applications are available online.

## Grasshopper Entrepreneur Scholarship

Grasshopper
197 First Avenue
Suite 200
Needham, MA 02494
Phone: 800-820-8210
Email: scholarships@grasshopper.com
https://grasshopper.com/entrepreneur-scholarship/
**Purpose:** To assist incoming first-year or current college students in undergraduate or graduate degree programs.
**Eligibility:** Applicants must attend an accredited American college, university or trade school. An essay of 500-700 words on the entrepreneurial-related topic provided is required.
**Amount:** $5,000.
**Number of Awards:** 1.
**Deadline:** August 30.
**How to Apply:** Applications are available online.

## Hagan Scholarship

Hagan Scholarship Foundation
P.O. Box 1225
Columbia, MO 65205
Email: scholarships@hsfmo.org
https://haganscholarships.org
**Purpose:** To help high-achieving, dedicated students who live in smaller counties.
**Eligibility:** Applicants must be U.S. citizens and be graduating seniors from a public high school located in a county with fewer than 50,000 residents. Students must be enrolling in a four-year college or university the first semester following high school graduation. Applicants must work 240 hours in the year prior to the start of each academic year.
**Amount:** Varies.
**Number of Awards:** 300.
**Deadline:** November 15.
**How to Apply:** Applications are available online.

## Horatio Alger Association Scholarship Program

Horatio Alger Association
Attn.: Scholarship Department
99 Canal Center Plaza
Suite 320
Alexandria, VA 22314
Phone: 703-684-9444
Email: association@horatioalger.org
https://scholars.horatioalger.org/
**Purpose:** To assist students who are committed to pursuing a bachelor's degree and have demonstrated integrity, financial need, academic achievement and community involvement.
**Eligibility:** Applicants must enter college the fall following their high school graduation, have at least a 2.0 GPA, be in need of financial aid ($55,000 or less adjusted gross income per family is preferred) and be involved in extracurricular and community activities. Students applying from Louisiana, Montana and Idaho have additional state specific requirements.
**Amount:** $25,000.
**Number of Awards:** 106.
**Deadline:** October 25.
**How to Apply:** Applications are available online.

## Humane Studies Fellowships

Institute for Humane Studies at George Mason University
3434 Washington Boulevard
MS 1C5
Arlington, VA 22201
Phone: 800-697-8799
Email: ihs@gmu.edu
http://www.theihs.org
**Purpose:** To award scholarships to students who are interested in the classical liberal/libertarian tradition of individual rights and market economies and wish to apply these principles in their work.
**Eligibility:** Applicants must be graduate students who are in any field and at any stage before completion of the Ph.D., law students, MBA students or other professional students. The fellowships can be used for study in the U.S. or abroad. Applicants must also be enrolled as full-time students at an accredited degree-granting institution. Students must be alumni of IHS programs and events.
**Amount:** Up to $15,000.
**Number of Awards:** Varies.
Scholarship may be renewable.
**Deadline:** February 8.
**How to Apply:** Applications are available online. There is a $25 application fee that is waived by applying by January 5.

## IAPMO Essay Scholarship Contest

International Association of Plumbing and
Mechanical Officials (IAPMO)
4755 E. Philadelphia Street
Ontario, CA 91761
Phone: 909-472-4100
Email: gaby.davis@iapmo.org
http://www.iwsh.org/hidden/iwsh-essay-
scholarship-contest/
**Purpose:** To share the "importance the
plumbing and mechanical industry plays in our
everyday lives."
**Eligibility:** Applicants must be current high
school seniors or enrolled or accepted as
full-time students in an accredited technical
school, community college, trade school,
four-year accredited college or university or an
apprentice program.
**Amount:** $500-$1,000.
**Number of Awards:** 3.
**Deadline:** April 30.
**How to Apply:** Applications are available
online. An essay of 800 to 1,600 words on the
topic provided is required.

## Jack Kent Cooke Foundation College Scholarship Program

Jack Kent Cooke Foundation
44325 Woodridge Parkway
Lansdowne, VA 20176
Phone: 800-941-3300
Email: scholarships@jkcf.org
http://www.jkcf.org
**Purpose:** To assist high school seniors with
financial need.
**Eligibility:** Applicants must plan to graduate
from a U.S. high school in the spring and plan
to enroll in an accredited four-year college
beginning in the fall following application.
Students must have a minimum 3.5 GPA and
have standardized test scores in the top 15
percent: SAT combined critical reading and
math score of 1200 or above and/or ACT
composite score of 26 or above. Applicants
must also demonstrate significant unmet
financial need. Family incomes up to $95,000
are considered. However, the majority of
recipients will be eligible to receive a Pell
grant.
**Amount:** Up to $40,000 per year for four
years.
**Number of Awards:** Up to 40.
Scholarship may be renewable.
**Deadline:** November 13.

**How to Apply:** Applications are available
online.

## James M & Erma T Freemont Foundation Scholarship Program

James M. & Erma T. Freemont Foundation
P.O. Box 82563
Hapeville, GA 30354
http://www.freemontfoundation.com
**Purpose:** To support students who
demonstrate involvement and leadership.
**Eligibility:** Applicants must be graduating
high school seniors, undergraduate or
graduate students. Students must demonstrate
outstanding academic achievement, leadership
and volunteerism in their community and
participation in extracurricular school activities.
**Amount:** Varies.
**Number of Awards:** Varies.
**Deadline:** February 2.
**How to Apply:** Applications are available
online.

## Jeannette Rankin Women's Scholarship Fund

Jeannette Rankin Foundation
1 Huntington Road
Suite 701
Athens, GA 30606
Phone: 706-208-1211
Email: info@rankinfoundation.org
http://www.rankinfoundation.org
**Purpose:** To support the education of low-
income women 35 years or older.
**Eligibility:** Applicants must be women
35 years of age or older, plan to obtain an
undergraduate or vocational education and
meet maximum household income guidelines.
**Amount:** Varies.
**Number of Awards:** Varies.
Scholarship may be renewable.
**Deadline:** Last day of February.
**How to Apply:** Applications are available
online or by sending a self-addressed and
stamped envelope to the foundation.

## John F. Kennedy Profile in Courage Essay Contest

John F. Kennedy Library Foundation
Columbia Point
Boston, MA 02125
Phone: 617-514-1649
Email: profiles@nara.gov

http://www.jfklibrary.org/Education/Profile-in-Courage-Essay-Contest.aspx

**Purpose:** To encourage students to research and write about politics and John F. Kennedy.

**Eligibility:** Applicants must be in grades 9 through 12 in public or private schools or be home-schooled and write an essay about the political courage of a U.S. elected official who served during or after 1956. Essays must have source citations. Applicants must register online before sending essays and have a nominating teacher review the essay. The winner and teacher will be invited to the Kennedy Library to accept the award, and the winner's teacher will receive a grant. Essays are judged on content (55 percent) and presentation (45 percent).

**Amount:** $100-$20,000.

**Number of Awards:** Up to 25.

**Deadline:** January 17.

**How to Apply:** Applications are available online. A registration form and essay are required.

## Josephine De Karman Fellowship

Josephine De Karman Fellowship Trust
P.O. Box 3389
San Dimas, CA 91773
Phone: 909-592-0607
Email: info@dekarman.org
http://www.dekarman.org

**Purpose:** To recognize students who demonstrate academic achievement.

**Eligibility:** Applicants must be undergraduate students entering their senior year or Ph.D. candidates nearing completion of their degree (all requirements except for the dissertation must be completed by January 31). Applicants may not be post-doctoral students. Special consideration is given to doctoral students in the humanities. The award is open to international students living in the U.S.

**Amount:** $14,000-$22,000.

**Number of Awards:** 8.

**Deadline:** January 31.

**How to Apply:** Applications are available online.

## LA Tutors Innovation in Education Scholarship

LA Tutors
9454 Wilshire Boulevard
Suite 600
Beverly Hills, CA 90212

Phone: 424-335-0067
Email: contact@latutors123.com
https://www.latutors123.com/scholarship/

**Purpose:** To reward innovation.

**Eligibility:** Applicants must be a high school or college student within the U.S. or Canada. A minimum 3.0 GPA is required. Students must be a citizen of, permanent resident of or hold a valid student visa in the U.S. or Canada. Applicants will have designed an innovative project that makes the difference in the lives of others. The project can include a website, series of blogs, an app, fundraising event, etc. An essay describing the goal of the project and providing supporting documentation is required. The contest is monthly.

**Amount:** $500.

**Number of Awards:** 12.

**Deadline:** Monthly.

**How to Apply:** Application is available online.

## Leaders and Achievers Scholarship Program

Comcast NBCUniversal
Comcast Leaders and Achievers Scholarship Program, Scholarship America
One Scholarship Way
Saint Peter, MN 56082
Phone: 800-537-4180
Email: leadersandachievers@scholarshipamerica.org
https://learnmore.scholarsapply.org/leadersandachievers/

**Purpose:** To provide one-time scholarship awards to graduating high school seniors. Emphasis is on students who take leadership roles in school and community service and improvement.

**Eligibility:** Students must be high school seniors with a minimum 3.0 GPA, be nominated by their high school principal or guidance counselor and attend school in a Comcast community. See the website for a list of eligible communities by state. Comcast employees, their families or other Comcast affiliates are not eligible to apply.

**Amount:** $2,500.

**Number of Awards:** 800.

**Deadline:** December 6.

**How to Apply:** Applications are available from the nominating principal or counselor.

## Leesa Social Impact Scholarship

Leesa
3704 Pacific Avenue
Suite 200
Virginia Beach, VA 23451
Phone: 844-335-3372
Email: scholarship@leesa.com
https://www.leesa.com/pages/scholarship
**Purpose:** To support exceptional students interested in social action.
**Eligibility:** Applicants must be accepted to or currently enrolled at an accredited college or university and have a minimum GPA of 3.0. Students must demonstrate a commitment to social action. Applicants must submit a video describing the role that social action has had upon their lives.
**Amount:** $1,000.
**Number of Awards:** 4.
**Deadline:** July 31, December 31.
**How to Apply:** Applications are available online.

## Life Lessons Scholarship Program

Life and Health Insurance Foundation for Education
1655 N. Fort Myer Drive
Suite 610
Arlington, VA 22209
Phone: 202-464-5000
Email: info@lifehappens.org
http://www.lifehappens.org
**Purpose:** To support students who have been affected financially and emotionally by the death of a parent.
**Eligibility:** Applicants must submit either a 500-word essay or a three-minute video describing the impact of losing a parent at a young age. The grand prize winner of the video contest is selected by an online public vote.
**Amount:** Up to $15,000.
**Number of Awards:** 31.
**Deadline:** March 1.
**How to Apply:** Applications are available online.

## Lions International Peace Poster Contest

Lions Club International
300 W. 22nd Street
Oak Brook, IL 60523-8842
Phone: 630-571-5466
Email: pr@lionsclubs.org
http://www.lionsclubs.org
**Purpose:** To award creative youngsters cash prizes for outstanding poster designs.
**Eligibility:** Students must be 11, 12 or 13 years old as of the deadline and must be sponsored by their local Lions club. Entries will be judged at the local, district, multiple district and international levels. Posters will be evaluated on originality, artistic merit and expression of the assigned theme.
**Amount:** $500-$5,000.
**Number of Awards:** 24.
**Deadline:** November 15.
**How to Apply:** Applications are available from your local Lion's Club.

## Live Mas Scholarship

Taco Bell Foundation
Email: info@livemasscholarship.com
http://www.livemasscholarship.com
**Purpose:** To support the "next generation of innovators, creators and dreamers."
**Eligibility:** Applicants must be a legal resident of the 50 United States and the District of Columbia, at least 16 years of age and no older than 24 years of age and on track to apply for or currently enrolled in an accredited post-high school/post-secondary educational programs (including accredited two-and four-year colleges, universities, vocational-technical and trade schools).
**Amount:** $5,000-$25,000.
**Number of Awards:** 100.
**Deadline:** January 23.
**How to Apply:** Applicants must submit a video (two minutes or less in length) that tells the story of their life's passion.

## Live Your Dream Awards Program

Soroptimist International of the Americas
1709 Spruce Street
Philadelphia, PA 19103
Phone: 215-893-9000
Email: siahq@soroptimist.org
http://www.soroptimist.org/awards/live-your-dream-awards.html
**Purpose:** To assist women entering or re-entering the workforce with educational and skills training support.
**Eligibility:** Applicants must be attending or have been accepted by a vocational/skills training program or an undergraduate degree program. Applicants must be the female head of household who provide the primary source of financial support for their families and demonstrate financial need. Applicants must

submit their application to the appropriate regional office.

**Amount:** Up to $10,000.

**Number of Awards:** Varies.

**Deadline:** November 15.

**How to Apply:** Applications are available online.

## LULAC National Scholastic Achievement Awards

League of United Latin American Citizens
1133 19th Street NW
Suite 1000
Washington, DC 20036
Phone: 202-835-9646
Email: scholarships@lnesc.org
http://www.lnesc.org

**Purpose:** To aid students of all ethnic backgrounds attending colleges, universities and graduate schools.

**Eligibility:** Applicants do not need to be Hispanic or Latino to apply. Applicants must have applied to or be enrolled in a college, university or graduate school and be U.S. citizens or legal residents. Students must also have a minimum 3.5 GPA and if entering freshmen a minimum ACT score of 29 or minimum SAT score of 1350. Eligible candidates cannot be related to scholarship committee members, the Council President or contributors to the Council funds. Since applications must be sent from local LULAC Councils, students without LULAC Councils in their states are ineligible.

**Amount:** $2,000.

**Number of Awards:** Varies.

**Deadline:** March 31.

**How to Apply:** Applications are available online.

## Marshall Memorial Fellowship

German Marshall Fund of the United States
1744 R Street NW
Washington, DC 20009
Phone: 202-683-2650
Email: info@gmfus.org
http://www.gmfus.org/transatlantic-leadership-initiatives/marshall-memorial-fellowship

**Purpose:** To provide fellowships for future community leaders to travel in Europe and to explore its societies, institutions and people.

**Eligibility:** Applicants must be nominated by a recognized leader in their communities or professional fields. They must be between 28 and 40 years of age and demonstrate achievement within their profession, civic involvement and leadership. They must be U.S. citizens or permanent residents or be permanent citizens of one of the 38 countries listed on the scholarship page. European applicants will visit the United States for their fellowship opportunities. Candidates should have little or no previous experience traveling through Europe. Fellows visit five or six cities and meet with policy makers, business professionals and other community leaders.

**Amount:** Varies.

**Number of Awards:** 75.

**Deadline:** September 27.

**How to Apply:** Applications are available online.

## Marshall Scholar

Marshall Aid Commemoration Commission
Email: info@marshallscholarship.org
http://www.marshallscholarship.org

**Purpose:** Established in 1953 and financed by the British government, the scholarships are designed to bring academically distinguished Americans to study in the United Kingdom to increase understanding and appreciation of the British society and academic values.

**Eligibility:** Applicants must be U.S. citizens who expect to earn a degree from an accredited four-year college or university in the U.S. with a minimum 3.7 GPA. Students may apply in one of eight regions in the U.S.

**Amount:** Varies.

**Number of Awards:** Up to 40.

**Deadline:** September 30.

**How to Apply:** Contact your regional center at the address listed on the website.

## Mensa Education and Research Foundation Scholarship Program

Mensa Education and Research Foundation
1229 Corporate Drive West
Arlington, TX 76006
Phone: 817-607-5577
Email: info@mensafoundation.org
http://www.mensafoundation.org

**Purpose:** To support students seeking higher education.

**Eligibility:** Applicants do not need to be members of Mensa but must be residents of a participating American Mensa Local Group's area. They must be enrolled in a degree program at an accredited U.S. college or university in the academic year after application. They must write an essay explaining career, academic or vocational goals.

**Amount:** Varies.

**Number of Awards:** Varies.

**Deadline:** January 15.

**How to Apply:** Applications are available online in September. Please do not write to the organization to request an application. An application form and essay are required.

## MILK United States Student Scholarship

Milk Books
Ironbank
Suite 404
150 Karangahape Road
Auckland, 1010
Phone: 424-389-3485
Email: scholarships@milkbooks.com
https://www.milkbooks.com/scholarship/united-states/

**Purpose:** To encourage students to be creative thinkers.

**Eligibility:** Applicants must be attending an educational college or university within the United States that have partnered with MILK Books. Students must either write or illustrate what creativity means as part of the application process.

**Amount:** $3,000.

**Number of Awards:** 1.

**Deadline:** May 31.

**How to Apply:** Applications are available online.

## Mometrix College Scholarship

Mometrix Test Preparation
3827 Phelan #179
Beaumont, TX 77707
Phone: (800) 673-8175
http://www.mometrix.com/collegescholarships/

**Purpose:** To support graduating seniors or students already enrolled in an accredited college or university.

**Eligibility:** Applicants must submit a 2,000 character (about 400 words) or less essay based on their test preparation practices. First, second and third place prizes are awarded.

**Amount:** $1,000.

**Number of Awards:** 3.

**Deadline:** May 15.

**How to Apply:** Applications are available online.

## Money Matters National Education Day Scholarships

American Payroll Association
660 North Main Avenue
Suite 100
San Antonio, TX 78205
Phone: 210-226-4600
Email: moreinfo@americanpayroll.org
https://www.nationalpayrollweek.com/money-matters-scholarship-entry/

**Purpose:** To reward students interested in financial literacy.

**Eligibility:** Applicants must study the Money Matters National Education Day Bring Home The Gold student workbook and complete a five-question quiz based on the material. Students who correctly answer all five questions on the quiz will be automatically entered in a drawing for the scholarships.

**Amount:** Up to $5,000.

**Number of Awards:** 3.

**Deadline:** September 30.

**How to Apply:** Applications are available online.

## Most Valuable Student Scholarships

Elks National Foundation Headquarters
2750 North Lakeview Avenue
Chicago, IL 60614
Phone: 773-755-4732
Email: scholarship@elks.org
https://www.elks.org/scholars/

**Purpose:** To support high school seniors who have demonstrated scholarship, leadership and financial need.

**Eligibility:** Applicants must be graduating high school seniors who are U.S. citizens and who plan to pursue a four-year degree on a full-time basis at a U.S. college or university. Male and female students compete separately.

**Amount:** $4,000-$12,500.

**Number of Awards:** 500.

Scholarship may be renewable.

**Deadline:** November 5.

**How to Apply:** Contact the scholarship chairman of your local Lodge or the Elks association of your state.

## National College Match Program

QuestBridge
120 Hawthorne Avenue
Suite 103
Palo Alto, CA 94301
Phone: 888-275-2054

Email: questions@questbridge.org
http://www.questbridge.org
**Purpose:** To connect outstanding low-income high school seniors with admission and full four-year scholarships to some of the nation's most selective colleges.
**Eligibility:** Applicants must have demonstrated academic excellence in the face of economic obstacles. Students of all races and ethnicities are encouraged to apply. Many past award recipients have been among the first generation in their families to attend college.
**Amount:** Full tuition plus room and board.
**Number of Awards:** Varies.
Scholarship may be renewable.
**Deadline:** September 27.
**How to Apply:** Applications are available on the QuestBridge website in August of each year. An application form, two teacher recommendations, one counselor recommendation (Secondary School Report), a transcript and SAT and/or ACT score reports are required.

## National D-Day Museum Online Essay Contest

National D-Day Museum Foundation
945 Magazine Street
New Orleans, LA 70130
Phone: 504-528-1944
Email: collin.makamson@
nationalww2museum.org
https://www.nationalww2museum.org/
students-teachers/school-programs
**Purpose:** To increase awareness of World War II by giving students the opportunity to compete in an essay contest.
**Eligibility:** Applicants must be high school or middle school students in the United States, its territories or its military bases. They must prepare an essay of up to 1,000 words based on a topic specified by the sponsor and related to World War II. Only the first 500 valid essays will be accepted.
**Amount:** Varies.
**Number of Awards:** Varies.
**Deadline:** December 27.
**How to Apply:** Applications are available online. An essay and contact information are required.

## National Honor Society Scholarship

National Honor Society
c/o National Association of Secondary School Principals
1904 Association Drive
Reston, VA 20191
Phone: 703-860-0200
Email: nhs@nhs.us
https://www.nhs.us
**Purpose:** To recognize NHS members.
**Eligibility:** Applicants must be senior National Honor Society members. Applicants must demonstrate character, scholarship, service and leadership.
**Amount:** $2,325-$20,125.
**Number of Awards:** 400.
**Deadline:** December 6.
**How to Apply:** Application forms are available from your local NHS chapter adviser.

## National Merit Scholarship Program and National Achievement Scholarship Program

National Merit Scholarship Corporation
1560 Sherman Avenue, Suite 200
Evanston, IL 60201-4897
Phone: 847-866-5100
http://www.nationalmerit.org
**Purpose:** To provide scholarships through a merit-based academic competition.
**Eligibility:** Applicants must be enrolled full-time in high school, progressing normally toward completion and planning to enter college no later than the fall following completion of high school, be U.S. citizens or permanent legal residents in the process of becoming U.S. citizens and take the PSAT/NMSQT no later than the 11th grade. Participation in the program is based on performance on the exam.
**Amount:** $2,500.
**Number of Awards:** Varies.
Scholarship may be renewable.
**Deadline:** October PSAT test date.
**How to Apply:** Application is made by taking the PSAT/NMSQT test.

## National Oratorical Contest

American Legion
Attn.: Americanism and Children and Youth Division
P.O. Box 1055
Indianapolis, IN 46206
Phone: 317-630-1249
Email: acy@legion.org
http://www.legion.org
**Purpose:** To reward students for their knowledge of government and oral presentation skills.

**Eligibility:** Applicants must be high school students under the age of 20 who are U.S. citizens or legal residents. Students first give an oration within their state and winners compete at the national level. The oration must be related to the Constitution of the United States focusing on the duties and obligations citizens have to the government. It must be in English and be between eight and ten minutes. There is also an assigned topic which is posted on the website, and it should be between three and five minutes.

**Amount:** $1,500-$18,000.

**Number of Awards:** Varies.

**Deadline:** Local American Legion department must select winners by March 18.

**How to Apply:** Applications are available from your local American Legion post or state headquarters. Deadlines for local competitions are set by the local Posts.

## National Pathfinder Scholarship

National Federation of Republican Women
124 North Alfred Street
Alexandria, VA 22314
Phone: 703-548-9688
Email: mail@nfrw.org
http://www.nfrw.org

**Purpose:** To honor former First Lady Nancy Reagan.

**Eligibility:** Applicants must be female college sophomores, juniors, seniors or master's degree students. Two one-page essays and three letters of recommendation are required. Previous winners may not reapply.

**Amount:** $2,500.

**Number of Awards:** 3.

**Deadline:** June 1.

**How to Apply:** Applications are available online. An application form, three letters of recommendation, transcript, two essays and State Federation President Certification are required.

## Newman Civic Fellow Awards

Campus Compact
45 Temple Place
Boston, MA 02111
Phone: 617-357-1881
Email: campus@compact.org
http://www.compact.org

**Purpose:** To provide scholarships and opportunities for civic mentoring to students with financial need.

**Eligibility:** Emphasis is on students who have demonstrated leadership abilities and significant interest in civic responsibility. Students must attend one of the 1,000 Campus Compact member institutions and be nominated by the Campus Compact member president. Applicants must be sophomores or juniors at four-year colleges or must attend a two-year college.

**Amount:** Varies.

**Number of Awards:** Varies.

**Deadline:** February 3.

**How to Apply:** Nominations must be made by the Campus Compact member president.

## Odenza Marketing Group Scholarship

Odenza Vacations
4664 Lougheed Highway
Suite 230
Burnaby, BC V5C5T5
Phone: 877-297-2661
http://www.odenzascholarships.com

**Purpose:** To aid current and future college students who are between the ages of 16 and 25.

**Eligibility:** Applicants must be U.S. or Canadian citizens who have at least one full year of college study remaining. They must have a GPA of 2.5 or higher. Selection is based on the overall strength of the essays submitted.

**Amount:** $500.

**Number of Awards:** Varies.

**Deadline:** March 30, September 30.

**How to Apply:** Applications are available online. An application form and two essays are required.

## OpenWater Student Scholarship

OpenWater
4401 Fairfax Drive
Suite 200
Arlington, VA 22203
https://www.getopenwater.com/scholarship/

**Purpose:** To encourage the next generation of entrepreneurs.

**Eligibility:** Applicants must be permanent residents of the U.S. and enrolling or currently enrolled as a full-time student seeking a bachelor's degree with a minimum grade point average of 3.3. Students must have a minimum ACT score of 24 or SAT score of 1680 and demonstrate leadership and good citizenship.

**Amount:** $1,500.

**Number of Awards:** 1.

**Deadline:** December 31.

**How to Apply:** Applications are available online.

## Optimist International Essay Contest

Optimist International
4494 Lindell Boulevard
St. Louis, MO 63108
Phone: 314-371-6000
Email: programs@optimist.org
http://www.optimist.org

**Purpose:** To reward students based on their essay-writing skills.

**Eligibility:** Applicants must be under 18 years of age as of December 31 of the current school year and application must be made through a local Optimist Club. The essay topic changes each year. Applicants compete at the club, district and international level. District winners receive a $2,500 scholarship. Scoring is based on organization, vocabulary and style, grammar and punctuation, neatness and adherence to the contest rules. The club-level contests are held in early February but vary by club. The deadline for clubs to submit their winning essay to the district competition is February 28.

**Amount:** $2,500.

**Number of Awards:** Varies.

**Deadline:** Early February.

**How to Apply:** Contact your local Optimist Club.

## Out of the Box Thinking Scholarship

Litter-Robot
2900 Auburn Court
Auburn Hills, MI 48326
Phone: 877-250-7729
Email: marketing@litter-robot.com
https://www.litter-robot.com/scholarship

**Purpose:** To encourage students who have a passion for pets and creating innovative ideas for pet care.

**Eligibility:** Applicants must be a current high school, undergraduate or graduate student in the U.S. An essay, pitch or summary about a pet innovation idea and how it was conceptualized is required.

**Amount:** $250-$1,250.

**Number of Awards:** 3.

**Deadline:** July 31.

**How to Apply:** Applications are available online.

## P.E.O. Program for Continuing Education

PEO International
3700 Grand Avenue
Des Moines, IA 50312
Phone: 515-255-3153
http://www.peointernational.org

**Purpose:** To assist women whose education has been interrupted.

**Eligibility:** Applicants must be women who are resuming studies to improve their marketable skills due to changing demands in their lives. They must have financial need and cannot use the funds to pay living expenses or repay educational loans. They must be sponsored by a P.E.O. chapter and be citizens and students of the United States or Canada. They must have had at least two consecutive years as a non-student in their adult lives and be able to complete their educational goals in two consecutive years or less. Doctoral degree students are not eligible.

**Amount:** $3,000.

**Number of Awards:** Varies.

**Deadline:** 10 weeks before the start of classes.

**How to Apply:** Applications are available from your local P.E.O. Chapter. An application form, income and expense statement and chapter recommendation are required. See website to locate nearest P.E.O. Chapter.

## Patriot's Pen Youth Essay Contest

Veterans of Foreign Wars
406 W. 34th Street
Kansas City, MO 64111
Phone: 816-968-1117
Email: kharmer@vfw.org
https://www.vfw.org/community/youth-and-education

**Purpose:** To give students in grades 6 through 8 an opportunity to write essays that express their views on democracy.

**Eligibility:** Applicants must be enrolled as a 6th, 7th or 8th grader in a public, private or parochial school in the U.S., its territories or possessions. Home-schooled students and dependents of U.S. military or civilian personnel in overseas schools may also apply. Foreign exchange students and former applicants who placed in the national finals are ineligible. Students must submit essays based on an annual theme to their local VFW posts. If an essay is picked to advance, the entry is judged at the District (regional) level, then the Department (state) level and finally at the National level. Essays are judged 30 percent on knowledge of the theme, 35 percent on development of the theme and 35 percent on clarity.

**Amount:** Up to $5,000.

**Number of Awards:** 54.

**Deadline:** October 31.

**How to Apply:** Applications are available online or by contacting the local VFW office. Entries must be turned into the local VFW office. Contact information for these offices can be found online or by calling the VFW National Programs headquarters at 816-968-1117.

## Pedro Zamora Young Leaders Scholarship

National AIDS Memorial Grove
870 Market Street, Suite 965
San Francisco, CA 94102
Phone: 415-765-0446
Email: mkennedy@aidsmemorial.org
https://aidsmemorial.org/programs/

**Purpose:** To support students with a commitment to ending HIV/AIDS.

**Eligibility:** Applicants must complete the application with a personal statement and a written essay describing their service or leadership in the fight against HIV/AIDS. Students must provide a letter of recommendation and transcripts demonstrating a minimum grade point average of 2.5.

**Amount:** $5,000.

**Number of Awards:** 10.

**Deadline:** May 31.

**How to Apply:** Applications are available online.

## Photo Essay Scholarship Contest

DirectTextbook.com
1525 Chemeketa Street NE
Salem, OR 97301
Phone: 503-930-4568
Email: service@directtextbook.com
https://www.directtextbook.com

**Purpose:** To assist students who submit photos.

**Eligibility:** Applicants must be U.S. citizens who are current two- or four-year college students and who have a minimum 2.0 GPA. Students must submit a photo based on the theme given.

**Amount:** $500.

**Number of Awards:** 6.

**Deadline:** January 16.

**How to Apply:** Applications are available online.

## Photography Scholarship Contest

Negative Population Growth
2861 Duke Street
Suite 36
Alexandria, VA 22314
Phone: 703-370-9510
https://npg.org/scholarships.html

**Purpose:** To support students who draw attention to the dangers of population growth.

**Eligibility:** Applicants must submit a photograph of a U.S. environmental feature along with a short explanation of how population growth is putting the environmental future at risk. Selection is based on the overall strength of the submission.

**Amount:** $1,500.

**Number of Awards:** 5.

**Deadline:** April 11.

**How to Apply:** Applications are available online.

## Pilot International Scholarship

Pilot International Foundation
102 Preston Court
Macon, GA 31210
Phone: 478-743-2245
http://www.pilotinternational.org

**Purpose:** To support students who are preparing for a career that focuses on caring for others.

**Eligibility:** Applicants must be an undergraduate student and pursuing a career that focuses on helping others.

**Amount:** Up to $1,500.

**Number of Awards:** Varies. Scholarship may be renewable.

**Deadline:** March 15.

**How to Apply:** Applications are available online.

## Pilot Pen G2 Overachievers Student Grant

Pilot Pen
3855 Regent Boulevard
Jacksonville, FL 32224
Phone: 904-645-9999
http://g2overachievers.com/enter

**Purpose:** To support students involved in community and public service.

**Eligibility:** Applicants must be ages 13 to 19 years old. Students must demonstrate

exceptional academics and a dedication to serving others and must write an essay describing how they are working to help others outside of the classroom.
**Amount:** $15,000.
**Number of Awards:** 1.
**Deadline:** December 31.
**How to Apply:** Applications are available online.

## Power Poetry Scholarships

Power Poetry
295 East 8th Street
Suite 3W
New York, NY 10009
Phone: 347-460-6741
Email: help@powerpoetry.org
http://www.powerpoetry.org
**Purpose:** To reward students who write a slam poem.
**Eligibility:** Applicants must be 25 or younger and a U.S. citizen. Students submit their poem online.
**Amount:** $1,000.
**Number of Awards:** 1.
**Deadline:** Varies.
**How to Apply:** Applicants must join the website and submit their poem online.

## Prudential Spirit of Community Awards

Prudential Spirit of Community Awards
Prudential Financial Inc.
751 Broad Street
Newark, NJ 07102
Phone: 973-802-4568
Email: spirit@prudential.com
https://spirit.prudential.com/
**Purpose:** To recognize students for their self-initiated community service.
**Eligibility:** Applicants must be a student in grades 5-12 and a legal resident of one of the 50 states of the U.S. or District of Columbia and be engaged in a volunteer activity.
**Amount:** Up to $5,000.
**Number of Awards:** 102.
**Deadline:** November 5.
**How to Apply:** Applications are available online.

## RealtyHop Scholarship

RealtyHop
355 Madison Avenue

4th Floor
New York, NY 10017
https://www.realtyhop.com/resources/scholarship
**Purpose:** To support students who demonstrate ambition, diligence, leadership and an entrepreneurial spirit.
**Eligibility:** Applicants must be graduating high school seniors or currently enrolled undergraduates seeking a bachelor's or associate's degree. Students must submit their application including an essay via their school email address.
**Amount:** $1,000.
**Number of Awards:** 2.
**Deadline:** April 30, August 31.
**How to Apply:** Applications are available online.

## Redfin Scholarship

Redfin
1099 Stewart Street
Suite 600
Seattle, WA 98101
https://www.redfin.com/resources/scholarship
**Purpose:** To support the pursuit of higher education.
**Eligibility:** Applicants must be U.S. residents. Students must have a minimum grade point average of 3.5 and be graduating high school seniors enrolling in an accredited post-secondary institution or current freshmen, sophomores or juniors at an accredited college or university.
**Amount:** $2,500.
**Number of Awards:** 2.
**Deadline:** August 1.
**How to Apply:** Applications are available online.

## Regeneron Science Talent Search

Regeneron Science Talent Search
Society for Science and the Public
1719 N Street NW
Washington, DC 20036
Phone: 202-785-2255
Email: sts@societyforscience.org
https://www.regeneron.com/science-talent-search
**Purpose:** To recognize excellence in science among the nation's youth and encourage the exploration of science.
**Eligibility:** Applicants must be high school seniors in the U.S., Puerto Rico, Guam, Virgin Islands, American Samoa, Wake or Midway

Islands or the Marianas. U.S. citizens attending foreign schools are also eligible. Applicants must complete college entrance exams and complete individual research projects and provide a report on the research.
**Amount:** Up to $250,000.
**Number of Awards:** 40.
**Deadline:** November 13.
**How to Apply:** Applications are available by request.

## RentHop Apartment Scholarship

RentHop
101 Avenue of Americas
18th Floor
New York, NY 10013
Phone: 913-982-6682
Email: college-scholarship@renthrop.com
https://www.renthop.com/college_scholarship
**Purpose:** To support undergraduate students who display an entrepreneurial spirit as they pursue their college education.
**Eligibility:** Applicants must be a graduating high school senior or an undergraduate pursuing a bachelor's or an associate's degree. Students will need to submit a 500-word essay on the topic provided.
**Amount:** $1,000.
**Number of Awards:** 2.
**Deadline:** April 30, August 31.
**How to Apply:** An application consists of the essay being emailed to RentHop via a school email address. If applicant doesn't have a school email address, proof of enrollment will need to be provided.

## Return 2 College Scholarship

R2C Scholarship Program
http://www.return2college.com/awardprogram.cfm
**Purpose:** To provide financial assistance for college and adult students with college or graduate school expenses.
**Eligibility:** Applicants must be college or adult students currently attending or planning to attend a two-year or four-year college or graduate school within the next 12 months. Students must be 17 years or older and U.S. citizens or permanent residents. The award may be used for full- or part-time study at either on-campus or online schools.
**Amount:** $1,000.
**Number of Awards:** Varies.
**Deadline:** January 31.

**How to Apply:** Applications are available online.

## Rhodes Scholar

Rhodes Scholarship Trust
Attn.: Elliot F. Gerson
8229 Boone Boulevard, Suite 240
Vienna, VA 22182
Phone: 703-821-5960
Email: amsec@rhodesscholar.org
http://www.rhodesscholar.org
**Purpose:** To recognize qualities of young people who will contribute to the "world's fight."
**Eligibility:** Applicants must be U.S. citizens between the ages of 18 and 24 and have a bachelor's degree at the time of the award. The awards provides for two to three years of study at the University of Oxford including educational costs and other expenses. Selection is extremely competitive and is based on literary and scholastic achievements, athletic achievement and character.
**Amount:** Full tuition plus stipend.
**Number of Awards:** 32.
**Deadline:** October 7.
**How to Apply:** Applications are available online.

## Samuel Huntington Public Service Award

Samuel Huntington Fund
Attn: Amy Stacy
National Grid
40 Sylvan Road
Waltham, MA 02451
Phone: 508-389-2000
Email: amy.stacy@nationalgrid.com
https://www.samuelhuntingtonaward.org
**Purpose:** To assist students who wish to perform one year of humanitarian service immediately upon graduation.
**Eligibility:** Applicants must be graduating college seniors, and must intend to perform one year of public service in the U.S. or abroad. The service may be individual work or through charitable, religious, educational, governmental or other public service organizations.
**Amount:** $15,000.
**Number of Awards:** Up to 3.
**Deadline:** January 17.
**How to Apply:** Applications are available online.

## Scholars Helping Collars Scholarship

P.L.A.Y.
246 2nd Street, Unit A
San Francisco, CA 94105
Phone: (855) 300-7529
https://www.petplay.com/scholarship/
**Purpose:** To reward graduating seniors with a passion for animal welfare.
**Eligibility:** Applicants must have a history of volunteer work to help animals in need. Students must submit an essay about how that volunteer work has impacted their lives and the importance of animal welfare. Selection is based on the overall strength of the submission.
**Amount:** $1,000.
**Number of Awards:** 3.
**Deadline:** February 28.
**How to Apply:** Applications are available online.

## Scholarship America Dream Award

Scholarship America Dream Award
One Scholarship Way
Saint Peter, MN 56082
Phone: 507-931-1682
Email: dreamaward@scholarshipamerica.org
https://scholarshipamerica.org/dreamaward/
**Purpose:** To assist students in their second year or higher of post-secondary education.
**Eligibility:** Applicants must be U.S. citizens or permanent or legal residents who received a high school diploma from a U.S. school. Students must be planning to complete a minimum of one full year of post-secondary education and be planning to enroll as full-time undergraduates at the sophomore level or higher for the coming academic year. Applicants must have a grade point average of 3.0 or better.
**Amount:** $5,000-$15,000.
**Number of Awards:** Varies.
Scholarship may be renewable.
**Deadline:** October 15.
**How to Apply:** Applications are available online.

## Scholarships for Student Leaders

National Association for Campus Activities
13 Harbison Way
Columbia, SC 29212
Phone: 803-732-6222
Email: info@naca.org
https://www.naca.org/FOUNDATION/Pages/Scholarships.aspx
**Purpose:** The NACA foundation is committed to developing professionals in the field of campus activities.
**Eligibility:** Applicants must be current undergraduate students who hold a significant campus leadership position, have made significant contributions to their campus communities and have demonstrated leadership skills and abilities.
**Amount:** Varies.
**Number of Awards:** Varies.
**Deadline:** December 31.
**How to Apply:** Applications are available online.

## Scholastic Art and Writing Awards

Scholastic Art and Writing Awards
557 Broadway
New York, NY 10012
Phone: 212-343-6100
Email: info@artandwriting.org
http://www.artandwriting.org/scholarships/
**Purpose:** To reward creative young writers and artists.
**Eligibility:** Applicants must be in grades 7 through 12 in U.S. or Canadian schools and must submit writing pieces or portfolios in one of the following categories: dramatic script, general writing portfolio, humor, journalism, nonfiction portfolio, novel, personal essay/memoir, poetry, science fiction/fantasy, short story and short short story.
**Amount:** Up to $10,000.
**Number of Awards:** Varies.
**Deadline:** Varies.
**How to Apply:** Applications are available online.

## ScienceSoft Scholarship

ScienceSoft
5900 South Lake Forest Drive
Suite 300
McKinney, TX 75070
Phone: 214-306-6837
Email: contact@scnsoft.com
https://www.scnsoft.com/about/scholarship
**Purpose:** To encourage students who are interested in artificial intelligence technologies.
**Eligibility:** Applicants must be full-time students of U.S. colleges and universities who have completed the first year of their studies as well as graduate students. Students must submit an essay on a provided topic.

**Amount:** Up to $2,000.
**Number of Awards:** 3.
**Deadline:** December 31.
**How to Apply:** Applications are available online.

## Second Chance Scholarship Contest

American Fire Sprinkler Association
12750 Merit Drive
Suite 350
Dallas, TX 75251
Phone: 214-349-5965
Email: scholarship@firesprinkler.org
https://www.afsascholarship.org/
secondchance/
**Purpose:** To help U.S. students pay for higher education.
**Eligibility:** Applicants must be U.S. citizens or legal residents and be high school graduates or GED recipients. They must be enrolled at an institution of higher learning no later than the spring semester of the upcoming academic year. American Fire Sprinkler Association (AFSA) staff and board member relatives are ineligible, as are past contest winners. Selection is made by random drawing from the pool of contest entrants.
**Amount:** $1,000.
**Number of Awards:** 5.
**Deadline:** August 31.
**How to Apply:** Contest entrants must read an informational article on fire sprinklers before taking a ten-question multiple choice test on the material covered in the article. The number of correct responses on the test is equal to the number of entries that will be made in the entrant's name, giving each entrant up to 10 entries to the random drawing that will determine the winners of the contest.

## Simon Youth Foundation Community Scholarship

Simon Youth Foundation
225 W. Washington Street
Indianapolis, IN 46204
Phone: 800-509-3676
Email: syf@simon.com
http://www.syf.org/scholarships/
**Purpose:** To assist promising students who live in communities with Simon properties.
**Eligibility:** Applicants must be high school seniors who plan to attend an accredited two- or four-year college, university or technical/vocational school full-time. Scholarships are awarded without regard to race, color, creed, religion, gender, disability or national origin, and recipients are selected on the basis of financial need, academic record, potential to succeed, participation in school and community activities, honors, work experience, a statement of career and educational goals and an outside appraisal. Awards are given at every Simon mall in the U.S.
**Amount:** $1,500.
**Number of Awards:** Varies.
**Deadline:** February 19.
**How to Apply:** Applications are available online. Only the first 3,000 applications that the organization receives are considered.

## Sixt Scholars Program

Sixt Rent a Car
1501 NW 49th Street
Suite 100
Fort Lauderdale, FL 33309
Phone: 954-703-2359
Email: noemi.montejo@sixt.com
https://www.sixt.com/sixt-scholars
**Purpose:** To assist high-school seniors who are involved in extracurricular activities.
**Eligibility:** Applicants must have a minimum 3.7 GPA on a 4.0 scale, be a graduating high school senior in the U.S. and plan to enroll full-time in a two- or four-year university. Only the first 500 applicants will be considered. Selection is based on factors including financial need and extracurricular activities.
**Amount:** $5,000.
**Number of Awards:** 5.
**Deadline:** November 30.
**How to Apply:** Application available online and must include a high school transcript.

## Sleeknote Scholarship

Sleeknote
Jens Baggesens Vej 90A
8200 Aarhus
Denmark, Email: mail@sleeknote.com
https://sleeknote.com/scholarship
**Purpose:** To help students who create a video essay.
**Eligibility:** Applicants must be currently enrolled in a high school, university or college and able to submit their application in English. Students must create a short original video essay discussing their chosen field of study and future plans.
**Amount:** $1,000.
**Number of Awards:** 2.
**Deadline:** September 30.

**How to Apply:** Applications are available online.

## Sodexo STOP Hunger Scholarship

Sodexo Foundation
9801 Washingtonian Boulevard
Gaithersburg, MD 20878
Phone: 800-763-3946
Email: stophunger@sodexofoundation.org
http://us.stop-hunger.org
**Purpose:** To aid students who have been active in the movement to eradicate hunger.
**Eligibility:** Applicants must be U.S. citizens or permanent residents. They must be students in kindergarten through graduate school who are enrolled at an accredited U.S. institution. They must have been active in at least one unpaid volunteer effort to end hunger during the past 12 months. Sodexo employees and previous recipients of this award are ineligible. Selection is based on the overall strength of the application.
**Amount:** $1,000-$5,000.
**Number of Awards:** Up to 25.
**Deadline:** February 28.
**How to Apply:** Applications are available online. An application form and supporting materials are required.

## Spark Energy

Spark Energy
12140 Wickchester Lane
Suite 100
Houston, TX 77079
Email: scholarship@sparkenergy.com
https://www.sparkenergy.com
**Purpose:** To assist graduating high school students who write about a "spark."
**Eligibility:** Applicants must be graduating high school seniors with a minimum GPA or 3.5 who have been accepted to a four-year college or university. Students must provide transcripts and essay along with their application.
**Amount:** $3,000.
**Number of Awards:** 1.
**Deadline:** August 31.
**How to Apply:** Applications are available online.

## Spirit of Anne Frank Awards

Anne Frank Center USA
1325 Avenue of the Americas
28th Floor
New York, NY 10019

Phone: 212-431-7993
Email: education@annefrank.com
https://www.annefrank.com/scholarships
**Purpose:** To reward students who lead the way in combating prejudice and injustice in their communities.
**Eligibility:** Students should be high school seniors, be U.S. citizens and plan on attending a four-year college or university in the fall of the upcoming academic year. Applicants must submit a 1,000-word essay characterizing their efforts and dedication toward achieving lasting change with regards to prejudice and intolerance.
**Amount:** $1,000-$5,000.
**Number of Awards:** 3.
**Deadline:** February 28.
**How to Apply:** Applications are available online and must be submitted along with the essay and two letters of recommendation.

## Spirit of Giving Scholarship

Wine Country Gift Baskets
Phone: 800-394-0394
Email: scholarship@winecountrygiftbaskets.com
https://www.winecountrygiftbaskets.com/information/scholarship.asp
**Purpose:** To encourage acts of kindness, service and giving.
**Eligibility:** Applicants must be high school seniors or currently enrolled students in an accredited U.S. certificate program, college, trade school or university who will be attending the program in the following year. Students must submit an essay relating to giving and service to others.
**Amount:** $1,000.
**Number of Awards:** 3.
**Deadline:** July 31.
**How to Apply:** Applications are available online.

## Stamps Scholars

Stamps Family Charitable Foundation Inc.
P.O. Box 98374
Atlanta, GA 30359-2074
Email: info@stampsfoundation.org
https://www.stampsfoundation.org/
**Purpose:** To support students pursuing higher education with their related expenses.
**Eligibility:** Applicants must be currently enrolled high school seniors, undergraduates or graduate students attending an accredited

college or university. Selection is based on the overall strength of the application as well as the following: academic achievement, leadership ability, integrity, perseverance, extracurricular activities and community involvement.

**Amount:** Varies.

**Number of Awards:** Varies.

**Deadline:** Varies.

**How to Apply:** Applications are available online. An application form, official transcripts and SAT and/or ACT scores are required.

## Stokes Educational Scholarship Program

National Security Agency (NSA)
Attn: MB3, Stokes Program
9800 Savage Road
Suite 6272
Ft. George G. Meade, MD 20755-6000
Phone: 410-854-4725
https://www.intelligencecareers.gov/icstudents.html?Agency=NSA

**Purpose:** To recruit those with skills useful to the NSA, especially minority high school students.

**Eligibility:** Students must be seniors at the time of application, be U.S. citizens, have a 3.0 GPA, have a minimum ACT score of 25 or a minimum SAT score of 1200 and demonstrate leadership skills. Applicants must be planning to major in computer science or computer/ electrical engineering.

**Amount:** Up to $30,000.

**Number of Awards:** Varies. Scholarship may be renewable.

**Deadline:** November 15.

**How to Apply:** Applications are available online.

## Stuck at Prom Scholarship

Henkel Consumer Adhesives
32150 Just Imagine Drive
Avon, OH 44011-1355
http://stuckatprom.com/

**Purpose:** To reward students for their creativity with duct tape.

**Eligibility:** Applicants must attend a high school prom as a couple in the spring wearing the most original attire that they make from duct tape. Both members of the couple do not have to attend the same school. Photographs of past winners are available on the website.

**Amount:** $1,000-$10,000.

**Number of Awards:** Varies.

**Deadline:** June 8.

**How to Apply:** Applications are available online. Contact information, release form and prom picture are required.

## Student Transportation Video Contest

American Road and Transportation Builders Association
1219 28th Street, NW
Washington, DC 20007
Phone: 202-289-4434
Email: lshair@artba.org
https://www.artba.org/foundation/student-video-contest/

**Purpose:** To support students from elementary through graduate school interested in the transportation industry in the United States.

**Eligibility:** Applicants must be currently enrolled elementary through graduate school students. They must produce a 2-4 minute video on some aspect of the transportation industry in the United States. Selection is based on creativity and the overall strength of the video.

**Amount:** $500.

**Number of Awards:** 2.

**Deadline:** October 31.

**How to Apply:** Videos must be uploaded to YouTube and a link to the video sent to ARTBA by the submission deadline. Submission forms are available online. A submission form, waiver, link to the video, enrollment verification and photo release form are required.

## Student View Scholarship

Student Insights
136 Justice Drive
Valencia, PA 16059
Phone: 724-612-3685
Email: jbecker@studentinsights.com
http://studentinsights.com

**Purpose:** To support graduating high school seniors regardless of academic achievement or need.

**Eligibility:** Applicants must complete an online survey and then they will be entered into a random drawing for an award.

**Amount:** Up to $4,000.

**Number of Awards:** 13.

**Deadline:** April 22.

**How to Apply:** Applications are available online.

## Student-Caregiver Scholarship

Caring.com
2600 South El Camino Real
Suite 300
San Mateo, CA 94403
Email: scholarship@caring.com
https://www.caring.com/caregivers/
scholarships-for-student-caregivers/
**Purpose:** To support students who also serve
as family caregivers.
**Eligibility:** Applicants must be U.S. citizens or
permanent residents who are graduating high
school seniors or currently enrolled full-time
students at an accredited two- or four-year
college in the U.S. Students must be caring for
a family member and must submit an essay or
video addressing their caregiver situation.
**Amount:** $1,500.
**Number of Awards:** 2.
**Deadline:** June 30.
**How to Apply:** Applications are available
online.

## StudentCam Competition

C-SPAN
Phone: 800-523-7586
Email: educate@c-span.org
http://www.studentcam.org
**Purpose:** To reward students interested in
government and societal issues.
**Eligibility:** Applicants must be either middle
school or high school students in the United
States, U.S. territories or the District of
Columbia. Students must follow rules for the
documentary competition. Applicants' entries
must reflect the current theme.
**Amount:** Varies.
**Number of Awards:** Varies.
**Deadline:** January 20.
**How to Apply:** Applications are available
online.

## Study Abroad Grants

Honor Society of Phi Kappa Phi
7576 Goodwood Boulevard
Baton Rouge, LA 70806
Phone: 800-804-9880
Email: awards@phikappaphi.org
http://www.phikappaphi.org
**Purpose:** To provide scholarships for
undergraduate students who will study abroad.
**Eligibility:** Applicants do not have to be
members of Phi Kappa Phi but must attend an
institution with a Phi Kappa Phi chapter, have

between 30 and 90 credit hours and have at
least two semesters remaining at their home
institution upon return. Students must have
been accepted into a study abroad program
that demonstrates their academic preparation,
career choice and the welfare of others. They
must have a GPA of 3.75 or higher.
**Amount:** $1,000.
**Number of Awards:** 75.
**Deadline:** March 15.
**How to Apply:** Applications are available
online. An application form, personal
statement, transcript, letter of acceptance and
two letters of recommendation are required.

## SuperCollege Scholarship

SuperCollege.com
Scholarship Dept. 673
2713 Newlands Avenue
Belmont, CA 94002
Email: supercollege@supercollege.com
http://www.supercollege.com/scholarship/
**Purpose:** SuperCollege donates a percentage
of the proceeds from the sales of its books to
award scholarships to high school, college,
graduate and adult students.
**Eligibility:** Applicants must be high school
students, college undergraduates, graduate
students or adult students residing in the
U.S. and attending or planning to attend any
accredited college or university within the
next 12 months. The scholarship may be used
to pay for tuition, books, room and board,
computers or any education-related expenses.
**Amount:** $1,000.
**Number of Awards:** 1.
**Deadline:** December 31.
**How to Apply:** Applications are available
online.

## Technology Addiction Awareness Scholarship

Digital Responsibility
3561 Homestead Road #113
Santa Clara, CA 95051-5161
Email: scholarship@digitalresponsibility.org
http://www.digitalresponsibility.org
**Purpose:** To help students understand the
negative effects of too much screen time.
**Eligibility:** Applicant must be a high school,
college, graduate or home schooled student
who is a U.S. citizen or legal resident. A
140-character message about technology
addiction is required to apply. The top 10
applications will be selected as finalists; finalists

will be asked to write a full length 500- to 1,000-word essay about technology addiction. Only online applications are accepted.
**Amount:** $1,000.
**Number of Awards:** 1.
**Deadline:** January 30.
**How to Apply:** Applications are available online.

## Telluride Association Summer Programs

Telluride Association
217 West Avenue
Ithaca, NY 14850
Phone: 607-273-5011
Email: tasp-queries@tellurideassociation.org
http://www.tellurideassociation.org
**Purpose:** Summer program to provide high school students with a college-level, intellectually enriching experience.
**Eligibility:** Applicants must be high school juniors. The association seeks applicants from a variety of socio-economic backgrounds and provides for their tuition and room and board during summer programs in New York and Michigan. Students are invited to apply either by receiving a score on the PSAT/NMSQT that is usually in the top 1 percent or by nomination by a teacher or counselor.
**Amount:** Summer program tuition and fees.
**Number of Awards:** Varies.
**Deadline:** January 13.
**How to Apply:** Applications are sent to nominated students.

## The Fountainhead Essay Contest

Ayn Rand Institute
P.O. Box 57044
Irvine, CA 92619
Phone: 949-222-6550
Email: essays@aynrand.org
https://www.aynrand.org/students/essay-contests
**Purpose:** To honor high school students who distinguish themselves in their understanding of Ayn Rand's novel "The Fountainhead".
**Eligibility:** Applicants must be high school juniors or seniors who submit a 800-1,600 word essay which will be judged on both style and content with an emphasis on writing that is clear, articulate and logically organized. Winning essays must demonstrate an outstanding grasp of the philosophical and psychological meaning of "The Fountainhead".

**Amount:** $50-$10,000.
**Number of Awards:** 59.
**Deadline:** May 28.
**How to Apply:** Essay is required for the contest. There is no application.

## TicketCity Annual College Scholarship Program

TicketCity
5912 Balcones Drive
Suite 102
Austin, TX 78731
Email: scholarship@ticketcity.com
http://www.ticketcity.com/ticketcity-annual-college-scholarship-program.html
**Purpose:** To help a student with their educational expenses.
**Eligibility:** Applicants must be U.S. citizens and be enrolled full-time as a freshman, sophomore or junior at an accredited U.S. four-year university. Students must have a GPA of 2.5 or higher. Selection is based on the strength of the application and overall creativity of applicant's essay.
**Amount:** $3,000.
**Number of Awards:** 1.
**Deadline:** December 1.
**How to Apply:** Applications are available online. An application and an essay which includes a picture or short video are required.

## Toyota Teen Driver Video Challenge

Toyota Teen Driver
One Discovery Place
Silver Spring, MD 20910
Phone: 800-323-9084
http://www.teendrive365inschool.com/teens/video-challenge
**Purpose:** To support teens who are interested in persuading their peers to drive safely.
**Eligibility:** Applicants must be at least 13 years old, in grades 9-12 and legal residents of the United States. Applicants must work by themselves or in teams of two to four members. Students must create a 30- to 60-second video aimed at teenage drivers about how important it is to drive safely. Selection of winners will be based on the creativity, content and presentation of the video.
**Amount:** Up to $15,000.
**Number of Awards:** 14.
**Deadline:** February 26.
**How to Apply:** Applications are available online.

## Travel Video Contest

InternationalStudent.com
224 First Street
Neptune, FL 32266
http://www.internationalstudent.com
**Purpose:** To support students who wish to pursue an international education or study abroad program.
**Eligibility:** Applicants must be at least 18 years old, be enrolled or currently enrolling in a college or university abroad. Students must submit a video describing a desired trip if they are currently studying abroad or describing a proposed study abroad if they are currently studying in their home country. Applicants must create a video that does not exceed four minutes, submit a fully completed online entry form and be prepared to document the entire experience in a weekly blog, if selected.
**Amount:** $4,000.
**Number of Awards:** 1.
**Deadline:** October 15.
**How to Apply:** Applications are available online.

## Tripz.com

Tripz.com
3422 Old Capitol Trail
Suite 193
Wilmington, DE 27101
Phone: 866-479-2819
https://www.tripz.com/scholarship.php
**Purpose:** To support students with an interest in promoting their communities.
**Eligibility:** Applicants must be U.S. citizens in their junior or senior year of high school or currently enrolled college students and have a minimum 2.5 GPA. Students must write an essay pertaining to tourism in their community.
**Amount:** $1,000.
**Number of Awards:** 4.
**Deadline:** March 31, June 30, September 31, December 31.
**How to Apply:** Applications are available online.

## Truman Scholar

Truman Scholarship Foundation
712 Jackson Place NW
Washington, DC 20006
Phone: 202-395-4831
Email: office@truman.gov
http://www.truman.gov
**Purpose:** To provide college junior leaders who plan to pursue careers in government, non-profits, education or other public service with financial support for graduate study and leadership training.
**Eligibility:** Applicants must be juniors, attending an accredited U.S. college or university and be nominated by the institution. Students may not apply directly. Applicants must be U.S. citizens or U.S. nationals, complete an application and write a policy recommendation.
**Amount:** Up to $30,000.
**Number of Awards:** 55-65.
**Deadline:** February 4.
**How to Apply:** See your school's Truman Faculty Representative or contact the foundation.

## Tuition Exchange Scholarships

Tuition Exchange
1743 Connecticut Avenue NW
Washington, DC 20009
Phone: 202-518-0135
Email: info@tuitionexchange.org
http://www.tuitionexchange.org
**Purpose:** To assist the children or other family members of the faculty and staff at participating colleges and universities to encourage employment of parents and guardians in higher education.
**Eligibility:** Eligibility varies by institution. Applicants must be family members of the home institution where they are applying. However specific details about employment status, years of service or other requirements are determined solely by the home institution.
**Amount:** Up to full tuition.
**Number of Awards:** 6,000.
Scholarship may be renewable.
**Deadline:** Varies.
**How to Apply:** Applications are available from the liaison officer at the home institution.

## U.S. Bank Scholarship Program

U.S. Bank
c/o U.S. Bank Office of Corporate Citizenship
1420 Kettner Boulevard
7th Floor
San Diego, CA 92101
Phone: 800-242-1200
http://www.usbank.com/community/financial-education/scholarship.html
**Purpose:** To support graduating high school seniors who plan to attend college.

**Eligibility:** Applicants must be high school seniors who plan to attend or current college freshmen, sophomores or juniors attending full-time at an accredited two- or four-year college and be U.S. citizens or permanent residents. Recipients are selected through a random drawing.

**Amount:** $20,000.

**Number of Awards:** Varies.

**Deadline:** October 27.

**How to Apply:** Applications are only available online.

## U.S. JCI Senate Scholarship Grants

U.S. JCI Senate
106 Wedgewood Drive
Carrollton, GA 30117
Email: tom@smipc.net
http://www.usjcisenate.org

**Purpose:** To support high school students who wish to further their education.

**Eligibility:** Applicants must be high school seniors and U.S. citizens who are graduating from a U.S. accredited high school or state approved home school or GED program. Winners must attend college full-time to receive funds. Applications are judged at the state level.

**Amount:** $1,000.

**Number of Awards:** Varies.

**Deadline:** January 24.

**How to Apply:** Applications are available from your school's guidance office.

## U.S. PIRG Fellowship

National Association of State Public Interest Research Groups
294 Washington Street
Suite 500
Boston, MA 02108
Phone: 617-747-4370
https://jobs.uspirg.org/fellowship.html

**Purpose:** To prepare future leaders for public service.

**Eligibility:** Applicants must commit to the two-year program. Students must demonstrate academic excellence, leadership experience and superior communication skills.

**Amount:** $26,500.

**Number of Awards:** Varies.

**Deadline:** Varies.

**How to Apply:** Applications are available online.

## Undergraduate Transfer Scholarship

Jack Kent Cooke Foundation Undergraduate Transfer Scholarship
44325 Woodridge Parkway
Lansdowne, VA 20176
Phone: 800-941-3300
Email: scholarships@jkcf.org
http://www.jkcf.org

**Purpose:** To help community college students transfer to and attend four-year universities.

**Eligibility:** Applicants must be a current student at an accredited U.S. community college or two-year institution with sophomore status by December 31 of the application year or a recent graduate. Students must plan to enroll full time in a baccalaureate program at an accredited college or university in the following fall and have a cumulative undergraduate grade point average of 3.5 or better on a 4.0 scale. Applicants must also demonstrate significant unmet financial need. Family income of up to $95,000 will be considered. However, the majority of scholarship recipients will be eligible to receive a Pell grant.

**Amount:** Up to $40,000.

**Number of Awards:** About 85. Scholarship may be renewable.

**Deadline:** November 20.

**How to Apply:** Applications are available online.

## United States Hispanic Leadership Institute Denny's Hungry for Education

United States Hispanic Leadership Institute Denny's Hunger for Education
Email: hungryforeducation@dennys.com
http://www.dennyshungryforeducation.com

**Purpose:** To support students who have ideas for fighting childhood hunger.

**Eligibility:** Applicants must be high school seniors or college students, be citizens of the United States or be living in the United States legally and have a 2.5 GPA. Students must write an essay as part of their application and have ideas on ending childhood hunger. Applicants may apply regardless or race or national origin.

**Amount:** $1,000.

**Number of Awards:** 8.

**Deadline:** December 13.

**How to Apply:** Applications are available online.

## Unpakt College Scholarship

Unpakt
555 W. 25th Street
Floor 3
New York, NY 10001
Phone: 212-677-5333
Email: scholarship@unpakt.com
http://www.unpakt.com/scholarship
**Purpose:** To support students who write about their future.
**Eligibility:** Applicants must be currently enrolled college students or recent graduates. Students must submit an application and essay discussing where they plan to move after graduation to start their professional life and why.
**Amount:** $1,000.
**Number of Awards:** 3.
**Deadline:** December 31.
**How to Apply:** Applications are available online.

## Urban Fellows Program

New York City Department of Personnel
1 Centre Street
Room 2425
New York, NY 10007
Phone: 212-386-0058
https://www1.nyc.gov/site/dcas/employment/urban-fellows.page
**Purpose:** To support high-achieving students pursue government and public service.
**Eligibility:** Applicants must have received their bachelor's degree within the last two years. Students must commit full-time to the nine month Fellowship and suspend any graduate study or outside work. Applicants must be eligible to work in the U.S.
**Amount:** $30,000.
**Number of Awards:** Varies.
**Deadline:** January 13.
**How to Apply:** Applications are available online.

## USMA Blake Family Metric Scholarship Award

U.S. Metric Association
P.O. Box 471
Windsor, CO 80550-0471
Phone: 779-537-5611
http://www.us-metric.org/usma-blake-family-foundation-metric-awards
**Purpose:** To support students who help promote metric awareness and usage.

**Eligibility:** Applicants must be high school seniors who plan to enter college in the fall after graduation. Selection is based on involvement in promoting metric awareness and usage in the U.S. An additional award is available to a non-student.
**Amount:** $2,500.
**Number of Awards:** 1.
**Deadline:** March 31.
**How to Apply:** Applications are available online.

## Voice of Democracy Audio Essay Contests

Veterans of Foreign Wars
406 W. 34th Street
Kansas City, MO 64111
Phone: 816-968-1117
Email: kharmer@vfw.org
https://www.vfw.org/community/youth-and-education
**Purpose:** To encourage patriotism with students creating audio essays expressing their opinion on a patriotic theme.
**Eligibility:** Applicants must submit a three- to five-minute audio essay on tape or CD focused on a yearly theme. Students must be in the 9th to 12th grade in a public, private or parochial high school, home study program or overseas U.S. military school. Foreign exchange students are not eligible for the contest, and students who are age 20 or older also may not enter. Previous first place winners on the state level are ineligible.
**Amount:** $1,000-$30,000.
**Number of Awards:** Varies.
**Deadline:** October 31.
**How to Apply:** Applications are available online but must be submitted to a local VFW post.

## VRG Scholarship

Vegetarian Resource Group
P.O. Box 1463
Baltimore, MD 21203
Phone: 410-366-8343
Email: vrg@vrg.org
http://www.vrg.org
**Purpose:** To reward high school seniors who promote vegetarianism.
**Eligibility:** Applicants must be graduating U.S. high school students who have promoted vegetarianism in their schools or communities. Vegetarians do not eat meat, fish or fowl. The award is based on compassion, courage

and commitment to promoting a "peaceful world through a vegetarian diet or lifestyle." Applicants should submit transcripts and at least three recommendations.
**Amount:** $5,000-$10,000.
**Number of Awards:** 3.
**Deadline:** February 20.
**How to Apply:** Applications are available online, by mail, by phone or by email. A typed document containing the application's information will be accepted.

## We The Future Contest

Constituting America
P.O. Box 1988
Colleyville, TX 76034
Phone: 888-937-0917
Email: constitutingamerica@yahoo.com
https://constitutingamerica.org/enter/
**Purpose:** To encourage students who are learning about the importance of the U.S. Constitution.
**Eligibility:** Applicants must be U.S. citizens or legal residents and middle, high school or college students. Students must submit an entry in one of the following categories: essay, song, entrepreneurial plan, short film, PSA, STEM or speech - all with the theme of the U.S. Constitution.
**Amount:** Up to $2,000.
**Number of Awards:** 8-10.
**Deadline:** September 17.
**How to Apply:** Applications are available online.

## Western Digital Scholarship Program

Western Digital Scholarships for STEM
c/o International Scholarship and Tuition Services Inc. (ISTS)
1321 Murfreesboro Road
Suite 800
Nashville, TN 37217
Phone: 855-670-ISTS
Email: contactus@applyists.com
https://www.westerndigital.com/company/corporate-philanthropy/scholarship-programs
**Purpose:** To assist students who have demonstrated an interest in STEM.
**Eligibility:** Applicants must be a high school senior or college freshman, sophomore or junior and must attend or plan to attend a full-time undergraduate program. Students must also demonstrate financial need.

**Amount:** Up to $5,000.
**Number of Awards:** 400.
Scholarship may be renewable.
**Deadline:** April 3.
**How to Apply:** Applications are available online. An application form and an essay are required.

## White House Fellows Program

White House
1600 Pennsylvania Avenue NW
Washington, DC 20500
Phone: 202-395-4522
Email: whitehousefellows@who.eop.gov
https://www.whitehouse.gov/get-involved/fellows/apply/
**Purpose:** To provide motivated students with first-hand experience working at high levels of federal government.
**Eligibility:** Applicants must be U.S. citizens who have completed their undergraduate education and demonstrate early professional achievement and evidence of leadership skills. Students must demonstrate commitment to public service and the ability to work as part of a team and provide three recommendations along with the application.
**Amount:** Varies.
**Number of Awards:** Varies.
**Deadline:** January 10.
**How to Apply:** Applications are available online.

## Young People for Fellowship

People For the American Way Foundation
Young People For
1101 15th Street NW
Suite 600
Washington, DC 20005
Phone: 202-467-4999
Email: mhall@pfaw.org
http://youngpeoplefor.org/fellowship/
**Purpose:** To encourage and cultivate young progressive leaders.
**Eligibility:** Applicants must be undergraduate students and be interested in promoting social change on their campuses and in their communities. Selection is based on the overall strength of the application.
**Amount:** Varies.
**Number of Awards:** Varies.
**Deadline:** December 31.
**How to Apply:** Applications are available online. An application form is required.

## Young Scholars Program

Jack Kent Cooke Foundation Young Scholars
Program
301 ACT Drive
P.O. Box 4030
Iowa City, IA 52243
Phone: 800-941-3300
Email: scholarships@jkcf.org
http://www.jkcf.org
**Purpose:** To help high-achieving students
with financial need and provide them with
educational opportunities throughout high
school.
**Eligibility:** Applicants must have financial
need, be in the 7th grade and plan to attend
high school in the United States. Academic
achievement and intelligence are important,
and students must display strong academic
records, academic awards and honors and
submit a strong letter of recommendation. A
GPA of 3.65 is usually required, but exceptions
are made for students with unique talents or
learning differences. The award is also based
on students' will to succeed, leadership and
public service, critical thinking ability and
participation in the arts and humanities. During
two summers, recipients must participate in
a Young Scholars Week and Young Scholars
Reunion in Washington, DC.
**Amount:** Varies.
**Number of Awards:** 60.
Scholarship may be renewable.
**Deadline:** March 23.
**How to Apply:** Applications are available
online and at regional talent centers. An
application form, parental release, financial
and tax forms, school report, teacher
recommendation, personal recommendation
and survey form are required.

## Young Women's Leadership Retreat Scholarship Essay Contest

Network of Enlightened Women
1360 E. Capitol Street NE
Washington, DC 20003
Phone: 423-838-4477
Email: amber@enlightenedwomen.org
https://enlightenedwomen.org/calling-
high-school-juniors-seniors-young-womens-
leadership-retreat-scholarship-essay-contest-
now-open/
**Purpose:** To inspire female high school
students to reflect on leadership.
**Eligibility:** Applicants must be female and
legal residents of the U.S. currently enrolled as
a high school junior or senior. Students must
write an essay discussing the opportunities and
challenges of emerging technology and social
media on current and future leaders.
**Amount:** $1,000.
**Number of Awards:** 1.
**Deadline:** April 30.
**How to Apply:** Applications are available
online.

## ZipRecruiter $3,000 Scholarship Challenge

ZipRecruiter
1453 3rd Street Promenade #335
11th Floor
Santa Monica, CA 90401
Phone: 404-936-1644
https://www.ziprecruiter.com/scholarship
**Purpose:** To promote the use of creativity in
the career search.
**Eligibility:** Applicants must be college students
at least 18 years of age who are legal residents
of the United States or its territories and
possessions. Students are to write an essay on
the topic provided. A minimum 2.5 GPA is
required.
**Amount:** $3,000.
**Number of Awards:** 1.
**Deadline:** October 31.
**How to Apply:** Applications are available
online.

## ABOUT THE AUTHORS

Harvard graduates and husband and wife team Gen and Kelly Tanabe are the founders of SuperCollege and award-winning authors of 14 books including: *The Ultimate Scholarship Book, 1001 Ways to Pay for College, How to Write a Winning Scholarship Essay, The Ultimate Guide to America's Best Colleges, Get into Any College, Accepted! 50 Successful College Admission Essays* and *501 Ways for Adult Students to Pay for College.*

Together, Gen and Kelly were accepted to every school to which they applied, including all the Ivy League colleges, and won more than $100,000 in merit-based scholarships. They were able to graduate from Harvard debt-free.

Gen and Kelly give workshops across the country and write the nationally syndicated "Ask The SuperCollege.com Experts" column. They have made hundreds of appearances on television and radio and have served as expert sources for *USA Today, The New York Times, U.S. News & World Report, New York Daily News, San Jose Mercury News, Chronicle of Higher Education, CNN* and *Seventeen.*

Gen grew up in Waialua, Hawaii. A graduate of Waialua High School, he was the first student from his school to be accepted at Harvard, where he graduated *magna cum laude* with a degree in both History and East Asian Studies.

Kelly attended Whitney High School, a nationally ranked public high school in her hometown of Cerritos, California. She graduated *magna cum laude* from Harvard with a degree in Sociology.

The Tanabes approach financial aid from a practical, hands-on point of view. Drawing on the collective knowledge and experiences of students, they provide real strategies students can use to pay for their education.

Gen and Kelly live in Belmont, California with their sons Zane and Kane.